D1250820

**Meramec Library
St. Louis Community College
11333 Big Bend Blvd.
Kirkwood, MO 63122-5799
314-984-7797**

WITHDRAWN

St. Louis Community College
at Meramec
Library

WITHDRAWN

REGIONAL PEACEKEEPING IN THE POST-COLD WAR ERA

Regional Peacekeeping
in the Post-Cold War Era

HILAIRE McCOUBREY

Professor in Law, University of Hull, United Kingdom

and

JUSTIN MORRIS

Lecturer in International Politics, University of Hull, United Kingdom

KLUWER LAW INTERNATIONAL
THE HAGUE / LONDON / BOSTON

A C.I.P Catalogue record for this book is available from the Library of Congress.

ISBN 90-411-1317-7

Published by Kluwer Law International,
P.O. Box 85889, 2508 CN The Hague, The Netherlands

Sold and distributed in North, Central and South America
by Kluwer Law International,
675 Massachusetts Avenue, Cambridge, MA 02139, USA

In all other countries, sold and distributed
by Kluwer Law International, Distribution Centre
P.O. Box 322, 3300 AH Dordrecht, The Netherlands

Printed on acid-free paper

All Rights Reserved
© 2000 Kluwer Law International
Kluwer Law International incorporates the publishing programmes of
Graham & Trotman Ltd, Kluwer Law and Taxation Publishers,
and Martinus Nijhoff Publishers.

No part of the material protected by this copyright notice may be reproduced or
utilized in any form or by any means, electronic or mechanical,
including photocopying, recording, or by any information storage and
retrieval system, without written permission from
the copyright owner.

Printed and bound in Great Britain by Antony Rowe Limited.

Table of Contents

Preface

The end of the Cold War, which had significantly shaped, or distorted, international relations and global security structures for nearly half a century, was inevitably taken to be the harbinger of radical change. In the initial enthusiasm of the Coalition action in the 1990-91 Gulf Conflict President Bush proclaimed a 'new world order' characterised by an international rule of law and effective law enforcement. The period of transition to a post-Cold War era of international relations and law has indeed been marked by radical developments and changes. Their character has, however, been neither so simple nor so naively optimistic as President Bush's anticipations seemed to suggest. Although the formal structure of the principal provisions of Chapters VII and VIII of the UN Charter is *prima facie* one of collective defence and security, the Cold War reality was a mixed system which combined these elements with a more 'traditional' balance of (Super)power system. The end of this system, with the eclipse of one of the Superpowers, imposed a practical burden of peace support upon the UN which it had always faced in theory but had not done so in practice. The post 1991 debacle in former Yugoslavia, Somalia, the African Great Lakes region and East Timor swiftly and painfully demonstrated that the UN organisation lacked the resources and infrastructure effectively to meet the enhanced demands being placed upon it. The idea that regional organisations and arrangements might fill the gap thus disclosed was prominent amongst the immediate responses to this problem and was most clearly set out in Boutros Boutros-Ghali's *Supplement to Agenda for Peace.* The role of the NATO led forces, IFOR, SFOR and KFOR in successive episodes of the former-Yugoslav crisis lent some support to this idea, but also illustrated some of its dangers. As the post-Cold War era has moved on, it has become manifest, as was indeed surely obvious *ab initio*, that whilst the regional options may have much to offer they can afford no simple or singular solution to the post-Cold War peace support crisis. It is the purpose of this book to explore both the potential and the limitations of regional agencies as significant peace support actors at the dawn of a new century and a new millennium.

The book has been written upon a trans-disciplinary basis, involving both international relations and international legal perceptions, proceeding upon the presumption that these disciplines are not ultimately separable. No attempt has been made to define the concept of a "region" but the self-definition implied by organisational membership has been accepted for the purposes of this analysis. The nature and the diversity of regional capacities are examined, as is the continuing importance of global control in arguments which can be traced back to the very genesis of the UN era. The ultimate conclusion that the key issue for the twenty first century is one of appropriate selection amongst options, within the meaning of article 53 of the UN Charter, need perhaps occasion little surprise. The nature of these options and the actual or potential processes of selection are, however, of vital importance in the initiation of a meaningful twenty first century defence and security debate. It is to this end that the present analysis is offered and whether its central thesis attracts agreement of dissent is of less importance than the generation of a serious debate upon an informed basis in preference to a grasping at whatever *ad hoc* 'solutions' may seem most immediately expedient in a moment of crisis.

H. McCoubrey   J. Morris
University of Hull, 17 September 1999

Acknowledgements

In preparing this book the authors have received much useful counsel and comment, especially, but not only, from personnel of the United Nations, National Governments, the various regional agencies, the International Peace Academy and members of the global academic and scholarly community. It would be both difficult and cumbersome to attempt a complete listing of those with whom the authors have consulted but it would be impossible not to mention some of those to whom a particular debt of gratitude is due. Particular thanks are due to: Martin Barber, Peter Boehm, James A. Burger, Arthur E. Dewey, Paul Durand, John Funstone, Max Johnstone, Bilahari Kausikan, Chetan Kumar, Tiyan Leong, Elisabeth Lindenmayer, David Malone, Sally Morphett, Chris Page, Peter Quilter, David Richardson, Leonard Sebastian, Elizabeth Spehar, Christopher Thomas, Ed Tsui, Margaret Voigt, Nancy Wildgoose and Philip Wilkinson.

In addition to these named individuals and organisations, the authors gratefully acknowledge the various financial and material assistance afforded to them in the course of their work upon this project by the University of Hull Research Fund, NATO and the British Academy. It remains only to say that none of the above people and organisations should necessarily be taken to share the authors' analyses and conclusions, all of which are offered entirely upon their own responsibility.

CHAPTER 1

The Concept of Collective Security

"[Collective security] began as a specialised concept, a technical term in the vocabulary of international relations. Collective security was the name given by the planners of a new world order after World War I to the system for the maintenance of peace that they intended as a replacement for the system commonly known as the balance of power. ... [However] since the concept gained prominence [it] has been appropriated as an honorific designation for virtually any and all multilateral activities that statesmen or scholars may regard, or wish to have regarded, as conducive to peace and order." [1]

Today one is as likely to find the term collective security applied to organisations such as NATO, the OSCE, ASEAN, the OAS and the OAU as to those to which it is more appropriate such as the League of Nations and the United Nations. For whilst the former group of organisations are clearly multinational in nature and are tasked, to varying degrees, with responsibilities in the area of regional security, it does not follow that they should necessarily be considered as examples of 'collective security'. The term must be lifted from the nomenclatural confusion which has come to exemplify a significant body of the international relations and security studies literature and the thinking which informs it and in particular it must be distinguished from 'collective defence', while acknowledging the often complex relationship which exists between the two concepts.[2] The apparent confusion between collective security and collective defence appears to have a number of explanatory factors, not least of which is that, at levels of both theory and practice, the defining and therefore distinguishing characters remain, at best, opaque. As Mark T. Clark notes:

"Advocates of collective security neither argue from a single political perspective nor promote a coherent, or at least consistent, view of what collective security is. Perhaps that is natural for an idea that has yet to take root in policy." [3]

This process of clarification, it should be stressed at the outset, is no mere matter of semantics. An organisation designed to perform a regional collective security role, or indeed a more general body designed to improve regional development and relations, is likely to possess a significantly different institutional framework, operational capacity and ethos to one intended as a collective defence organisation. In addition, regional organisations will inevitably be shaped by the political, economic and cultural dynamics peculiar to the part of the world in which they operate. This may appear as obvious as it is important and yet all too often it is overlooked. It follows from this that any work which seeks to study the relationship between global collective security and regional organisations must be clear as to the nature of the organisations with which it is dealing and sensitive to the dangers of espousing generalised solutions to specific problems.

COLLECTIVE SECURITY, COLLECTIVE DEFENCE
AND THE BALANCE OF POWER

Notwithstanding the need to distinguish between collective security and collective defence, it should be noted that both concepts share significant similarities beyond mere nomenclature. In particular, within both forms of organisation member states commit themselves to assist one another in case of attack and, in so doing, potential victims of aggression hope, and indeed expect, to increase their defensive strength – and hence increase their overall security – through concerted action. However, in the case of collective defence, the participant states invariably seek to defend themselves against a pre-defined enemy, be it actual or potential, and in so doing they are usually able to define a territorial sector within which they seek to operate. As a result, members of a defensive alliance are able to develop contingency plans based on a relatively limited number of conflict scenarios. In contrast, collective security is geared toward deterring and, where necessary, defeating acts of aggression by any and every state which offends against the particular peace the preservation of which constitutes the basic rationale of the organisation. The underlying ethos of collective security is premised upon the notion of the 'indivisibility of peace' which requires that states perceive all acts of aggression as being detrimental to their interests irrespective of whether they are directly targeted.[4]

Understood in these terms collective defence can be viewed as a means by which states, operating within the confines of a balance of power mechanism, seek to improve their security through collaborative action. Collective security on the other hand constitutes, at least theoretically, a rejection of simple balance of power logic and an embrace of an alternative mechanism which, its advocates proclaim, provides a more stable (and many would add morally superior) guarantee of peace. It should here be noted, however, that advocacy of collective security does not amount, as it is often alleged, to a blindness which prevents an appreciation of the importance of power in the international realm.[5] In fact the concept seeks, through co-operation, to direct power to ensure that potential aggressors are deterred from using force against other states. It is upon this notion of a manipulation of the balance of power that collective security is said to be able to provide a more stable international environment than can be secured through a process of the balancing of power involving collective defence alliances.[6]

The twentieth century has witnessed two attempts to attain peace through institutions which employ, to a substantial degree, the mechanism of collective security. The perceived failure of the first of these, the League of Nations, remains inextricably linked with the outbreak of the Second World War and led to a conclusion, however erroneous, on the part of many that collective security was itself a fundamentally flawed theory. Nevertheless, 1945 witnessed the establishment of a new global organisation, the United Nations, and this too sought to evoke the theory of collective security in its quest for peace. Yet despite their common theoretical underpinnings, the League of Nations and the United Nations adopted markedly different approaches to their prescribed task. In so doing they illustrate the breadth of the concept of collective security, whilst simultaneously demonstrating the centrality to such organisations of the notion of 'all against one' in accordance with which each member of the organisation must obligate itself to join a coalition to oppose any other member of the organisation which adopts a policy of aggression. According to Inis Claude, the original version of collective security as advocated by US President Woodrow Wilson, was envisaged as involving:

> "the creation of an international system in which the danger of aggressive warfare is to be met by the avowed determination of virtually all other states to exert pressure of every necessary variety – moral, diplomatic, economic and military – to frustrate attack upon any state ... The scheme is collective in the fullest sense; it purports to provide security *for* all states, *by* the action of all states, *against* all states that might challenge the existing order by the arbitrary unleashing of their power."[7]

The system to which Claude here refers may be referred to as one of 'ideal collective security' and may be seen to exhibit at least three distinguishing characteristics: firstly it is characterised by *certainty*. The 'avowed determination' to which Claude refers manifests itself in an institutional framework which places member states under a strict obligation to act against *any* aggressor state within their midst. This obligation constitutes the defining feature of collective security, the notion that, in the face of an attack upon one state, all other states within the organisation must rally to the victim's defence and in so doing must make secure the peace upon which the organisation is built and in the name of which it serves. The constitution of such an organisation should, therefore, spell out in unequivocal terms the obligations inherent in membership and the international acts deemed unacceptable. As Claude explains:

> "Collective security is a design for providing the certainty of collective action to frustrate aggression – for giving to the potential victim the reassuring knowledge, and conveying to the potential law-breaker the deterring conviction, that the resources of the community

will be mobilised against any abuse of national power. The ideal permits no *ifs* or *buts*."[8]

The second characteristic of ideal collective security organisations is that they should be able to call upon member states to utilise as many of the tools of international politics as are available to them. Member state must be willing to resort not only to moral and diplomatic censure on behalf of the endeavour, they must also be prepared to employ economic and ultimately military sanctions. This is not, of course, to suggest that collective security rejects non-military forms of conflict resolution, indeed collective security is often closely associated with mechanisms providing for pacific settlement of disputes and also with attempts to secure lower levels of armament. It is, nevertheless, central to a system of collective security that where the necessity arises, the organisation is capable of calling upon its membership to provide a military force of sufficient potency to deter or oppose military aggression. This characteristic, which we may refer to as *utility*, when coupled with that of *certainty*, presents collective security in its most unequivocal form and yet in so doing raises problems in terms of both attainment and execution, for if membership of a collective security organisation requires the acceptance of automatic and binding commitments to use all available means to oppose aggression irrespective of its perpetrator, states will be dissuaded from joining by the inevitability of conflict. Furthermore the inclination of states to accept theoretical obligations may very well exceed their willingness to live up to these burdens when required to do so in practice. Thus, whatever rhetorical commitments are made, states may calculate that involvement in collective action, particularly when such an undertaking involves economic and military sanctions, is too expensive and the rewards too abstract and meagre. Such an absolutist approach to collective security is likely therefore to experience difficulties in maintaining its prestige, legitimacy – and ultimately its operational efficiency – as it raises expectations only to be found lacking when called upon to perform its allotted role.

One final problem worthy of note with respect to both *utility* and *certainty* is that, even assuming that states are prepared to subscribe to a system of ideal collective security which seeks to deter aggression through the provision of a specific response to a prohibited act, such an organisation risks implicitly stipulating those actions which will not induce a remedial response. States wishing to pursue an expansionist policy may therefore be able to act in such a way that they gain their objectives without incurring censure from the collective security organisation. This may at first sight seem an overly doctrinaire or legalistic line of reasoning, but in fact such arguments in part lay behind the evasion of the imposition of sanctions against Japan following its invasion of China in 1936 [9] and behind the decision not to define what constitutes an 'act of aggression' within the terms article 39 of the Charter of the United Nations [10]. At the San Francisco Conference it was successfully argued that any attempt to provide such a definition would be doomed to failure, in part because it would not be possible to devise a definition which could cover every possible case – particularly given progress in the techniques of warfare – but also because any such definition would make it possible for a would-be aggressor to utilise the definition to their own ends and so to evade indictment. [11]

The final characteristic of ideal collective security, a consequence of its essentially introverted nature, is that of *universality* or *inclusivity*. In addition to the fact that the greater the size of the membership the greater the potential force that the organisation can wield, it should be recalled that collective security organisations seek to deter and oppose aggressors from *within* their ranks, and it therefore follows that the ideal version of such an institution counts as many states as possible amongst its membership. Unlike collective defence, collective security does not seek to make security preparations against a pre-identified state or group of states; it does not aim to address a specific threat to world peace, but rather seeks to preserve world order generally and to defend the prevailing territorial and political landscape against any state or group of states which would strive to overturn it. It follows that membership of the organisation should be as extensive as possible as it endeavours to provide security for all, against all. This requirement, however, raises significant practical problems, since the size of the membership of an organisation is likely to prove inversely proportionate to its ability to determine its objectives, functions and powers. Prospective members will, therefore, be forced into compromises likely to result in an institutional framework which, while not as ambitious as some may wish, is at least acceptable to the vast majority. In short, a 'lowest common denominator' mentality prevails. Moreover, assuming the establishment of an essentially universal organisation, difficulties prevail regarding the maintenance of internal organisational political cohesion, the sustenance of which is crucial to operational efficacy. An all encompassing membership is likely, therefore, to give rise to further problems since the ability of an organisation to deduce and express the collective will of its membership is also likely to be subject to a relationship of inverse proportionality to the number of members involved. While a general consensus over action is crucial to the longevity of any such organisation, the larger the membership the more elusive such agreement is likely to prove.

THE PREREQUISITE CONDITIONS OF COLLECTIVE SECURITY

Difficulties inherent in establishing a collective security mechanism approximating to the 'ideal type' are numerous, but in addition to these all forms of collective security organisation, 'ideal' or otherwise [12], are dependent for their success upon the existence of certain prerequisites. For collective security to operate successfully, it is essential that the international system be characterised by a sufficiently diffuse distribution of military power that no state has the capacity to stand against a coalition established by the community to oppose its aggressive behaviour. Collective security seeks not to oppose like force with like, as in a balance of power system, but to field overwhelming opposition to aggression. The presence of any state or group of states which can prevent the realisation of this aim undermines the collective endeavour. This crucial precondition creates obvious difficulties, not least because, uncertain of the commitment of fellow member states, those who seek to oppose aggression through the workings of a collective security mechanism are likely to have to rely upon a coalition of force which is smaller in actuality than in principle. The greater the power of the potential adversary, the more equivocal the support for the collective response is likely to be. Collective security may, therefore, be capable of policing and where necessary opposing the actions of lesser and medium powers, but is less so when faced with the expansionist intentions of a major power. Such logic underpinned the comment of the Mexican delegate at the UN's founding conference in San Francisco in 1945 that what was being established was a 'world order in which the mice could be stamped out but in which the lions would not be restrained.' [13] It should also be noted here that the ability of a collective security mechanism to deter aggression is dependant, as are all deterrence mechanisms, upon the rationality of those operating within the system. A state which does not rationally weigh up the odds may choose to commence with a policy of military hostility even when it is faced with an overwhelming adversary and certain defeat. In such situations conflict may be inescapable, though it is certain to prove futile and the *status quo* will be preserved. It is also worthy of note that in such circumstances collective security is likely to fare no worse, and potentially much better, than would a balance of power system.

    A second prerequisite of collective security is that there must exist agreement regarding the prevailing geo-political situation. The goal of collective security is inherently conservative; it seeks not simply to preserve peace but to preserve a particular peace which exists at a particular moment in time. It is, therefore, required that no power, and especially that no major power, pursue a foreign policy directed, for either ideological or geo-strategic reasons, to the overturning of the prevailing international order. As Henry Kissinger famously observed:

"Stability ... has commonly resulted not from a quest for peace but from a generally accepted legitimacy. 'Legitimacy' as here used should not be confused with justice. It means no more than an international agreement about the nature of workable agreements and about the permissible aims and methods of foreign policy. It implies an acceptance of the framework of the international order by all major powers, at least to the extent that no state is so dissatisfied that, like Germany after the Treaty of Versailles, it expresses its dissatisfaction in a revolutionary foreign policy. A legitimate order does not make conflicts impossible, but it limits their scope. Wars may occur, but they will be fought *in the name of* the existing structure and the peace which follows will be justified as a better expression of the 'legitimate', general consensus."[14]

While Kissinger's conclusion may have been reached in specific reference to a system of peace maintenance based upon a 'concert' of the great powers, it is no less applicable to both a balance of power system and collective security. Indeed, the very nature of the latter makes, as the experience of the League of Nations demonstrates all too vividly, the dedication of the major powers an indispensable pre-condition. It also requires that the prevailing peace is one the continuation which states, and in particular the great powers, deem as being in their interest. This brings us to the third and final pre-requisite of collective security.

The concept of collective security requires that the major powers 'enjoy a minimum of political solidarity and moral community.' [15] It is crucial that they exhibit unanimity amongst themselves in the name of the collective organisation and the particular peace which it serves, and that they be willing to act together in the name of the international community which they lead. States, and in particular the major powers, must be prepared to act in such a way that, in the words of Charles and Clifford Kupchan, 'national self-interest becomes equated with, but not subjugated to, the welfare and stability of the international community.' [16] Collective security requires that states perceive peace as being indivisible and that they understand the international system to be one within which, in the words of Inis Claude 'the fabric of human society has become so tightly woven that a breach anywhere threatens disintegration everywhere ... collective security demands what is essentially a factual agreement; it then imposes a related normative framework: loyalty to the world community.' [17] In less abstract terms this aspect of collective security was well captured in the words of the Haitian delegate who, when addressing the Assembly of the League of Nations on the issue of the Italian invasion of Abyssinia commented that "Great or small, strong or weak, near or far, white or coloured, let us never forget that one day we may be someone's Ethiopia." [18]

COLLECTIVE SECURITY AND THE BALANCE OF POWER:
STRENGTHS AND WEAKNESSES

Advocates of collective security suggest that it reduces the uncertainties associated with alliance formation and in so doing also increases the probability that any aggressor will be faced with a preponderant, rather than an approximately equal, opposing force thus more effectively deterring aggression. This argument, in addition to revealing the paucity of the criticism that collective security pays insufficient account of the importance of power, also points to what is often cited as a fundamental flaw in balance of power theory, namely its inability to satisfactorily address the contradiction inherent in the relationship between effectiveness and symmetry. Under a system of balance of power, in order for one side of the balance to feel that its security is being effectively maintained, it is required that the balance be characterised by a state of disequilibrium, that is, that there exists an imbalance within which one side holds a sufficient preponderance of power to deter any potential attack by the other. Such a situation results in acute insecurity for the other side, yet where the balance is a genuine one characterised by symmetry, neither party feels effectively secure since either may consider attack a viable option where the odds are approximately even. A collective security mechanism, in contrast to one dependant upon a simple balance of power, seeks to manipulate the balance to ensure that preponderant power is permanently amassed in favour of the maintenance of the accepted *status quo*.

It is argued that collective security further reduces the potential for aggressive acts through the manner in which it serves to increase transparency and in so doing assists in the identification of aggressor states, both actual and potential. Collective security also benefits from an ability not only to institutionalise international co-operation, but actually to promote it. In this argument lies the counter to a common criticism of collective security, namely that it can only work when there exists among the great powers a high prevalence of co-operation and that at such times collective security is not, in any case, required. The grounds for mounting a defence against such a criticism are to be found in the substantial body of neo-liberal institutionalist literature, which suggests that international institutions, including collective security mechanisms, whilst initially requiring such co-operation, subsequently come to normalise and thus perpetuate co-operative behaviour. [19] This is achieved through a mechanism which, accepted by participating member states, seeks not only to constrain behaviour, but also to shape future expectations. States are thus socialised into conforming with normatively prescribed patterns of behaviour, the primary aim of which is to reduce conflict through the prohibition of acts of aggression between states.

This argument does not, however, answer satisfactorily the question of how states are to be enticed into such a mechanism at the outset. Why should states agree to constrain their behaviour and to reject the option of recourse to force? The answer can only be provided through the establishment of an order which satisfies the aspirations of states (and once again privilege must here be given, however reluctantly, to the position of the great powers) at least to the extent than the vast majority are willing to work within the system rather than resorting to force in an attempt to overturn it in pursuit of their perceived national interests. The success of the venture must, however, negotiate an initial hurdle which requires something of a diplomatic 'leap of faith' on the part of participating states, for if collective security is to succeed it requires that member states adopt and pursue policies based upon the notion that their security is guaranteed by the collective venture of which they are a part. If they fail to do this, through, for example, entry into a covert alliance directed against a particular state or group of states, their actions are likely to undermine the collective security mechanism, so reducing the probability of success. Hence, states must act upon the basis that the system works, not because they have evidence of this, but because to do otherwise is to ensure failure. In the world of power politics and national security states must act with a degree of prudence which, in the absence of guarantees, mitigates against participation in such risky ventures; collective security, at least in its uncompromising 'ideal' form, asks too much of the responsible statesman.

Contesting the claimed benefits of collective security are those who argue for a continuing provision of security through the traditional means of defensive alliances and who criticise collective security as being both unfeasible and, in certain situations, dangerously destabilising. According to Richard Betts:

> "The protean character of collective security reflects the fact that many who endorse it squirm when the terms are specified or applied to awkward cases. This has occurred with all incarnations of the idea. The main problem is the gap between the instinctive appeal of the idea in liberal cultures as they settle epochal conflicts, and its inherent defects in relations among independent states as they move from peace toward war."[20]

The first and in many ways most fundamental criticism to be levelled at collective security, indeed a criticism of the whole of what E. H. Carr so notoriously termed the utopian approach to the discipline of international relations, is that it is based upon a notion of what *ought* to be, rather than upon one of what *is* actually attainable. In his famous critique of the inter-war period Carr wrote:

> "It took its rise from the great and disastrous war ... The passionate desire to prevent war determined the whole initial course and direction of the study. ... It has been in the initial stage in which wishing prevails over thinking, generalisation over observation, and in

which little attempt is made at a critical analysis of existing facts or available means. In this stage, attention is concentrated almost exclusively on the end to be achieved."[21]

Through the prioritisation of desire and intention over attainable reality, proponents of collective security fail to recognise that it could only function successfully in circumstances in which it will never be called upon to act to maintain peace, and that where major threats arise the edifice crumbles and conflict and insecurity ensue. The logic of the argument is as simple as it is persuasive, namely that where states are in a relationship in which co-operation is possible, conflict is unlikely, yet where conflict is a significant likelihood the prospect for co-operation is, at best, limited. While counter-arguments exist [22], this powerful critique of collective security is one which even its most ardent advocates find hard to deflect, particularly in situations in which the vital interests of major powers come into conflict.

Critics of collective security continue their assault by suggesting that, in the unlikely scenario in which a collective security mechanism does act to oppose aggression, it will be less effective in so doing than states acting, either unilaterally of multilaterally, within a balance of power mechanism. Within a balance of power system states are constantly acting to ensure their own security, either alone or in partnership with allies, investing time, money, and diplomatic energy in such endeavours. Such preparations are incompatible with a system of collective security within which no state can be singled out in advance as an aggressor and no state can be treasured as an ally in concert with which others pledge in advance to act. Within a system of collective security, therefore, states must act in an *ad hoc* manner, as and when circumstances demand. According to Henry Kissinger '[n]o arrangement would be more likely to create conditions in which one nation can dominate ... For if everybody is allied with everybody, nobody has a special relationship with anybody. It is the ideal situation for the most ruthless seeking to isolate potential victims' [23] Moreover, given that collective security seeks to act through a coalition of forces, its effectiveness is further reduced, with the total force contributed likely to be less than the sum of its parts. While it is true to say that alliances within a balance of power also work on the basis of coalition forces, within formalised defensive alliance structures the investments noted above in terms of time, money and political will serve to develop an infra-structure likely to mitigate against the negative aspects of such coalition action. In contrast, the forces fielded in the name of collective security, *ad hoc* and inevitably ill-prepared as it must necessarily be, must work to overcome problems of co-operation and interoperability in a conflict environment which is far from conducive to such a process.

A second criticism of collective security is that it is an inherently legalistic, conservative and *status quo* oriented mechanism, the resulting inflexibility of which is ill-suited to an international environment governed by the 'laws of politics' [24] and characterised by a constantly changing distribution of power. The dangers inherent in adopting an approach incapable of adapting to the mercurial nature of international politics is well captured by Inis Claude in commenting that:

> "To adopt a rigid formulation of future policy in international relations is to ignore the infinite variety of circumstances, the flux of contingency, the mutability of situations, which characterise that field and to abdicate the function of applying statesmanlike rationality to problems as they arise."[25]

While collective security seeks to preserve a particular peace embodying a particular territorial settlement, it is invariably the case that within such a settlement, there will be a number of dissatisfied states which seek to overturn the *status quo*. In situations where states opt to pursue what Kissinger refers to as 'revolutionary foreign policies' and where they choose to do so by non-pacific means, collective security requires that states oppose such action. However, third parties to a conflict may be called upon to make judgements as to the merits of a case which, over the passage of time, have faded and become far from clear, thus jeopardising the collective mechanism. As Roland Stromberg comments,

> "The problem is not, as the Wilsonians imagined, one of suppressing an infrequent case of diabolism, a clear case of law and decency *versus* the criminal aggressor. ... To determine the aggressor is really to decide who is the bad nation. And a general law can never do this."[26]

Moreover, if a collective security system is perceived as being insufficiently flexible to be able to accommodate legitimate calls for the adjustment of the *status quo*, third parties may be further disinclined to stand by their collective security commitments. Even more threateningly, where the dissatisfied state is a great power, perhaps one defeated at the culmination of the most recent of 'epochal conflicts' the termination of which gave rise to the existing order, the collective security mechanism may become unsustainable in its original form as the dissatisfied power regenerates and comes to assume once more its great power status.

Not wholly unconnected to the above point, the automicity and universality required by collective security is also problematic. Collective security requires of states that they oppose aggression wherever and by whomsoever and it does not allow for calculations of national interest in the same way that a balance of power mechanism does. As Inis Claude writes:

> "If collective security is to operate impartially, governments and peoples must exhibit a fundamental flexibility of policy and sentiment. France must be as ready to defend Germany as Belgium against aggression, and Britain must be equally willing to join in collective sanctions against the United States or the Soviet Union. In short, collective secu-

rity recognises no traditional friendships and no inveterate enmities, and permits no alliances *with* or alliances *against*." [27]

The willingness of states to make such commitments, and to stand by them once made, is not demonstrated by historical experience, but rather, as Hans J. Morgenthau states with regard to the League of Nations, history suggests that collective action was (and will) only be undertaken 'in the rare instances when either the interests of the great powers among its members were not affected or the common interests of the most influential among them seemed to require it'. [28] Moreover, a further consequence of this universality and automicity is that it may serve to escalate conflict, with major global powers being dragged in to small scale, regional disagreements which could, in other circumstances, have been left to burn themselves out.

> "... Indeed collective security has not been notable for any keen awareness of potential sources of trouble; it has shown a rather lamentable tendency to wait until some breach of peace occurs and then pounce on it with 'punitive' action. It has always been known that apparently trivial disputes *may* involve the danger of a big war. But collective security seems to assert dogmatically that this is true of every case. ... Force is not a universal panacea, but a dangerous remedy which ought to be reserved for certain rare and otherwise incurable maladies." [29]

Finally, with regard to the automicity inherent in collective security, it is worth noting that such advanced commitment as is required, raises questions not only of prudence and political judgement, but also of democratic governance, since a statesman may be obligated to undertake action which is opposed by the domestic electorate which (s)he represents. Thus while, through the (relatively brief) course of its history, collective security has come to be associated with liberal-democracy, there is in this sense at least, a profound contradiction between the ideals which such an ideology encapsulates and the demands of collective security.

COLLECTIVE SECURITY IN PRACTICE

The various difficulties associated with formulating a collective security system approximating to that which Claude refers to as 'ideal' in type suggest the need to develop mechanisms which place less onerous burdens upon member states, but which nevertheless derive the benefits inherent in a collectivised approach to peace rather than one which is solely dependant upon a balance of power. A system which fetters states in regard to security policy, which commits them to act when there may exist strong political and strategic reasons for doing otherwise, and yet which lacks efficacy in the realm of military action and ultimately is unable to guarantee security for even its most loyal participants, is not one which can be suggested as offering a genuine alternative to defensive alliances operating within a balance of power. However, it is possible to adapt the 'ideal' in order to produce a system which is at once both more effective and flexible and yet which is able to institutionalise (and ultimately therefore to increase the possibility of normalising) non-forceful modes of dispute settlement and to mobilise a preponderance of force to oppose aggression where necessary. Such an organisation seeks to invoke the spirit of collective security whilst accepting and, as far as possible accommodating, the tendency of great powers to act not in unison but in opposition through a balancing of power.

While the theory of 'ideal' collective security does not allow for the existence of collective defence organisations – for to do so would be to identify adversaries prior to any act of aggression – such defensive arrangements are not in themselves contrary to the spirit of collective security subject, of course, to their renunciation in word and deed of any aggressive intent. Just as in almost any system of municipal law a victim of assault, prior to the arrival of the police, is permitted to use reasonable force in self defence and is entitled to receive assistance in so doing from third parties, so within a collective security mechanism states may act to defend themselves, either unilaterally or acting in concert with others. In the latter situation the collective defence may be based upon an *ad hoc* arrangement, but equally it may involve recourse to a pre-existing formalised defensive alliance. Such an arrangement, allowing for the operation of collective defence organisations within a broader framework of collective security, is found in the case of the United Nations under article 51. [30]

A further dilution of the 'ideal' notion of collective security presents itself in the accommodation of a 'concert' based element to the provision of security. [31] According to Charles and Clifford Kupchan:

> "Concert-based collective security relies on a small group of major powers to guide the operation of ... [the] ... security structure. This design reflects power realities – an essential condition for a workable structure – while capturing the advantages offered by collective security." [32]

Concerts thus replace the *universality* of 'ideal' collective security with an exclusivity of great power membership and in so doing (and while acting as a behavioural yoke upon those within) also reject introversion and seek instead to impose their numerically limited collective will upon states outside of their number which pursue aggressive policies. Concert based systems are also less likely to adhere to the principle of certainty which characterises collective security in its 'ideal' form, since states enjoying great powers status are more likely than others to demand the flexibility of policy which this curtails. Concerts, therefore, proceed on the basis of negotiation between the great powers, rather than in accordance with pre-ordained rules and it follows from this that the membership may decide upon any form of response ranging from military engagement to total inaction. Voting systems are likely to be inapplicable, with consensus being required in order to maintain the cohesion of a body which, given the status of the individual members, cannot function successfully other than on the basis of unanimity.

As with 'ideal' collective security, concert based systems, while enjoying significant advantages in certain regards – namely their sensitivity to the dynamics of power and their inherent flexibility of response – also exhibit certain shortcomings and these are likely to be far more manifest in today's world of relatively democratic international relations than during the high point of concert governance immediately following the Napoleonic Wars. Flexibility of response may prove to be somewhat double-edged in its implications, since it undermines the deterrent effect of a certain unequivocal response. Perhaps more significantly though, concerts, through their attempt to impose the judgement and will of the few upon the actions of the many, lack the legitimacy required of a system of global governance for the twenty-first century. In a post-colonial world of sovereign equals, this form of overt imposition is no longer politically acceptable and it is at best questionable as to whether it is practically sustainable.

It follows from the preceding discussion that while neither 'ideal' collective security nor a concert system are either sustainable or desirable, both have significant attributes and should, therefore, be harnessed as major components of a collective security mechanism which also allows states to exercise a right of self defence, either individually or collectively. It is this form of hybrid system which is enshrined in the Charter of the United Nations, itself the product a process of development which can be clearly traced back, *inter alia*, to the League of Nations and the Concert of Europe before. The United Nations Security Council, with 'primary responsibility for international peace and security' bestowed upon it by article 25 of the Charter, functions in a manner not dissimilar to a concert, comprising as it does the permanent members which were, at the time of the organisation's founding in 1945, the principal victorious powers and ten (originally seven) non-permanent members chosen from among the General Assembly. Nevertheless, in theory at least, the Security Council is under a strict obligation to act on behalf of the whole membership when carrying out its duties and while in practice some may question the adherence of key members of the Council to this principle, it is absolute under the terms of the Charter and to this end, states may, in accordance with article 31, address the Council over security issues where their interests are 'specially affected'. The clear separation of powers between the Security Council and the General Assembly was established, the experience of the League fresh in the memories of the drafting parties, to ensure that 'prompt and effective' action could be taken when and where necessary, yet the relationship between the two organs has often been characterised by tension and suspicion, a trait which is not least notable today.

A further dilution of 'ideal' collective security is found in the discretion which the Security Council enjoys in carrying out its duties under the Charter. While the mandatory language of article 39 states that the '... Security Council shall determine the existence of any threat to the peace, breach of the peace, or act of aggression ...' the political rather than legal nature of the Council clearly presupposes an ability to exercise political and strategic judgement in making such a determination. The Council accordingly enjoys discretion in making such a determination, but once made, it is under a duty to take the enforcement measures necessary to restore international peace and security. Such an interpretation of the Council's role and powers is supported by the *travaux prépartoires*, not least in significance amongst which is the rejection of any inclusion of a definition of aggression against which the conduct of states could be assessed. [33]

The UN system is also at variance with the theory of collective security, at least in its unadulterated form, in that it makes specific provision for the existence of collective defence arrangements under article 51 and, less problematically in theoretical terms, 'regional arrangements or agencies' under the provisions of Chapter VIII of the Charter. As will be discussed throughout the course of this book, numerous such organisations exist and all claim in their founding documents to operate in conformity with the UN Charter. What is worthy of discussion at this juncture, however, is the manner in which these various hybridous organisations aspire to perform roles which include elements of both collective security and collective defence and in so doing demonstrate the fluid and at times overlapping practical nature of the two concepts. To recognise here the inter-linked manner in which these two concepts come to manifest themselves in practice is not to contradict the need, expressed at the outset of this chapter, to distinguish between the two in theory. Rather it is to acknowledge that, in the absence of a practice which can accommodate theoretical absolutes, they often take operational form within the same composite institutional framework. A brief consideration of some of the organisations to be discussed later in this text will suffice to clarify this point.

As has already been made clear, the United Nations, whilst the organisation most obviously developed in accordance with the principles of collective security, also seeks to utilise other mechanisms, not least the balance of power which is so often depicted as the antithesis of collective security, in its attempts to stabilise the international environment. The UN privileges the role of the great powers, enshrining it within a mechanism which in many ways approximates to that of a concert, and allows states, in practice if not in the language of the Charter, considerable freedom in exercising the right, either individually or collectively, of self-defence. The Charter also provides, under article 53, for the UN to 'utilise ... regional arrangements [and] agencies' which, in the absence of a definition of such, in practice has involved regional organisations with a wide range of remits and roles, including those originally designed to undertake a wholly defensive function.

The North Atlantic Treaty Organisation (NATO) is one such organisation which, initially established to fulfil a defensive role in the face of a perceived threat from the Soviet Union and its Warsaw Pact allies during the Cold War, has now expanded its operational remit to that of a much more broadly based security institution. [34] Under article 5 of the North Atlantic Treaty, signatory states agree, in the event of an armed attack against one or more of their number, to assist the victim state(s), by military means if necessary, in order to restore peace in the Atlantic area as defined by article 6. During the more than four decades of the Cold War the conflict scenario envisaged by NATO was clear, and extensive provision and planning was carried out in order to deter possible Soviet aggression. This task constituted the totality of the alliance's role, indeed within the context of the Cold War, it would have been unacceptable for NATO to perform any wider security function, as bi-polar tensions precluded either side in the conflict from fulfilling any wider role allotted to them. Sensitivities were such that any involvement by NATO (or the Warsaw Pact) in conflicts arising outside of the immediate parameters of the Cold War would have risked the possibility of dangerously destabilising the international order and as such the defensive alliances most closely associated with the Cold War were effectively disbarred from any form of participation in UN action under Chapter VIII.

The end of the Cold War resulted in a radical transformation in the international environment and no where is this more clearly evident than in the manner in which NATO has come to expand its operational remit. With the collapse of the Soviet Union and a much enfeebled Russia beholden to its former western adversaries for financial and political support, NATO currently enjoys a freedom to pursue a wider political and strategic agenda than ever before in its history. According to NATO's Strategic Concept agreed at the North Atlantic Council meeting in Washington D.C. in April 1999,

"The Alliance is committed to a broad approach to security, which recognises the importance of political, economic, social and environmental factors in addition to the indispensable defence dimension. This broad approach forms the basis for the Alliance to accomplish its fundamental security tasks effectively, and its increasing effort to develop effective cooperation with other European and Euro-Atlantic organisations as well as the United Nations." [35]

This more expansive security role, including cooperation with the United Nations, is most evident in the assistance which NATO provided to UNPROFOR in the former-Yugoslavia and in the UN mandated but NATO dominated IFOR/SFOR operation in Bosnia-Herzegovina. A still more radical departure from its traditional role and ethos can be seen in recent NATO action in Kosovo which took place in the absence of a UN mandate and in the face of Russian opposition and which clearly demonstrates the Alliance's determination to ensure and secure – within Europe at least – a post-Cold War international environment which accords with NATO's political and strategic values and interests. Such operations, undertaken as they have been beyond the territorial limits of article 6 of the North Atlantic Treaty, suggests a future role for the Alliance as a 'security exporter' rather than as the mere defensive arrangement which was initially envisaged by the organisation's founders.

The Organisation of American States (OAS), with a history spanning almost two-hundred years, has in its own way in more recent times experienced a change in role no less profound than that of NATO. [36] Given the breadth of the purposes and principles stipulated in the Charter of the OAS, the organisation cannot accurately be termed either one of collective security or collective defence, for while the Charter bestows upon the organisation both such roles [37], it also provides in articles 2 and 3 for cooperation in areas such as political, economic, social and cultural development. The organisation should therefore be understood as one the aims of which are to promote western hemispheric cooperation and development in a variety of areas. The espousal of these various objectives within the Charter of the OAS has, throughout the organisation's history, given rise to considerable discord among member states as to which of the activities should receive priority, disharmony which has primarily taken the form of disagreement between the Southern and Central American states on the one hand and the United States on the other.

During the earliest phases of the development of the Inter-American system the USA sought to expand commercial relations with its southern neighbours and to this end to develop within the system means of pacific dispute resolution and defence against extra-hemispheric intervention. While the Latin American states showed general enthusiasm for these policies, concerns over European intervention soon came to be overshadowed by a fear of the Great Power to the north as it sought hemispheric security through pursuit of the Monroe Doctrine and the even more invasive Roosevelt Corollary. A multilateralisation of the former and an abandonment of the latter served, to some extent, to placate fears during a period of relative harmony of interests which ran throughout the 1930s and extended until the end of World War II. Divergent goals and conflicting interests emerged once more, however, as, with the onset of the Cold War, the US sought to manipulate the OAS in pursuit of its own security concerns, while the Latin American states sought economic development through regional cooperation. A degree of convergence arose during the latter half of the 1960s as Washington sought to induce governmental compliance through the provision of military, economic and social assistance as part of its continuing endeavours to prevent the spread of communism to the Americas. With South America suitably 'secured', the US conducted its Central America policy on a unilateral basis, not infrequently through the use of covert and at times overt force, but with very little recourse to the Inter-American system. The end of the Cold War had a profound impact upon the OAS, as did the process of hemispheric democratisation which preceded it, but which is not wholly independent of it. In a fundamentally changed security environment military concerns have given way to other challenges, in themselves no less daunting, involving tackling endemic poverty, securing democratic government and combating organised crime, much of it related to the trade in illegal drugs. That these are the issues which now dominate the OAS agenda is testament to the extent to which the organisation has had to adapt during its long history, and while the shadow cast from the north looms as large as ever, it is hoped that, in the absence of a global adversary, the USA can play a more positive role at the outset of the twenty-first century.

As a single factor – the proximity of the USA – has served to condition almost all aspects of the OAS' existence, so colonialism has shaped that of the Organisation of African Unity (OAU). [38] As with the OAS, the OAU seeks to operate neither as a collective security or defence organisation, but rather as an institution designed to promote continental cooperation and unity on a far broader basis. Article 2(1) of the Charter of the OAU states that:

> "The Organization shall have the following purposes:
> a. To promote the unity and solidarity of the African states;
> b. To co-operate and intensify their collaboration and efforts to achieve a better life for the peoples of Africa;
> c. To defend their sovereignty, their territorial integrity and independence;
> d. To eradicate all forms of colonialism from Africa; and
> e. To promote international co-operation, having due regard to the Charter of the United Nations and the Universal Declaration of Human Rights."

In the manner in which the OAU has sought, often with limited success, to pursue these purposes the import of the continent's colonial past is pervasive, to the extent that even the states which make up the organisation are territorially constituted along colonially determined lines. [39] The desire to rid itself of extra-continental interference goes much of the way to explaining many of the principles central to the operation of the OAU, including, in accordance with article 3(2), non-interference in the internal affairs of states and non-alignment with political blocs, enshrined in article 3(7) of the OAU Charter. Paradoxically, the instability inherent in a state system imposed by former colonial powers often made non-alignment impossible, as governments struggling to maintain control over states which were at once both factious and factitious sought support from superpower patrons only too willing to provide it as part of their wider Cold War ideological ambitions. [40] The OAU thus failed to prevent external penetration of Africa, though this took place in the form of 'assistance' to governments rather than overt conquest, as in the previous phase of continental history. The organisation also proved powerless to act in the face of African conflict at both an inter and intra-state level, as Cold War machinations too powerful to oppose came to dominate political practice.

The above factors fuelled and combined with other problems, such as poverty, debt, corrupt government and grossly unfavourable climatic conditions to prevent the realisation of the ideals spelt out in the Charter of the OAU. The end of the Cold War does not represent a panacea for Africa's ills, but rather an opportunity to begin to address them in an environment more conducive to their cure. The ending of Apartheid also had a significant impact on the African, and in particular the southern-African, political and strategic environment, transforming a major security concern into a powerful potential asset. Much here depends upon the manner in which South Africa meets the challenges, both domestic and external, of the post-Apartheid era and, in the context of southern Africa, upon on the acclimatisation of neighbouring states to a radically different sub-regional setting. Despite these unquestionably beneficial changes, at present the much vaunted notion of 'African solutions to African problems' places too great a burden upon an inadequate organisational infrastructure and too little emphasis upon the possibility of genuinely symbiotic collaboration, but the OAU and other, sub-regional, actors such as the South African Development Community (SADC) and the Economic Community of West African States (ECOWAS), acting in collaboration with the UN and with other more affluent and developed regional actors, possess at least the potential to address the varied and various problems which face their continent. With regard to its security role, the vastness of the continent and the diversity of the membership almost certainly precludes the OAU from acting as an emergency crisis management mechanism and limitations in terms of operation capacity disbar a direct military role, but the organisation can act constructively as a political forum and possibly through the provision, subject to UN Charter restrictions, of continent-wide mandates to sub-regional actors involved in peace keeping and enforcement.

The Cold War had a significant impact upon the region of Southeast Asia and yet in many ways it differed markedly from those of the regions briefly discussed above. [41] As did Africa, though clearly not Western Europe and the Americas, Southeast Asia fell outside of any agreed sphere of influence during the Cold War and as such governments there, while often espousing the principles of non-alignment, found themselves subject to the covert and overt influence of the Cold War protagonists. Unlike any other region however, for the nations of Southeast Asia the Cold War was, in many regards, a three rather than two-way confrontation, with the People's Republic of China a significant additional actor. Given these factors and the additional problems inherent in the complex and often unstable internal make-ups of the states concerned, Southeast Asia proved an inappropriate venue for a regional collective defence organisation, as the rapid effective demise of the South East Asia Treaty Organization (SEATO), premised upon Western European conceptions of Cold War security requirements, aptly demonstrated. Within the context of Southeast Asian relations such defensive alliances were viewed as placing too great an emphasis upon the military aspect of security while failing to address equally – if not more – important issues such as economic development and internal stabilisation. Moreover, through their prior identification of adversaries, collective defence organisations have a divisive impact which runs contrary to the consensual political culture of Southeast Asia.

The Association of Southeast Asian Nations (ASEAN) thus affords a rather different perspective upon the potential for regional peace support from that offered by traditional military alliances, its founding document, the Bangkok Declaration, avoiding any reference to either collective security or collective defence. The Association conceptualises security in far broader terms and, through the much vaunted consensus based 'ASEAN way', has sought to develop consensus and in so doing to build peace and confidence for the aversion of any possible regional conflict, whilst also seeking to avert external intervention in the region. The establishment in 1993 of the ASEAN Regional Forum (ARF) in many ways represents the extension of the ASEAN way into a somewhat more overt security structure which includes the overwhelming majority of powers in, or with an interest in, the region including the USA, the PRC and Japan. While the ARF is somewhat more focused upon traditional security issues, it should not be viewed as a fully-fledged collective security organisation, still less a defensive alliance, rather as an extension of the process of peace and confidence building which has been the most notably achievement of the ASEAN way. As the situation in East Timor in the late summer of 1999 demonstrates, neither ASEAN nor the ARF provide the region of Southeast Asian with a workable military institution capable of dealing with conflicts, be they intra or inter-state, which have developed to the level of armed hostilities and a collective response to such is only possible on an *ad hoc* basis. While this is a significant shortcoming, it should be noted that

ASEAN's achievement's have not been inconsiderable and the Association's contribution to the development and stabilisation of the region should not be underestimated.

The brief foregoing discussion demonstrates the diversity of regional organisations, each having been shaped by a complex combination of factors specific to the region in which it functions. The aims, practices, strengths, weaknesses and future potential of each institution cannot be fully understood outside of the unique context within which it has developed and now operates. No organisation exists in a form which accords to the ideal theoretical models discussed during this chapter, but this should not be taken to suggest that the models are themselves without value, but rather that no single model can account for the diversity of experience and circumstance that such adherence would require. The distinct conceptual underpinnings of collective security and collective defence, however, are significant insofar as the perception of an organisation's membership that they are creating and participating in one or other form of endeavour signifies not only its intended purpose, but also its likely operational capacity and future potential. That these are likely to differ widely from organisation to organisation is a theme to which we shall return throughout this text.

NOTES

1. I.L. Claude Jnr, *Swords into Plowshares* (4th Ed.), (McGraw-Hill: New York, 1984), p.247
2. The idea of a 'security community', which Karl Deutsch defines as existing when, between a group of states, 'there is [a] real assurance that the members of that community will not fight each other physically, but will settle their disputes in some other way', will not be discussed as the 'assurance' to which Deutsch refers involves a set of normative assumptions not inherent in the concept of collective security. See K. W. Deutsch, A. Burrell and R. A. Kann, *Political community in the North Atlantic Area: international organization in the light of historical experience*, (Princeton: Princeton University Press, 1997).
3. M. T. Clark, 'The Trouble with Collective Security', p. 237.
4. For further discussion of the distinctions between collective defence and collective security see A. Wolfers, *Discord and Collaboration: Essays on International Politics*, (Baltimore: Johns Hopkins Press, 1962), pp.181-204.
5. For a general critique of the theoretical underpinnings of collective security see E.H. Carr, *The Twenty Years Crisis 1919-1939*, (Basingstoke: Macmillan, 1991); H. J. Morgenthau, *Politics Among Nations: The Struggle for Power and Peace*, (New York: McGraw Hill, 1993). For a more specific critique of collective security see R.M. Stromberg, 'The Idea of Collective Security', *Journal of the History of Ideas*, Vol. 17(2), 1956, pp. 250-63; R.K. Betts, 'Systems for Peace or Causes of War? Collective Security, Arms Control, and the New Europe', *International Security*, Vol. 17(1), 1992, pp.5-43 and M.T. Clark, 'The Trouble with Collective Security', *Orbis*, Vol. 39(2), 1995, pp.237-58
6. See below for a discussion of the merits and demerits of collective security and balance of power mechanisms.
7. I.L. Claude, *Power and International Relations*, (New York: Random House, 1962), p.110.
8. I.L. Claude, *Swords into Plowshares* , p.252-3

9. In this case the Lytton Commission, established by the League of Nations to investigate the Chinese claim that Japan had acted in violation of its obligations under the League Covenant, effectively argued that Japan had not so acted because it had not committed an act of war. See E. H. Carr, *International Relations Between the World Wars (1919 – 1939)* (London: Macmillan, 1967) pp.167-70.

10. See Chapter 2 for further discussion of the provisions of the Charter of the United Nations.

11. See L. M. Goodrich and E. Hambro, *Charter of the United Nations: Commentary and Documents* (2nd Ed), (London: Stevens and Sons Limited: 1949), pp.262-4.

12. See later for discussion of collective security mechanisms which deviate from the 'ideal' model discussed here.

13. Quoted I.L. Claude, *Power and International Relations*, p. 159.

14. H. A. Kissinger, *A World Restored: Metternich, Castlereagh and the Problems of Peace 1812-22*, (Boston: Houghton Mifflin Co., 1957), p.1.

15. K. Thompson, 'Collective Security Re-examined', *American Political Science Review*, Vol. 27(3), 1953, p. 761.

16. C.A. & C. A. Kupchan, 'Concerts, Collective Security and the Future of Europe', *International Security*, Vol. 16(1), 1991, pp. 124-5.

17. I.L. Claude, *Swords into Plowshares* , pp. 250-1.

18. Quoted in F. P. Walters, *A History of the League of Nations*, Vol. II (London: Oxford University Press, 1952), p. 653.

19. For an elaboration of this debate, see 'The false Promise of International Institutions', *International Security*, Vol.19(3), 1994/95, pp.5-47; R.O. Keohane and L.L. Martin, 'The Promise of Institutionalist Theory', *International Security*, Vol. 20(1), 1995, pp.39-52 and C.A. Kupchan and C.A. Kupchan, 'The Promise of Collective Security', *International Security*, Vol. 20(1), 1995, pp.52-61.

20. R.K. Betts, 'Systems for Peace or Causes of War? Collective Security, Arms Control, and the New Europe', p.6

21. E.H. Carr, *The Twenty Years Crisis 1919-1939*, p.8

22. See C.A. and C.A. Kupchan, 'The Promise of Collective Security'.

23. H. Kissinger, cited in R.K. Betts, 'Systems for Peace or Causes of War? Collective Security, Arms Control, and the New Europe', p. 18.

24. See For a famous exposition of this view see H. J. Morgenthau, *Politics Among Nations: The Struggle for Power and Peace*, pp. 4-16.

25. I.L. Claude, *Swords into Plowshares* , p.278.

26. Stromberg, 'The Idea of Collective Security', p. 255.

27. I.L. Claude, op cit., p.255.

28. H.J. Morgenthau, cited in C. Archer, *International Organizations*, (London: Routledge, 1992), p.83.

29. R. Stromberg, 'The Idea of Collective Security', pp. 258-9.

30. See Chapter Two for a detailed discussion of the UN Charter system.

31. For further discussion, and with particular reference to the Concert of Europe, see I. Clark, *The hierarchy of states: Reform and resistance in the international order*, (Cambridge: Cambridge University Press, 1989).

32. C.A. and C.A. Kupchan, 'The Promise of Collective Security', p. 116.

33. See above and L. M. Goodrich and E. Hambro, *Charter of the United Nations*, pp.264-72.

34. For a detailed discussion of European security architecture see Chapter 4.

35. NATO Document NAC-S(99)65, *The Alliance's Strategic Concept*, 24 April 1999, Paragraph 25.

36. For a detailed discussion of the Inter-American system see Chapter 5. NOTE: All references to the Charter of the OAS refer to the 1997 amended version of the document.

37. See Articles 28 and 27 of the Charter of the OAS

38. For a detailed discussion of African regionalism see Chapter 6.

39. This is, of course, also true of many Latin American states, but here the impact of the colonial experience appears to have been eroded by the passage of time with much of the Western Hemisphere having been decolonised during the early part of the Eighteenth Century.

40. For a discussion of the problematic nature of statehood in Africa see R. H. Jackson, *Quasi-states: sovereignty, international relations and the Third World*, (Cambridge: Cambridge University Press,

1990); see also B. Buzan, *People, States and Fear: An Agenda for International Security Studies in the Post-Cold War Era*, (London: Harvester Wheatsheaf, 1991).

41. For a detailed discussion of the development and operation of regional institutions in Southeast Asia see Chapter 7.

CHAPTER 2

Peacemaking and Enforcement under the UN Charter

When in 1945 the work of drafting the UN Charter commenced it was sought to continue and to strengthen the concept of collective security which had been adopted by the former League of Nations. [1] In this respect the principal distinction between the League and the new organisation lay in the supposedly decisive role of the UN Security Council, conceived as a body capable of swift and effective response to threats to, and breaches of, the peace in distinction from the vacillations of the League. In the UN system the powers of the Security Council and the General Assembly are clearly distinguished, in contrast with the more 'weakly' conceived structures of the League, and it is the former which is supposed to be central to the post-1945 collective security structure. This is made clear by articles 24 and 25 of the UN Charter. Article 24(1) provides explicitly that,

> "In order to ensure prompt and effective action by the United Nations, its Members confer on the Security Council primary responsibility for the maintenance of international peace and security, and agree that in carrying out its duties under this responsibility the Security Council acts on their behalf."

Article 25 then adds that,

> "The Members of the United Nations agree to accept and carry out the decisions of the Security Council in accordance with the present Charter."

The emphasis upon speed and efficacy of response, understandable in the aftermath of the catastrophic failure of collective security in the outbreak of the Second World War, [2] is obvious and this is also reflected in the structure of the Security Council itself. It is intended to have a small enough membership to facilitate the necessary rapid decision-making for the maintenance and/or restoration of international peace and security, with, in theory, the veto power of its Permanent Members [3] serving to ensure the political support of the major Powers for its decisions. [4] The right of veto is affirmed by article 27(3) of the Charter which requires the 'concurring votes of the permanent members' for all non-procedural decisions. [5] The pragmatic reason for this is explained by a Statement on the Voting Procedure in the Security Council issued on 7 June 1945, [6] which states in paragraph 9 that,

> "In view of the primary responsibilities of the permanent members, they could not be expected, in the present condition of the world, to assume the obligation to act in so serious a matter as the maintenance of international peace and security in consequence of a

decision in which they had not concurred. Therefore [provision is made] ... in respect of non-procedural matters, for unanimity of the permanent members ... ".

To this degree the UN system might be thought to be only one of 'partial' collective security. Given the preponderance of power held by the great powers of the day and the realisation that the wartime consensus between them was already under intense strain, the veto was explicitly included to ensure that the UN could never be placed in a position whereby it was forced to call upon its members to undertake enforcement action against a great power. Stalemate would be preferable to such a situation, for any attempt to police the behaviour of the great powers would inevitably lead to major conflict. Moreover this was the understanding and preferred position not only of the great powers but also of the lesser powers, the latter having no desire to enter into such a conflict in the name of the UN. As the Indian delegate to the San Francisco Conference stated,

> "The veto power ... is ... an implicit guarantee to all members that they will not be asked to wage a war, in the name of the United Nations, against any of the big powers." [7]

In this light the criticism sometimes voiced of the UN Charter and the collective security concept which it embodies as idealistic and impractical may be seen to be ill-founded since the relevant provisions do, and were intended to, take account of the real underlying power structures. The drafters of the Charter proceeded not upon the basis that consensus would be maintained and the veto would not be called upon, but upon the understanding that disagreements might occur and that where this was the case the Security Council would in practice be incapacitated. I.L. Claude remarks that,

> "The conclusion is inescapable that a conscious decision was made at San Francisco to avoid any attempt or pretence at subjecting the major powers to collective coercion. ... The security scheme of the Charter .. was conceived as an arrangement for collective action against relatively minor disturbers of the peace, in cases where the great powers were united in the desire to permit or take action." [8]

There was, thus, always a political 'price' to be paid for a workable system of collective security, the clear lesson of the imperative of great power involvement learnt from the experience of the League of Nations. However, the UN was inevitably weakened in cases where a permanent Member might not be a guarantor of international peace and security but in reality a threat thereto. This, in the Cold War era, was to be a difficulty for a number of states in the 'back yards' of the Superpowers, as also in cases where one or other of the permanent members felt important interests to be at stake. Nonetheless, it is probably the case that without the veto power the Security Council would not have been permitted to function at all, leading, potentially, to an entire collapse of post-War collective security with incalculable consequences. The power to veto Security Council resolutions was insisted upon by all of those

powers which participated in the initial drafting stages of the Charter. As Inis
Claude observes,

> "The veto provision was not an illiberal rule insisted upon by the Soviet Union over the
> opposition of the more progressive-minded great powers of the West. ... Indeed, Secre-
> tary of State Hull, in discussing a preliminary draft Charter with a group of Senators in
> May 1944, asserted that the veto principle was incorporated in it 'primarily on account
> of the United States,' and, with respect to the proposed Security Council, that 'our Gov-
> ernment would not remain there a day without retaining its veto power.'" [9]

In this, as in other matters, the practical outcome was severely influenced by
the Cold War ideological confrontation for most of the first half century of the
UN's existence. This was, hardly surprisingly, not only the case for the use,
and abuse, of the permanent members' veto power but also for the general
operation of the collective security system set out by the UN Charter. It is
therefore necessary in any legal or political analysis of this system to understand the divergences between its intended mode of operation and its subsequent practical working.

THE OPERATION OF UN COLLECTIVE SECURITY

The UN Charter makes provision for the maintenance of international peace
and security primarily by Chapter VII, comprising articles 39-51, particularly
in Articles 39-42. Article 39 provides that,

> "The Security Council shall determine the existence of any threat to the peace, breach of
> the peace, or act of aggression and shall make recommendations, or decide what meas-
> ures shall be taken in accordance with Articles 41 and 42, to maintain or restore interna-
> tional peace and security."

Just what constitutes a 'threat to the peace' for this purpose has in the past
been a subject for debate, [10] especially as regards the distinction between
this and a dispute 'the continuance of which is likely to endanger the maintenance of international peace and security' within the meaning of articles 33
and 34 of Chapter VI of the Charter. [11] The latter situation permits the
Security Council only to make 'recommendations' under article 36, whereas
a finding under article 39 leads almost, if not quite, inevitably to mandatory
action.

The historic practice of the Security Council suggests that the nature of
what constitutes a threat to international peace and security has changed
significantly. Originally conceived in essentially statist terms, emphasis was
placed upon the prohibition of the use of force at an inter-state level while
internal use of force was deemed to be beyond the purview of the Security
Council. Article 2(4) of the Charter prohibits Member States using force 'in
their *international* relations' while article 2(7) forbids UN involvement 'in

matters which are essentially within the domestic jurisdiction of any state' subject to the proviso that this principle shall not prejudice the application of Chapter VII, article 39 of which refers specifically to the maintenance or restoration of *international* peace and security. During the Cold War years there was little derogation from the principle that domestic use of force was a matter lying within the sovereign capacity of States, with the embryonic exception of the Spanish Question [12] and the Southern Rhodesian and South African situations. [13] The end of the Cold War has, however, diminished the political sensitivities which gave this question its essential significance and the result has arguably been a broadening of the concept of a threat to peace. The responses to the situations in Bosnia-Herzegovina, Somalia, Haiti, the Great Lakes region of Africa, all appear to confirm this proposition. N.D. White suggests that the essence of established usage of the term 'threat to peace' is,

> "that the situations have at their core the use of armed force, either internal or international. The integrity of the concept has been maintained by many of the recent uses of the terms by the Security Council, covering issues such as threats of force (provocative action directed by Iraq against Kuwait), widespread violations of international humanitarian law (including 'ethnic cleansing' in Bosnia), massive humanitarian crises (caused by the genocide in Rwanda in 1994 which led to related problems in Burundi and Zaire in 1996), and breach of a Security Council arms embargo (relating to Rwanda)." [14]

Inevitably the making of a determination that there is a threat to, or breach of, [15] the peace or an act of aggression will depend in practice at least as much upon political factors as upon strictly legal criteria, especially where the interests of permanent members may be involved. Once such a determination has been made the Security Council may make recommendations with a view to the restoration of international peace and security. It may also, under article 40, call upon the parties involved in the situation to comply with 'such provisional measures as it deems necessary or desirable' for the prevention of any aggravation of the problem. If the situation appears to demand further action the Security Council may proceed to impose sanctions under articles 41 and 42. Article 41 provides that,

> "The Security Council may decide what measures not involving the use of armed force are to be employed to give effect to its decisions, and it may call upon the Members of the United Nations to apply such measures. These may include complete or partial interruption of economic relations and of rail, sea, air, postal, telegraphic, radio and other means of communication, and the severance of diplomatic relations."

Ultimately, measures involving the use of force may be authorised under article 42, which provides that

> "Should the Security Council consider that the measures provided for in Article 41 would prove inadequate or have proved to be inadequate, it may take such action by air, sea, or land forces as may be necessary to maintain or restore international peace and security.
> ..."

The relationship between articles 41 and 42 has become a source of contention, especially since the end of the Cold War and the resulting potential increase in the practical efficacy of the Security Council as an institutional actor. It has been suggested that the relationship between the two provisions is sequential, so that the potential efficacy of economic sanctions imposed under article 41 must be exhausted before the use of force can be authorised under article 42. Nothing in the substance of the two provisions would appear to sustain this argument, other, perhaps, than the numerical implication of a staged sequence of responses, and it seems that the idea rests to a large degree upon the assumption that economic sanctions are necessarily to be seen as a more humanitarian preliminary response prior to resort to armed 'enforcement' measures. Whilst this argument undoubtedly has some *prima facie* attraction, its basic assumptions have, in the 1990s, been revealed to be at best questionable. The effects of the sanctions imposed upon Iraq after the 1990-91 Gulf Conflict and of those imposed upon Haiti have demonstrated painfully that the supposedly humanitarian first option may in fact be quite the reverse in its impact. [16] These experiences strongly suggest that the imposition of economic sanctions may have very little effect upon the governments and leadership cadres at which and whom they are aimed, whilst having a potentially devastating effect upon the civilian populations under the rule of such governments who may, indeed, be seen as the first and principal victims of a delinquent regime. [17] The representation of economic sanctions as necessarily more humane than military options is called further into question by the development of so-called 'smart' weapons systems with their capacity of highly specific targeting and consequent minimisation of collateral injury and damage. It is true that such weapons systems are in no sense a panacea and however accurate the targeting may be there will always remain the question of accuracy of the information upon which it is founded – a point demonstrated by the Amirayah Bunker incident during the 1990-91 Gulf Conflict. [18] Nonetheless recent experience strongly suggests that the simple idea of a staged progression of increasingly harsh or robust measures in the application of articles 39 to 42 of the UN Charter has become both naive and increasingly unsustainable. In this, ever more complex, context the question of the proper relationship, and indeed progression as between, articles 41 and 42 comes to rest more and more upon the application of political, strategic and ethical criteria in given circumstances rather than upon legal technicality.

Where, under article 42, the Security Council determined that military sanctions were necessary it was originally intended that such action would be undertaken by Forces under UN command and control taken from units held on stand-by by Member States for this purpose in accordance with article 43 of the Charter. This provides that,

"(1) All Members of the United Nations, in order to contribute to the maintenance of international peace and security, undertake to make available to the Security Council, on its call and in accordance with a special agreement or agreements, armed forces, assistance, and facilities, ...

(2) Such agreement or agreements shall govern the numbers and types of forces, their degree of readiness and general location, and the nature of the facilities and assistance to be provided." ...

This never happened. [19] Along with much else in the original UN peace support vision, the idea of forces held in readiness for UN deployment under article 43 agreements was effectively destroyed by the collapse after 1945 of the wartime inter-Allied consensus – which was in any event never so extensive as some appear to have believed – and its succession by Cold War tensions and suspicions. This was, if anything, even more the case with the provision of article 45 for the holding available of national air force contingents in immediate readiness for 'urgent military measures ... for combined international enforcement action'. The UN Military Staff Committee provided for in article 47 of the Charter was set up, but its functions are necessarily rather limited. It does, to a degree, fulfil the advisory function vis a vis the Security Council provided for in article 47(1), but the provision of article 46 that,

"Plans for the application of armed force shall be made by the Security Council with the assistance of the Military Staff Committee."

and of article 47(3) that,

"The Military Staff Committee shall be responsible under the Security Council for the strategic direction of any armed forces placed at the disposal of the Security Council."
...

have become for all practical purposes dead letters. It may in practice be said, perhaps a little harshly but nonetheless in essence truly, that the UN Military Staff Committee has become a general staff without an army.

The absence of 'article 43' forces is of some potential legal significance, and it has indeed been argued that without such forces the Security Council cannot legally proceed to enforcement measures under article 42. The point of this is that an article 42 decision would appear to be mandatory in the sense that the Security Council can 'take ... action by air, sea or land forces' and without necessarily available forces it could not do so. [20] Such a strict linkage between articles 42 and 43 can, however, be argued to be excessively legalistic and restrictive, if the view is taken that the provisions of article 43, and article 45, are *facilitative* in their relation to article 42 rather than a *prerequisite* for its operation. It has been argued elsewhere that,

"it is incorrect to state that there is an inextricable link between articles 42 and 43 in the sense that it would be a misuse of power for the [Security] Council to decide on the use of military measures under articles 39 and 42 without any *a priori* agreements under article 43. It would appear acceptable for the Council to use the power granted to it in article 42 without the mechanisms that were designed to make the imposition of military coercion a practical option. If an alternative practical option emerges such as an *ad hoc* coalition prepared to act under UN authority then it would appear to be *prima facie* lawful." [21]

In fact, quite apart from the absence of the readily available forces anticipated to be made available by Member States under the provisions of articles 43 and 45, the Cold War impediments to effective decision making by the Security Council rendered the use of article 42 so sensitive that it has rarely been directly referred to. Instead, a carefully non-specific reference to 'measures under Chapter VII' has generally been preferred when use of force has been authorised. In practice this may not have mattered very much, although it generated a rather sterile academic debate as to whether such action is in fact authorised under article 42 or upon some infinitely extensible interpretation of article 39. In any event UN peacekeeping forces in the Cold War were in practice comprised of contingents provided *ad hoc* by volunteer States in each situation and this system of 'emergency' last minute provision created major problems of interoperability and of command and control [22] illustrated even in the post-Cold War era by the experiences of UNPROFOR in former-Yugoslavia. In the present context the absence of pre-designated units for UN service leads to some blurring of the type of action to be taken under Chapter VII and that to be authorised for 'regional arrangements' under Chapter VIII. The difference in practice is likely to be rather slight but the issue may have some significance for the technical shape of any future regional peace support paradigms and is as such considered below.

There must also, however, be considered the further question of when a Security Council authorisation for the use of force ceases to be effective. In most cases the answer will clearly be when the objective mandates has been achieved and the authorisation has thereby been rendered *functus officio*. In some cases, however, this may be less than clear. D.D. Carron remarks that,

> "The [UN] Charter is silent on the means of termination ... of actions taken by the Security Council. Nonetheless, interpreting the Charter so as to ensure its effectiveness leads quite clearly to the position that it is for the Council itself to end or modify its actions. The United States and the United Kingdom, in supporting this interpretation of the Charter in the context of the gulf war, cited the fact that the sanctions against Rhodesia were terminated by Security Council resolution." [23]

This view may also be seen reflected in the Operation Desert Fox air strikes launched by the US and the UK against Iraq on 17 December 1998 following repeated obstruction by the Ba'ath regime of arms inspections imposed by the UN after the 1990-91 Gulf Conflict. The legal logic of Carron's position appears sound but gives rise to complex political questions and also leaves open the issues which might arise from ambiguities within Security Council resolutions, themselves often the result of necessary political compromise. UN Security Council Resolution 687 of 3 April 1991, setting out the conditions for the formal cease-fire at the end of the 1990-91 Gulf Conflict, provided by paragraph 8 that Iraq was required 'unconditionally' to accept the destruction and removal of, *inter alia*, all chemical and biological weapons and the means of their production 'under international supervision'. The obstruction of inspections was clearly a violation of the cease fire agreement and equally clearly raised the prospect of armed enforcement measures. It must, however, also be noted that paragraph 34 of Security Council Resolution 687 provides that the Council,

> "Decides to remain seized of the matter and to take such further steps as may be required for the implementation of the present resolution and to secure peace and security in the area."

This at least implies that any renewal of military enforcement action should have been referred to the Security Council, although with what potential result must be a matter for rather doubtful speculation.

The action was highly controversial and led Russia and China to accuse the US and the UK of 'aggression' and to a withdrawal of Russian ambassadors from Washington DC and London, in moves strongly reminiscent of the politics which afflicted the Security Council in the Cold War era. These reactions were no doubt excessive in view of sustained Iraqi intransigence over arms inspections, but the question still arises as to whether Operation Desert Fox did in fact have implicit Security Council authorisation and upon this there must be significant doubt. This question relates to action taken, at least notionally, on behalf of the UN, but the issues raised could become even more problematic in the context of possibly extended regional security problems in which peace enforcement or general support actions might be undertaken. The nature of the difficulties were further illustrated by the Kosovo crisis in March 1999 [24] when NATO undertook air strikes against Serbian forces in an effort to end quasi-genocidal 'ethnic cleansing' in the Albanian majority populated territory of Kosovo. In a clear humanitarian emergency and situation of threat to peace the UN Security Council was left unable to authorise robust action on its own behalf, because of the certainty of a Russian and Chinese veto, but also refused on 26 March 1999 to accept a Russian motion denouncing the NATO action as unlawful. The end result is that early development of post-Cold War peace support is left in extreme cases in a politico-legal limbo which cannot in the long or even medium term be tolerated.

To some degree these difficulties may be see as an aftermath of the Cold War confrontation which undoubtedly distorted, and in significant degree impeded, the peace support practice and capacities of the Security Council with, amongst its other consequences, a much enhanced resulting emphasis upon the self defence provision of article 51 of the UN Charter preserving the 'inherent' right of individual and collective self-defence in the event of an armed attack. [25]

PEACE SUPPORT ACTION AND THE UN GENERAL ASSEMBLY

A further question arises with regard to the relationship between the UN Security Council and the General Assembly in respect of peace support operations. In particular there must be considered the question of whether the Assembly has any *independent* power to authorise such operations. Article 11(2) of the UN Charter provides that,

> "The General Assembly may discuss any questions relating to the maintenance of international peace and security brought before it by any Member of the United Nations, or by the Security Council, or by a State which is not a Member of the United Nations in accordance with Article 35 ..., and, except as provided in Article 12, may make recommendations with regard to any such questions to the State or States concerned or to the Security Council or both. Any such questions, on which action is necessary, shall be referred to the Security Council by the General Assembly either before or after discussion."

Article 14 then provides that,

> "Subject to the provision of Article 12, the General Assembly may recommend measures for the peaceful adjustment of any situation ... which it deems likely to impair the general welfare or friendly relations among nations, including situations resulting from a violation of the provisions of the present Charter ..."

The caveat referred to by reference to article 12 is that the General Assembly may not make such recommendations to the Security Council in relation to a given situation whilst it is exercising its functions under the Charter in dealing with it, unless the Council so requests. The question of the General Assembly's capacities was considered by the International Court of Justice in the *Expenses case* [26] which arose from the financing of UNEF 1 in the Middle East and ONUC in the Congo, the General Assembly having mandated the first *ab initio* and taken over the latter. In considering whether the costs of these operations were properly 'expenses of the [UN] organization to be borne by the Members ...' within the meaning of article 17(2) of the UN Charter, the International Court of Justice found in an Advisory Opinion that the General Assembly must be presumed to have the power to mandate such operations in the absence of powerful contrary argument. However, it also emphasised that the power to authorise *coercive* action vests in the Security Council alone. In this context it should be noted that the powers conferred upon the General Assembly by articles 11 and 14 of the Charter specifically in relation to threats to or breaches of the peace amount to no more than a capacity to make *recommendations* to the Security Council. There is no suggestion that the Assembly could override the Council in respect of coercive measures and the concluding sentence of article 11(2) makes it clear that decisions are to be made by the Council and not the Assembly. Certainly, the latter could not itself authorise measures under Chapter VII, a point confirmed by the International Court of Justice in the *Expenses case*. As N.D. White remarks,

"Article 11(2) enables the General Assembly to find a 'threat to the peace', a 'breach of the peace' or an 'act of aggression' and to make recommendations thereon to restore international peace, a power concurrent with that of the Security Council under Article 39. It is a recommendatory power only, any coercive measures under Chapter VII requiring a mandatory decision can only be adopted by the Security Council." [27]

It may be added that any contrary conclusion would threaten to reintroduce one of the basic weaknesses of the League of Nations in vesting collective security decisions in a large and unwieldy body incapable in many cases of the decisive action often required. Such a reversion would, as explained above, [28] run seriously counter to the original purposes which informed the initial creation of the Security Council. A point reinforced by the difficulties occasioned by the (ab)use of the veto power during the Cold War, and potentially afterwards, even within the supposedly swiftly and effectively acting Security Council mechanism.

In the early days of the Cold War increasing concern over the impediment to effective Security Council action represented by ideologically motivated use of the veto power in the Council led to a number of endeavours to use the General Assembly as a means of circumventing the Council where it was prevented from taking action for the maintenance or restoration of international peace and security. These included the development of the so-called 'little assembly' which was a mechanism by which the Assembly could be convened at any time to consider, *inter alia*, such matters, whether or not it was in regular session. This process, which was in practice frustrated by Soviet obstruction, still left the power of recommendation with the full Assembly as provided for in the Charter and in that sense may be considered to have been more dramatic in appearance than in its real impact.

Somewhat more potentially significant was the 'Uniting for Peace' Resolution. [29] Paragraph 1 of this Resolution provides that the General Assembly,

"Resolves that if the Security Council, because of lack of unanimity of the permanent members, fails to exercise its primary responsibility for the maintenance of international peace and security in any case where there appears to be a threat to the peace, breach of the peace, or act of aggression, the General Assembly shall consider the matter immediately with a view to making recommendations to members for collective measures, in-

cluding in the case of a breach of the peace or act of aggression, the use of armed force
where necessary, to maintain or restore international peace and security. ..."

If not in session at a relevant time the General Assembly was to meet in
emergency session within 24 hours of a request therefore. [30] A Peace
Observation Commission and a Collective Measures Committee were set up
and remain in formal existence. The Assembly has acted under this resolution
on a number of occasions, most recently in 1982. [31] It is arguable that the
Uniting for Peace Resolution in itself is little more than a particular mechanism for the implementation of the capacity expressly granted to the Assembly
by article 11(2) of the Charter, even if the language of alternative action
stretches the meaning of that provision to the extreme. The question of actual
authorisation of military measures is much more doubtful – essentially for the
reasons already suggested above – although, as N.D. White remarks, [32] the
UN as such clearly has the power to authorise such measures and the question
of the General Assembly's powers in this regard may be little more than an
internal institutional question. Nonetheless, the creation of doubt in this area
is not desirable and the defects of the decision making processes of the former
League of Nations in this regard perhaps sound a warning note with regard to
the Uniting for Peace Resolution. In practice it has not been an issue of great
relevance since the early 1980s and seems unlikely to play any major role in
presently developing peace support paradigms.

REGIONAL DEFENCE AND SECURITY PROVISION UNDER THE UN CHARTER

From the outset it had been anticipated that regional organisations would play
a significant role in the maintenance of peace and security within the UN
system, although there was debate as to the nature and significance of that role
– especially as between the globalist and regionalist visions of security
provision after the Second World War. [33] In the structuring of the UN
system a globalist approach was ultimately favoured with the regional
organisations and defensive alliances very clearly subordinated to the United
Nations organisation, not least for the avoidance of the quasi-imperialism and
hegemonism which was very clearly implicit in, e.g., the Churchillian vision
of the regionalist option. [34]

Provision for regional security is made by Chapter VIII of the UN Charter,
comprising articles 52-54. Article 52(1) of the UN Charter provides that,

"Nothing in the present Charter precludes the existence of regional arrangements or
agencies for dealing with such matters relating to the maintenance of international peace
and security as are appropriate for regional action provided that such arrangements or
agencies and their activities are consistent with the Purposes and Principles of the United
Nations."

A local or regional security or defence organisation, such as NATO, is therefore entirely legitimate, whereas an organisation which was dedicated in whole or part to military aggression would not be so by virtue, *inter alia*, of its actual or potential breach of the fundamental imperative contained in article 2(4) of the Charter. The Charter does not define a 'regional arrangement or agency' for this purpose but in practice this is of little importance since the United Nations has adopted an *ad hoc* approach to this question and has considered such organisations as meet given regional needs to fall within the meaning of article 52.

The key provision for the present purpose is article 53(1) of the UN Charter, which provides that,

"... The Security Council shall, where appropriate, utilize such regional arrangements or agencies for enforcement action under its authority. But no enforcement action shall be taken under regional arrangements or by regional agencies without the authorisation of the Security Council."

The omitted section makes redundant reference to action against the former-Axis Powers in the context of the aftermath of the Second World War. The provision made by this article is, of course, additional to any exercise of the inherent right of collective self-defence preserved by article 51. The drafting of the provision is interesting on at least two levels. In the first place it will be noted that the phrasing is *mandatory* rather than permissive, i.e. the Security Council *shall*, rather than *may*, make use of regional arrangements or organisations in appropriate cases. This reinforces an obligation imposed on UN member states by article 33(1) which states that parties to a dispute shall seek pacific settlement of disputes through, *inter alia*, recourse to regional agencies or arrangements. Secondly it is emphasised that where such bodies are used in circumstances other than self -defence they may only proceed with Security Council authorisation – that is to say that there is delegation of action but not of control. [35] The essential point is well stated by J.G. Merrills, who comments, in a somewhat broader context of international dispute resolution, that,

"It is ... widely recognised that regional organisations cannot remove the Security Council's ultimate responsibility for the maintenance of international peace and security. ... despite its pre-eminence, it is only in special cases that the Security Council will attempt to displace a regional organisation when the latter is seised of a dispute." [36]

This basic principle is reinforced by the requirement of article 54 that the Security Council must at all times be kept fully informed of action taken or planned by regional arrangements or agencies for the maintenance of international peace and security. This latter is a general requirement and applies as much to action undertaken in the context of collective self-defence under article 51 as to any other.

While it is clear, therefore, that when acting under Chapter VIII regional agencies undertaking enforcement action are subject to the authority of the Security Council, what is less clear is what measures a regional organisation may take other than when acting in this role. The Charter fails to make clear whether the term 'enforcement action' as used in Chapter VIII has the same meaning as 'enforcement measures' as used in Chapter VII. If these terms have the same meaning it would suggest that it would be *ultra vires* for a regional body to undertake coercive non-military measures such as imposing economic sanctions without first gaining Security Council authorisation. This interpretation appears to be supported by a reading of the *travaux prepara-toires* and is favoured by writers such as Hans Kelsen. [37] However State practice is indicative of support for the alternative viewpoint, in particular suggesting that economic sanctions may legitimately be imposed by regional organisations. During debates over the imposition of economic sanctions by the OAS against Cuba in 1962 this line of argument was generally supported on the grounds that the term 'enforcement' naturally connotes a use of force and given that individual states can legally sever economic relations one with another it logically follows that they also have a collective right so to do. [38] Irrespective of the question of the legality of the imposition of economic sanctions it is, however, clear that the policing of such measures, almost certainly involving force, would fall strictly within the purview of the Security Council. This is a point which Boutros Boutros-Ghali made clear during the early stages of the conflict in former-Yugoslavia in respect to the possibility of NATO/WEU [39] enforcement of EU sanctions.

Article 53 in particular is crucial to the future of regional peace support action in any developing new post-Cold War peace support paradigm, or paradigms. In the post Cold-War context, with the increasing emphasis upon regional peace support action as a means of alleviating the burden of peace support demands which the under-resourced UN organisation has proved unable to sustain, a broadly based and flexible view of article 53 has become a necessity. As M.N. Shaw remarks,

> " [As to the appropriateness of regional action] recent events have demonstrated a broader measure of flexibility akin to the widening definition of what constitutes a threat to international peace and security. ... Practice in the post-Cold War era has amply demonstrated the increasing awareness by the Security Council of the potentialities of regional organisations. References in resolutions of the Council have varied in this regard. Some have specifically mentioned, commended or supported the work of named regional organisations without mentioning Chapter VIII, others have referred explicitly to Chapter VIII, while others have stated that the Council is acting under Chapter VIII." [40]

The ambiguities of reference to both Chapter VII and Chapter VIII of the Charter in this context is of considerable technical, but possibly rather slight practical, significance. N.D. White and O. Ulgen remark that,

"The thin line between military actions under Chapter VII and those under Chapter VIII is seen to be even more illusory when considering the legal basis of NATO actions in Bosnia under UN authority. The Resolutions ... can either be seen as deriving from Chapter VIII, thereby treating NATO as a 'regional arrangement', or as an authorisation to each ... Member State of NATO, as well as other contributors to IFOR, to form a multilateral force under Chapter VII. Both of these are equally plausible, thereby illustrating the overarching decentralised model based on simple UN authorisation." [41]

Both the advantages and the dangers of such 'decentralised' regional action have been clearly evidenced by, even the so far relatively brief, post-Cold War experience. The experiences of Haiti [42] and former-Yugoslavia [43] have arguably been of particular significance.

THE RELEVANCE OF ARTICLE 51

Whatever way forward is ultimately found in a new peace-support paradigm, or, as this book suggests, peace-support paradigms, much will inevitably depend upon the nature and capacities of the available regional organisations and alliances. These organisations are infinitely diverse in character and basis but for many, if not indeed all, the defensive alliances generated during the Cold War era article 51 of the UN Charter is central to their claimed remit and functions, although it is by no means necessarily so for regional organisations more generally. Article 51 provides that:

"Nothing in the present Charter shall impair the inherent right of individual or collective self-defence if an armed attack occurs against a Member of the United Nations, until the Security Council has taken the measures necessary to maintain international peace and security."

This provision was in some respects an afterthought in the drafting of the UN Charter and was not included in the 1944 Dumbarton Oaks proposals. It was added primarily at the instance of the South American States at San Francisco to preserve regional security and national defence mechanisms in the face of the potential impact of the retention of the veto power in Security Council proceedings and, specifically, with an eye to the perceived danger of hemispheric US hegemonism. It was intended to retain the lawfulness of immediate military response to military aggression [44] and was expanded to include collective as well as individual self-defence. However, as a result of the Cold War impediments to the effective operation of the Security Council, article 51 became in practice the most significant legal provision for response to aggression.

Unfortunately the provision was quite inadequately drafted for this much expanded role. Amongst the many controversies surrounding it are, inevitably, those of just what right of self-defence is 'inherent' – although clearly the doctrine found in the *Caroline case* [45] is modified by, *inter alia*, the 1928 Pact of Paris and article 2(3)(4) of the UN Charter, when an armed attack is deemed to 'occur' for this purpose and what Security Council 'measures' terminate its applicability. [46] The general question of 'self defence' lies beyond the remit of the present analysis but the emphasis upon article 51 as a defence vehicle in the Cold War era gave it a considerable significance in the moulding of regional organisations and defensive alliances which is of great importance in the present context.

The nature of the right to form a 'collective' for purposes of self-defence is not specified by the article. Some have indeed cast doubt upon the idea that such collectivity could actually be an 'inherent', in the sense of long-standing customary, right at all. Thus, D.W. Greig writes that,

> "It could hardly have been suggested that self-defence as a collective was an inherent right, i.e. had been long established in customary international law. The ideas that an attack against one member of an alliance was expressly deemed, by the treaty of alliance, to constitute an attack against all others was, at the time, a recent phenomenon. Nevertheless, because it provided the cause for concern that led to the inclusion of Article 51, with its specific relevance to collective self-defence, in the Charter, the strong inference is that Article 51 must be interpreted in the light of that recent practice." [47]

It is in fact possible to argue that the idea of collective self-defence has, at least in some forms, claims to a greater antiquity than is here suggested, as, e.g., in the proper understanding of the Islamic concept of *Jihad*. [48] Be that as it may, the 'practice' acknowledged by Greig developed decisively after 1945 and can be seen, e.g., in article 6 of the 1947 Rio Inter-American Treaty of Reciprocal Assistance, and with express reference to article 51 in article V of the 1948 Brussels Treaty – as amended by the 1954 Paris Protocol II – pertaining to the WEU, article 5 of the 1949 North Atlantic Treaty pertaining to NATO and article 4 of the 1955 Warsaw Pact.

There has been debate as to whether any particular nexus is required to establish a right to collective self-defence. Some writers have taken the view that a close community of interest is required. [49] If collective self-defence is regarded as merely a group extension of the right of each State to defend itself there might well be a persuasive logic to this argument, but it may in practice be suggested to run counter to the basic notion of UN collective security. It is not stretching the spirit of the UN Charter too far to suggest that an attack upon one state is an assault upon the basic norms of security attaching to all States. Examples of practice abound. The call for assistance by the Emir of Kuwait upon the occasion of the Iraqi invasion on 2 August 1990 [50] was not limited to neighbouring States but there has been no suggestion that this precluded reference to article 51. The same is to some degree true of defensive alliances, even though there is usually some degree of common interest, however diffuse it may be. In fact as M.N. Shaw suggests,

"By such [regional] agreements, an attack upon one party is treated as an attack upon all, thus necessitating the conclusion that collective self-defence is more than a collection of individual rights of self-defence, but another creature altogether." [51]

The International Court of Justice considered the criteria for a valid exercise of the right of collective self-defence in the *Nicaragua case*, a decision which has a considerable significance in the context of regional peace support action, including the concern with the potential for regional hegemonism.

The case arose from US funding of the Contra rebel forces against the Sandanista regime in Nicaragua and the Court found, although the US was not represented in the substance of the case, that this support amounted to an unlawful intervention and employment of force against Nicaragua, relying for this view upon the 1965 Declaration on Non-Intervention, the 1970 Declaration on Friendly Relations and the definition of 'aggression' in General Assembly Resolution 3314 of 1974. Of particular interest in the present context is the finding of the Court that even if it were proven that the Nicaraguan government had been supplying arms to rebels in El Salvador, which the court considered not to have been established, this would not have justified US intervention in Nicaragua as an exercise in collective self-defence within the meaning of article 51. As regards collective self-defence the court concluded that,

"in customary international law ... there is no rule permitting the exercise of collective self-defence in the absence of a request by the State which regards itself as the victim of an armed attack. ... [T]he requirement of a request by the State which is the victim of the alleged attack is additional to the requirement that such a State should have declared itself to have been attacked." [52]

The general conclusion would therefore seem to be that there are conjoined requirements for the exercise of a right of collective self-defence of (1) an armed attack and (b) a request for assistance by the victim State. Whether these requirements are truly 'customary' may be debated, but they do concord with the logic of the UN Charter. For article 51 to be applicable at all an armed attack must, in some sense, 'occur', equally to intervene militarily in the affairs of another State without its consent, even in the dire case of an invasion, would be a *prima facie* breach of the article 2(4) ban upon use of force. If this were not the case there would clearly be a danger of aggression under the cover of 'assistance'. It may also be remarked in parenthesis that the process of request may itself be open to abuse. Plain evidence for this may be seen in the Soviet intervention in former-Czechoslovakia and in the Iraqi invasion of Kuwait, both of which were, allegedly, undertaken at the 'request' of a puppet regime which had been installed for just that purpose. The Court's remarks in the *Nicaragua case* were in this respect addressed to *ad hoc* requests for military assistance, self-evidently the existence of treaties of alliance containing collective security guarantees, such as the 1949 North

Atlantic Treaty, would greatly clarify the situation in the circumstances to which they applied.

A further issue arises in the understanding of the meaning of the 'measures' to be taken by the Security Council which would terminate the application of the article in a given situation. The reference in the article to 'measures necessary to maintain international peace and security' is less than helpful. The term 'measures' clearly refers back to article 39 of the Charter under which the Security Council is to determine,

> "what measures shall be taken in accordance with Articles 41 and 42, to maintain or restore international peace and security."

So the 'measures' for this purpose are either those short of armed force to be authorised under article 41 or action involving armed force to be authorised under article 42. This, however, still leaves open a very wide spectrum of options. A resolution, for example, to interrupt postal, telegraphic and radio communications with an aggressor Power – an unlikely but legally possible response, might appear to be a 'measure' which would legally terminate the effect of article 51. This would, however, be absurd in practice since such an action would have very slight, if indeed any, impact upon a continuing course of aggressive warfare. As Greig remarks,

> "The common sense of the situation suggests that a State is not obliged to cease acting in self-defence against an aggressor which is continuing with an offensive until the measures, its own or those employed by the Security Council, prove effective. The use of the word "necessary" in Article 51 would seem to reinforce such an interpretation." [53]

This may readily be accepted, but there remain, nonetheless, significant ambiguities. There was some debate in the context of the Coalition action in the 1990-91 Gulf Conflict as to the relation between article 51 and UN-authorised action. Security Council Resolution 661 of 6 August 1990, imposing economic sanctions against Iraq, expressly affirmed,

> "the inherent right of individual or collective self-defence in response to the armed attack by Iraq against Kuwait in accordance with Article 51 of the Charter"

and this was taken by both the USA and UK to mean that the right of action pursuant to the Emir's request for assistance under article 51 endured notwithstanding any UN Security Council action. It is clearly the intention of Chapter VII of the Charter that once 'necessary measures' have been adopted by the Security Council, including economic measures under article 41, article 51 shall cease to be applicable. At the same time in the actual conditions of modern international relations it is hardly realistic to expect that a State actively fighting invasion with or without allied assistance, which in the relevant case Kuwait was not, should cease to do so merely because economic sanctions have been declared. Nonetheless the UN Secretary-General made clear in a statement issued on 8 November 1990 that military action could, in the light of the article 41 measures, only be taken with UN authorisation. [54] In the particular context this view was probably correct, although the question remains to some degree moot. However, in most cases the question is unlikely to arise in quite this form. In the circumstances of collective self-defence envisaged by, e.g., the 1949 North Atlantic Treaty in the case of NATO, it is inconceivable that the Security Council would wish, or even be able, to interpose economic sanctions in the midst of a major armed conflict. In the case of the possible development of a post-Cold War regional peace support paradigm, or paradigms, it must be supposed that UN authorisation would anyway have been secured in any circumstances other than those clearly falling under article 51 on the one hand or those involving merely consensual operations on the other.

COMMAND AND CONTROL IN MULTI-NATIONAL FORCES

Issues of command and control are inevitably a source of potential difficulty for any multi-national force, whether based upon an *ad hoc* military alliance or within the formal structures of an organisation such as NATO or upon a UN mandate. Whatever the structural basis, however, a force requires clarity of direction both as to its objectives and as to its chain of command and responsibility at both strategic and tactical levels. In his *Supplement to Agenda for Peace* Boutros Boutros-Ghali stressed the need to distinguish between different levels of authority. He refers specifically to the Security Council's responsibility for overall political direction, the Secretary-General's role of providing executive direction and command and to command in the field which the Secretary-General entrusts to the Chief of Mission, namely the Special Representative, Chief Military Observer or Force Commander. [55] He adds that,

> "It is as inappropriate for a chief of mission to take upon himself the formulation of his/her mission's overall political objectives as it is for the Security Council or the Secretary-General in New York to decide on matters that require a detailed understanding of operational conditions in the field." [56]

Herein lay one of the principal difficulties which bedevilled UNPROFOR. It was burdened with constantly shifting mandates and directives from New York which were in part mutually incompatible and sometimes even in conflict. It was expected, as a 'Protection Force', *inter alia*, to secure delivery of humanitarian relief supplies, whilst also acting as a peace-keeping force and, increasingly, as an enforcement force. These roles would not sit well together for any armed force and especially not for a multinational 'Blue

Helmet' Force with all the command and control problems which have long been associated with such forces. [57] These include in particular the difficulties of a force commander who, in practice, has to negotiate even at a tactical level with subordinate national contingent commanders who themselves look over their shoulder to the, possibly quite divergent, agendas of their national governments. As Boutros Boutros-Ghali remarks in *Supplement to Agenda for Peace,*

> "... commanders in the field are, as a matter of course, instructed to consult the commanders of national contingents ... [h]owever, such consultations cannot be allowed to develop into negotiations between the commander in the field and the troop-contributing Governments, whose negotiating partner must always be the Secretariat in New York."
> [58]

Sadly, however, in practice – through contingent commanders – UN Force Commanders have all too frequently been placed in precisely this position.

This is especially problematic in the context of the level of force which may be used and the circumstances in which it may be employed. This is, of course, a matter specified in detail in Rules of Engagement, but even these can lead to problems of interpretation inconceivable in a national, or even multinational allied, armed force. In the case of UNPROFOR it would seem that the principle of engagement was founded upon self-defence and, as Peter Rowe, in reference to published British statements, remarks,

> "The [United Kingdom Parliamentary] Defence Committee [Report] relied upon a statement from the UN Secretary General that any force used in self-defence was "deemed to include situations in which armed persons attempt by force to prevent United Nations troops from carrying out their mandate." [59]

The circumstances in which force could be used by UNPROFOR were admittedly extended significantly by reference to UN Security Council Resolution 836 of 4 June 1993 [60] in relation to the protection of designated 'safe areas' in Bosnia Herzegovina, but there remained a broad impression amongst those actively opposed to UNPROFOR operations that its response capacity was limited together with a strong sense of the divergences of opinion between the various nations contributing contingents to it.

LEGAL REGULATION OF UN AND UN-AUTHORISED FORCES

A number of final issues arise in the law governing the emplacement and conduct of UN and UN-authorised Forces. Military operations by foreign armed forces, even 'Blue Helmet' or UN-authorised Forces, in the territory of a State inevitably raise delicate legal problems. This was so throughout the first half-century of UN peace support experience and is likely to become, if anything, even more so in a new or varied peace support paradigm involving a larger use of regional or sub-regional organisations. A non-consensual enforcement action, such as that undertaken by UNOSOM II in Somalia or by the Coalition forces in the 1990-91 Gulf Conflict will not, of course, either require or receive the consent of the State against which the action is being taken. Consensual peace support operations will, however, need such consent in some form. Surprisingly, this has traditionally been dealt with rather vaguely in Status of Forces Agreements (SOFAs). [61] The mutual undertakings on the part of the UN Force to respect 'local laws and regulations; and on the part of the 'host' State to respect the international nature of the force at least imply such consensuality. This vagueness has, sadly, proved in some cases to be highly deleterious in its effects. One of the many obstacles faced by UNPROFOR in former-Yugoslavia in the operation of its complex and shifting mandates was the fact that it clearly did not have the consent of some of the factions, in some cases little more than bandits, who were opposing it. This was, of course, a symptom of the ambiguous position in which UNPROFOR was placed as a 'peacekeeping' force in a situation in which there was no peace to keep.

Interestingly the NATO-led IFOR Force in former-Yugoslavia was placed in a much more robust position. The provision for the force in Annex IA of the 1995 Dayton Peace Accord, expressly referred to in UN Security Council Resolution 1031 of 15 December 1995 which set up the Force, provided in particular that restrictions upon the freedom of movement of IFOR units or other obstruction of its functions would lead to military action against the perpetrators. Although the presence of IFOR was in principle consensual, this point emphasises the role of the force, in effect, as an Enforcement Force. In so far as the IFOR/SFOR forces in former-Yugoslavia may be considered one of the early models for 'regional' peace support action in a developing new paradigm this may be significant as a pointer towards future development in the context of 'peacekeeping' strictly so-called, although clearly not in that of overt 'peace enforcement' actions. Again, however, attention must be drawn to the wide diversity of regional organisations and the improbability of many, including specifically the OAS, engaging in non-consensual operations at all.

In other respects forces operating under the aegis of regional organisations or defensive alliances will face significantly fewer legal complexities than 'traditional' Blue Helmet Forces. This is especially the case for the application of the laws of armed conflict. There has for many years been debate, of an apparently rather sterile but actually highly significant nature, upon the applicability or otherwise of the humanitarian *jus in bello* to UN Forces engaged in combat. [62] The question turns upon the technical issue of whether it is possible for the United Nations to be in a condition of armed conflict, and therefore belligerency, with a State. The fundamental point was put well in the 1960s by Finn Seyersted, in commenting that,

"The most important political obstacle is the general feeling that a *United Nations action*, even if governed by the same laws as war in its traditional sense, *must be clearly distinguished from war*, and the apprehension that accession by the United Nations to the conventions on warfare might blur the distinction." [63]

To put the question another way, is it possible or desirable for those charged with the maintenance and enforcement of international law, peace and security to be placed on a legally co-equal footing with those against whom their action is directed?

In 1962 U Thant entered into correspondence with the International Committee of the Red Cross (the ICRC) upon this subject and confirmed that,

"UNO [the United Nations Organisation] insists on its armed forces in the field applying the principles of the 1949 Geneva Conventions as scrupulously as possible." [64]

It may be noticed that the reference here is specifically to the 1949 Geneva Conventions and not, e.g., to the 1899 and 1907 Hague Conventions or other provisions of the humanitarian *jus in bello*. Granted, however, that the letter was addressed to the ICRC and, of course, written before the conclusion of, e.g., the 1977 Additional Protocols, it may reasonably be concluded that the arguments which apply to the 1949 Geneva Conventions apply no less to the whole corpus of international humanitarian law.

The UN is not, however, formally party to any of the *jus in bello* treaties. A number of attempts have been made to draft provisions clarifying this issue, including, notably, the 1971 Zagreb Resolution of the Institute of International Law on Conditions of Application of Humanitarian Rules of Armed Conflict to Hostilities in which United Nations Forces may be Engaged. Article 2 of this draft provides expressly for the application of the norms of the *jus in bello* by UN Forces engaged in combat and if formally adopted, which it has not yet been, would afford a useful formal affirmation of the practice which is in reality adopted but which as a matter of principle is still left in some degree in a condition of undesirable ambiguity.

The question of the application of humanitarian rules and principles by forces in combat with UN forces is currently left in an even more ambiguous situation. The issue came into public prominence in June 1995 when soldiers serving with UNPROFOR were taken prisoner by Bosnian-Serb forces, whilst a number of Bosnian-Serb fighters were held prisoner by a French UNPROFOR unit in another sector. In light of the fact that the UNPROFOR personnel were not strictly speaking fighting with a 'party to the conflict' within the meaning of article 4A(1) of 1949 Geneva Convention III pertaining to prisoners of war, the ICRC declared that the 'captured' UNPROFOR personnel were not strictly 'prisoners of war'. It may, nonetheless, be argued that they were in an analogous position and certainly entitled to humane treatment under the provisions of 1949 Geneva Convention IV as, for this purpose, quasi-'civilian' internees, if not under 1949 Geneva Convention III as 'prisoners of war'. This was the situation of the small British military mission in Kuwait, present there in a non-combatant capacity, at the time of the Iraqi invasion in 1990 at the time when there was no armed conflict between Iraq and the United Kingdom. Once Operation Desert Storm commenced, involving UK forces, they would then have become entitled to prisoner of war status.

The personnel of 'regional' forces engaged in combat in the course of 'enforcement' action under UN authorisation must be presumed to be entitled to prisoner of war status pursuant to article 4A(1) of 1949 Geneva Convention III upon capture. It must, upon the same logic, also be the case that the humanitarian *jus in bello* applies to operations carried out by such forces in such circumstances, both as regards their duties and their entitlements with regard to the conduct of opposing forces.

There will remain the problem of different regulations and possibly different levels of national treaty commitment, beyond the limits of customary law – which in fact includes the preponderance of the established *jus in bello*. This, however, is a potential question for any multinational force, even for those coming from organisations with considerable joint operational experience such as NATO. It is one of the many issues deriving ultimately from the question of interoperability which has in varying degrees bedevilled UN, regional and sub-regional forces throughout the modern era. Sufficient interoperability is a *sine qua non* for effective multi-national operational efficacy, perfect interoperability is, however, improbable outside the limits of a single nation force and this seems likely to remain the case whatever peace support paradigm, or paradigms, may finally emerge from the post-Cold War era.

NOTES

1. See Chapter 1.
2. Even if in reality this was more a failure of political will on the part of the principal sponsoring Powers of the League than an inherent inadequacy of its *legal* instruments.
3. Essentially the victorious Powers in the Second World War, i.e., the USA, former USSR (whose seat is now held by the Russian Federation), the UK, France and China – a grouping which, more than half a century after the end of the Second World War, is in the late 1990s a matter for controversy – see below.
4. In accordance with Article 5 of the League Covenant decisions of the Council were to be made on the basis of unanimity unless otherwise specifically stated. In contrast the UN Security Council, in accordance with Article 27(3) makes decisions 'by an affirmative vote of nine members including the

concurring votes of the permanent members'. It should however be noted that in accordance with Security Council practice an abstention is deemed to be a 'concurring' vote.

5. For discussion of this see S.D. Bailey, *Voting in the Security Council* (xxx, 1969), pp.18-37.

6. UNCIO Document 852, III.1/37(1). The full text can also be found in F. Knipping, H. von Mangoldt and V. Rittberger, eds., *The United Nations System and its Predecessors* (Oxford University Press, 1997), Vol. I, at pp.618-621.

7. Cited by I.L. Claude, Jnr., *Power and International Relations* (Random House, 1962), p.161.

8. Ibid., at pp. 161-2.

9. I.L. Claude, *Swords into Plowshares*, 4 ed., (McGraw Hill, 1984), p.143.

10. With regard to the debates at San Francisco see, L.M. Goodrich and E. Hambro, *Charter of the United Nations: Commentary and Documents* (Stevens, 1949), pp. 262-265.

11. The narrower term 'aggression' can be more closely defined by reference to General Assembly Resolution 3314 (XXIX) of 14 December 1974 on the Definition of Aggression, although this in fact does little more than state the obvious.

12. SCOR. 1st Yr., 1st Ser., pp.370-6.

13. For discussion of these three instances see R. Higgins, *The Development of International Law through the Organs of the United Nations* (Oxford University Press, 1963), pp. 77-106.

14. N.D. White, *Keeping the Peace* (Manchester University Press, 1997), p.45

15. D.J. Harris makes the point that, rather oddly, *breaches* of the peace have only been found to have occurred in the instances of the Korean War, the 1982 Falklands Conflict, the 1980-88 Gulf War and the 1990-91 Gulf Conflict, see *Cases and Materials on International Law*, 5 ed., (Sweet and Maxwell, 1998), p.945

16. For a detailed discussion of the sanctions issue in the 1990-91 Gulf Conflict see L. Freedman and E. Karsh, *The Gulf Conflict 1990-1991*, 1993, pp. 129-228; For an analysis of the Security Council debates over the imposition of sanctions in Haiti see J. Morris, 'Force and Democracy: UN/US Intervention in Haiti', *International Peacekeeping*, Vol 2 (1995), p.391 at pp.403-406.

17. For discussion of the potential impact of economic sanctions see N.D. White, "Collective Sanctions: An Alternative to Military Coercion?" (1994) XII *International Relations*, 75.

18. For discussion of 'smart weapons' in the 1990-91 Gulf Conflict see F.J. Hampson 'Means and Methods of Warfare in the Gulf' in P. Rowe, ed., *The Gulf War 1990-91 in International and English Law* (Routledge/Sweet and Maxwell, 1993), pp.89-110.

19. For discussion see E. Grove, 'UN Armed Forces and the Military Staff Committee: A Look Back' *International Security* Vol. 17 No. 4, (1993), pp. 172-82.

20. See J.P. Cot and A. Pellet, eds., *La Charte des Nations Unies* (Economica, 1985), pp.709-11.

21. H. McCoubrey and N.D. White, *The Blue Helmets: Legal Regulation of United Nations Military Operations* (Dartmouth, 1996), p.13

22. For discussion see ibid., Chapters 6 and 7.

23. D.D. Carron, 'The Legitimacy of the Collective Authority of the Security Council' (1993) 87 *American Journal of International Law*, p.552 at p.578.

24. For discussion see chapter 4.

25. For discussion, see below.

26. (1962) ICJ. Reps, 151, see especially comments at pp,162-5.

27. N.D. White, *Keeping the Peace* (Manchester University Press, 1997), p.151.

28. See Chapter 1.

29. UN General Assembly Resolution 377(V) of 3 November 1950.

30. Ibid., paragraph 1.

31. D.J. Harris, op.cit., at p.970, cites 12 instances. The most recent was the Question of the Occupied Arab Territories – occasioned by an almost automatic US veto of any discussion of the issue in the Security Council.

32. N.D. White, *Keeping the Peace: The United Nations and the Maintenance of International Peace and Security*, 2 ed., (Manchester University Press, 1997), p.175

33. For discussion see Chapter 1

34. See I.L. Claude, op.cit., at p.113

35. For discussion see M. Akehurst, 'Enforcement Action by Regional Agencies, with Special Reference to the Organisation of American States' (1967) 42 *British Yearbook of International Law*, 175.
36. J.G. Merrills, *International Dispute Settlement* (Grotius, 1991), pp.228-9.
37. See H. Kelsen, *The Law of the United Nations* (Stevens, 1950).
38. See M. Akehurst, op.cit., at pp195-6.
39. See M. Weller, 'The International Response to the Dissolution of the Socialist Federal Republic of Yugoslavia', *American Journal of International Law*, (1992), Vol. 86, p.583.
40. M.N. Shaw, *International Law*, 4 ed., (Cambridge University Press, 1997), pp.882-884.
41. N.D. White and O. Ulgen, 'The Security Council and the Decentralised Military Option: Constitutionality and Function' (1997) XLIV *Netherlands International Law Review*, p.379 at p.389
42. For discussion of these instances see Chapters 3 and 5.
43. For discussion of this see Chapters 3 and 4.
44. See R.M. Russell and J.E. Muther, *A History of the United Nations Charter* (Brookings Institute, 1958), pp.696-706.
45. (1837) Moore's Digest of International Law, Vol.2, p. 412; British and Foreign State Papers, Vol 29, pp.1137-8, Vol 30., pp.195-6.
46. For discussion see D.W. Greig 'Self-Defence and the Security Council: What does Article 51 Require?'(1990) 42 *International and Comparative Law Quarterly*, pp. 366-424; also H. McCoubrey and N.D. White, *International Law and Armed Conflict* (Dartmouth, 1992), Chapter 6.
47. Op.cit., at p.371.
48. See Chapter 1.
49. See e.g., L. Oppenheim, *International Law*, 7 ed., (1952), Vol. 2, p.155.
50. See *Keesing's Record of World Events* (1990), pp.37631 ff.
51. M.N. Shaw, *International* Law, 4 ed., (Cambridge University Press, 1997) p.794.
52. *The Nicaragua case (Merits)* (1986) International Court of Justice Reports, p.14, Judgment at paragraph 199.
53. D.W. Greig, op.cit., at p.389.
54. For discussion see H. McCoubrey and N.D. White, 'International Law and the Use of Force in the Gulf (1991) X *International Relations*, p.347 at pp.352-4; also, T.M. Franck and F. Patel, 'UN Police Action in Lieu of War; the Old Order Changeth' (1991) 85 *American Journal of International Law*, p.63; C. Warbrick, 'The Invasion of Kuwait by Iraq' (1991) 40 *International and Comparative Law Quarterly*, p.482 and W.M. Reisman, 'Some Lessons from Iraq' (1991) 16 *Yale Journal of International Law*, p.203.
55. *Supplement to Agenda for Peace*, paragraph 38.
56. Ibid., paragraph 38.
57. See H. McCoubrey and N.D. White, *The Blue Helmets: Legal Regulation of United Nations Military Operations* (Dartmouth, 1996), Chapter 7.
58. *Supplement to Agenda for Peace*, paragraph 42.
59. P. Rowe, 'The United Nations Rules of Engagement and the British Soldier in Bosnia' [1994] 43 *International and Comparative Law Quarterly*, p.946 at p.948.
60. UN Doc. S/INF/49.
61. For discussion of the general issue see P.J. Rowe, *Defence: The Legal Implications* (Brassey's Defence Publishers, 1987), Chapter 6.
62. For detailed discussion of this see H. McCoubrey and N.D. White, *The Blue Helmets: Legal Regulation of United Nations Military Operations* (Dartmouth, 1996), Chapter 8.
63. F. Seyersted, *United Nations Forces in the Law of War and Peace* (A.W. Sijthoff, 1966), p.387.
64. Published in the *International Review of the Red Cross*, January 1962.

CHAPTER 3

The UN Between Paradigms:
Regional Devolution of Peace Support

The late 1980s and early 1990s involved a major shift in the patterns of global international relations which had a major, and continuing, impact upon world and regional security architecture. The end of the Cold War ideological confrontation between the USA, the former-USSR and their respective client states arguably represented at least as significant a change in the patterns of international relations as those which resulted from the First and Second World Wars and the development of the Cold War itself. At the same time the changes in the People's Republic of China which followed the death of Mao Zedong and the purging of the Jiang Qing group, leading to a major economic and foreign relations reorientation within a continuing authoritarian tradition symbolised by the events of Tienanmen Square, together with the ending in 1994 of the *apartheid* regime in South Africa and the processes of democatization in Southern and Central America contributed to a general reshaping of security concerns which have made the world at the outset of the 21st century very significantly different from its condition through the second half of the 20th century. The assumptions which had in practice, if not in theory, underlain the first half century of UN experience were largely displaced, forcing a radical rethinking of position on the part of the UN itself and many, if not all, of the regional organisations and defensive alliances. Indeed for some of the regional bodies accommodation to the new post-1980s situation has involved a process of virtual reinvention. For both the UN and the regional organisations and alliances this process of reconceptualisation has demanded a radical shift both in the perception of the nature of peace support action and the means of its implementation.

At the beginning of this period of transition there were optimistic anticipations of the peace support capacity of the UN itself when relieved from previous Cold War, and associated balance of power impediments, but these proved rapidly *in practice* to have been both naive and grossly unrealistic. The early success of action by the UN-sanctioned Coalition in the 1990-91 Gulf Conflict raised what proved to be exaggerated expectations, but later and more problematic actions, including those of UNPROFOR in former-Yugoslavia and UNOSOM in Somalia, led, by the same token, to a possibly excessive perception of UN 'failure', which may to some degree be seen as a consequence of original undue anticipations both within and beyond the UN. Be that as it may, there is a strong case to be made out that the UN after the Cold War was faced with an increased demand for peace support action for which neither its previous experience nor the resources actually or potentially available to it had well prepared the organisation. The consequent search for alternative and effective modes of operation forms a large part of the dynamic of the post-Cold War reorientation of peace support policy and practice.

Amongst the possible approaches a much increased reliance upon regional organisations and defensive alliances has been emphasised in the continuing debate. In *Supplement to Agenda for Peace* Boutros Boutros-Ghali stated that,

"Cooperation between the United Nations and regional organizations takes a number of forms. ... If those experiments [i.e. devolved peace support actions] succeed, they may herald a new division of labour between the United Nations and regional organizations, under which the regional organization carries the main burden but a small United Nations operation supports it and verifies that it is functioning in a manner consistent with positions adopted by the Security Council. ..." [1]

This is not, however, so simple or entirely so desirable a move as was initially *prima facie* supposed. There are inevitable pragmatic problems in the vast diversity of structure and capacity as between such organisations. [2] To this extent the experience of the transition from UNPROFOR to the NATO-led IFOR/SFOR forces in former-Yugoslavia may be considered to have been unfortunate. Whilst the NATO-led forces had considerable initial success – even if questions arise as to whether they were put in at the right time [3] and as to the ultimate effectiveness of the operation in the broader context of the Yugoslav crisis, as shown in the Kosovo situation in early 1999 – in terms of its operational experience, infrastructure, command and control practice and consequent military efficacy NATO is in many ways atypical of regional organisations. Strictly speaking it does not even consider itself to be a 'regional organisation' but merely a defensive alliance, even if in practice its post-Cold War redevelopment has significantly broadened that remit. Moreover NATO is unique in this context in that historically its membership comprised stable, representative democracies with clear subordination of military to civilian direction. [4] This is by no means universally the case, indeed typically it is not the case, and not all regional organisations, or their leading member states, are politically or strategically acceptable to other states, even in their defined area of operation. Linked with this is the shadow of regional hegemonism which was a cause for concern in the debates conducted at the outset of the UN era. Beyond this lies as a major issue for the UN the question of ultimate political control. Regional organisations and arrangements have long been recognised as having a valuable but unequivocally subordinate role in peace support and peace enforcement under Chapter VIII of the UN Charter [5] and it is important that their role remains that of *delegates* rather than *UN-alternatives* in the post-Cold War *jus ad bellum*. The issue was flagged up in actions such as Operation Desert Fox in December 1998 and the NATO air strikes against Serbia in the Kosovo crisis in March 1999 in the context of the extent of required prior consultation with and approval of the UN Security Council. [6]

The impact of the end of the Cold War has affected the global spectrum of security concerns and not only the immediately most obvious European and Atlantic sectors. There has been a considerable rethinking of security issues in the ASEAN area and in the broader Asia/Pacific context, as also in Africa where the future role of the OAU and the developing potential of ECOMOG and the South African Defence Community (SADC) raise major questions. This is also the case for the OAS, not least as the waning of the perceived communist threat has engendered highly significant debate upon a broadening of the concept of security to include, *inter alia*, the protection of democratic regimes from violent displacement. In some areas, including those of the tense confrontations between India and Pakistan, and in the Middle East, [7] there are no regional organisations capable of a peace support role. These many variable factors preclude any simple or singular solution to the dilemma of the UN in post-Cold War peace support action. It is therefore necessary that any assessment deals with the regions and their potential in terms of the local conditions and institutional infrastructures prevailing in each instance in order that an adequate view may be formed in the first place as to whether a genuinely new paradigm of peace support is being formed and, if so, what form or forms this is likely to take

REGIONAL PERSPECTIVES AND CAPACITIES

Regional security organisation in the Western European and Atlantic sector has, as indicated above, developed in many ways atypically, but is still taken to some degree as a paradigmatic example of the forms of regional security. Devised as a collective defence organisation and intended primarily to face up to the perceived threat posed by the USSR and its Warsaw Pact allies, NATO military action is fundamentally predicated upon article 5 of the North Atlantic Treaty. Resting upon the inherent right of self-defence preserved in the UN Charter, this provides for collective defence amongst the member states if an attack occurs upon any of them within the geographic limits of Europe or North America defined in article 6 of the treaty.

Whilst the threat which the organisation was originally created to counter has largely disappeared, the article 5 commitment remains its basic raison d'être, though the geographic parameters imposed by article 6 in relation to the collective defence commitment, while remaining in force, are likely to be liberally interpreted. Nonetheless, Article 6 does serve to complicate NATO endeavours to redefine its role through the potential addition of non-Article 5 operations. Since 1990 NATO has been engaged in a major review of its role and future, expected to culminate in the 1999 Washington Conference. In-area peace support operations not involving a direct attack upon NATO territory are seen as part of the organisation's future role, deriving at least in part from the experience of IFOR and SFOR in former-Yugoslavia. This case demonstrates NATO's willingness to expand its operational remit beyond that laid out in the treaty, action being undertaken even though the threat to the areas of defined NATO concern must be considered somewhat remote. The North Atlantic Treaty is, to a degree, like the UN Charter, a living document requiring some flexibility of interpretation if it is to remain functional in radically changing circumstances.

Amongst the concerns arising from the Yugoslav experience is an imperative need for clear directional mandates, including effective exit strategies, and an avoidance of the type of UN micro-regulation which was a major weakness of the former UNPROFOR force. A dual key system of command and control would be considered unacceptable, although if this was demanded by the political leadership it would have to be tolerated. It is also argued that minimization of 'mission creep', which might embroil NATO forces in activities for which they are ill-suited and little trained, will be a vital continuing policy concern. Experience also suggests that mandating is likely to prove a contentious issue. NATO, in common with any other such organisation contemplating such action, technically requires a UN, or possibly an OSCE, mandate if it wishes to undertake non-consensual, non-article 5 operations. It should be noted, however, that the potential of the OSCE now appears very limited, its membership is too numerous, its procedures too cumbersome and its bureaucracy too ineffective for it to be able to play such a role.

However, there is a divergence of views within NATO as to whether action without a mandate could ever be taken, an issue which led to both internal and external controversy over NATO military action against Serbia in March 1999. Some member states, notably the USA, are of the view that given sufficiently compelling strategic and political imperatives, action in the absence of such a mandate would be acceptable. This position is at variance with that of France, while the United Kingdom leans toward the American view, though with some reservations. It is not possible, given these divergent positions, to develop an overarching framework within which to assess the likelihood of future NATO peace support operations in the absence of a UN mandate. Similarly the issue of consent may have to be dealt with on a case-by-case basis, depending upon political and strategic dynamics and the nature and military power of the *de jure* government and of the other actors in the crisis, however, for the reasons set out above and in Chapter 2 the *prima facie* supposition must be that outwith article 51, non-consensual coercive operations would in almost all situations require a mandate apart, perhaps, from very short term emergency response. The delicacies of assessment were, again, clearly indicated by the Kosovo crisis.

In parallel with the rethinking of the role of NATO, the Western European Union (WEU) has not so much been involved in a process of reinvention as in one of reincarnation. The WEU was in origin a Western European precursor to NATO in which the five signatories to the 1948 Treaty of Brussels – Belgium, France, Luxembourg, the Netherlands and the United Kingdom – agreed to a system of European collective defence designed to deter potential aggression from a resurgent Germany and the developing Soviet bloc. This concept was swiftly broadened to include the vitally significant Atlanticist dimension, a bone of contention for France ever since. The consequent conclusion of the 1949 North Atlantic Treaty and the establishment of NATO effectively superseded the WEU, the security functions of which were transferred to NATO in 1950.

The winding down of the Cold War and an increasing sense in US domestic politics that Europe should to a greater degree shoulder its own defence, coupled with an increasing corporate consciousness within the EU, led to a revival of the WEU in the 1980s, notably at the 1984 Rome Conference. The broad intention was set out in a 1987 policy document, *Platform on European Security,* which is viewed by the UK as offering 'a means of strengthening the European pillar of the [NATO] Alliance and of giving concrete form to Europe's security and defence.' [8] Others have perceived a role for the WEU which is at once both more ambitious and more amorphous, including a potential, in effect, to be the security arm of the EU. It is clear that the WEU would prefer to maintain an existence separate from the EU, but the key question for its future is that of capability.

The potential remit of the organisation is, rather ambitiously, set out by the 1992 Petersburg Declaration of the WEU. This excludes self-defence, which is seen as NATO's core remit, but includes peacekeeping, humanitarian and rescue missions and crisis management. NATO for its part does not see humanitarian and rescue missions as forming part of its tasks but might be willing to share assets and infrastructure if the WEU became involved in such an operation. The WEU Council has designated S.E. Europe, the Mediterranean basin and Africa as areas of special interest. The rather startling inclusion of the latter apparently arose in response to concerns over Francophone Africa and specifically the Great Lakes crisis. Even assuming the availability of suitable military assets, however, it must seriously be doubted whether European forces could have a large role in sub-Saharan peace support, granted the historical 'baggage' of colonialism and the modern emphasis upon Africanization of such operations. In this respect the experience of the French-led Operation Turquoise in Rwanda was far from encouraging.

The ultimate role of the WEU remains to be seen, but its potential as a major peace support actor is considered with marked scepticism outside the organisation. It is difficult to avoid the thought that much of the impetus for revived interest in the WEU derives from French anti-Atlanticist policy in European defence, but the WEU may ultimately find a role between NATO and EU in peace support, although hardly upon the scale suggested by the Petersberg principles.

During the years of the Cold War the Soviet Union played a very limited role in peacekeeping operations. [9] The demise of the USSR brought with it, at least temporarily, a major change in attitude toward peacekeeping on the part of is 'successor' state, the Russian Federation. In an initial burst of enthusiasm for UN peacekeeping Moscow undertook eight new peacekeeping missions between 1992 and 1997 and as part of its new approach for the first time dispatched troops to participate in peacekeeping operations. However, Russia has not maintained this level of participation and since the Spring of 1998 has dramatically reduced its peacekeeping forces by 80 percent. At the time of writing Russia ranks a relatively lowly sixteenth amongst contributors to UN peacekeeping operations and, with the exception of its continued participation in SFOR and KFOR, shows signs of reverting to a Soviet-style, limited participation, observer only, UN peacekeeping stance. There has indeed been evidence of a return to balance of power politics associated with the instability of the Yeltsin government and an upsurge of militant national-ism evidenced in the Chechen crisis and in Russian attitudes towards both the continuation of the Iraq and former-Yugoslav crises in the late 1990s. Moscow has been active in unilateral and multilateral actions, often under the ostensi-ble guise of the Commonwealth of Independent States (CIS). In fact, for every Russian soldier deployed on UN or UN sanctioned peacekeeping missions outside of the CIS, between three and five have been deployed within the region.

Problematically, while Russian activities in UN or UN sanctioned opera-tions have met with a generally positive response, those undertaken outside of these parameters, often with the absence of effective international scrutiny and control, may present cause for greater concern. The deployment of troops prior to the establishment of cease-fires, the partial manner in which they have often been seen to act and their willingness to resort to force in excess of that usually deemed appropriate for peacekeeping purposes has led many to conclude that Russia is far from the ideal candidate as a regional peacekeeper. The potential for fellow-CIS member states to mount effective opposition in the face of Russia's apparent hegemonic regional ambitions is, at best, limited and the OSCE and the UN may find the task of restraining Moscow little easier.

Fears of regional hegemonism have also predominated in the OAS. During the period of the Cold War US fears of communist encroachment into the western hemisphere led to a distortion of OAS security concepts and in many cases the installation or support of highly repressive non-democratic regimes. The hemisphere's highly institutionalised collective security apparatus came to serve as a means of legitimising Washington's regional foreign policy objectives to the exclusion of other concerns. However, the end of the Cold War has led to a major revision of the perceptions and objectives of the OAS, coinciding with, and indeed strengthening, the democratization of Southern and later Central America. No longer preoccupied with the perceived communist threat, the organisation has turned to a broadened concept of security. This does not exclude traditional inter-State security concerns, at least in part because, as militaries cease looking inward, they might potentially begin to look across frontiers. However, issues such as human rights, democratization and economic and social development are now high on the OAS agenda. In particular the maintenance of norms of democratic govern-ance has come to be seen as part of the security agenda, as has a realisation that democracy is reliant upon a socio-economic base across the region in which all sectors of society can see real benefit.

Despite the dramatic changes which the western hemisphere has witnessed in the last decade, national and institutional historical experience continues to colour the manner in which the OAS and its member states view their future role. Thus, as regards peace support action, the OAS sees itself as having a persuasive rather than an enforcing or coercive role. The experience of action in Guatemala, the Dominican Republic and more recently in Grenada, Panama and Haiti has tended strongly to disincline the organisation from involvement in military intervention. Despite this, the organisation has developed a mechanism designed to further develop democratic ideals and to deal with threats to democracy should they arise. The basis of this mechanism is laid down in OAS General Assembly Resolution 1080 and the OAS membership most recently reiterated its commitment to this cause at the Second Summit of the Americas held in Santiago in April 1998. However an extreme reluctance to resort to the use of force is likely to prevail, though in the most extreme circumstances the OAS might be willing to refer the violent over-throw of a democratic government to the UN Security Council. Perhaps inevitably given the regional historical context the organisation emphasises peace building rather than peace enforcement and effective military/civilian liaison in confidence building measures. It has developed some considerable experience in this area, most notably during the seven year support and verification mission in Nicaragua which ended in June 1997. The future of peace support in the region would seem therefore to involve a central role in peace and confidence building by the OAS but in the end a reliance upon the UN for more robust action. Recent OAS thinking also recognises that the capacities of both the UN and the OAS itself are limited and that an enhanced role for sub-regional organisations may also become necessary in hemispheric peace support. [10] It must however be said that here, more than anywhere else, any action, by the UN or the OAS, would still rest upon at least the acquiescence of the USA as the inevitably dominant hemispheric power.

Peace support operations in Africa have been fraught with difficulty in part because of the colonial legacy and the varieties of historical 'baggage' which this imports, but also because of external Cold War related manipulation which contributed markedly to political instability in the region. This unhappy background has engendered a general consensus within and outwith Africa that the best way forward is an African solution to African problems in which a combination of action by regional organisations and coalitions of willing African states may be most efficacious. Establishing how and by whom such 'African' solutions are to be implemented is, however, highly problematic.

A starting point must be found in the OAU, the Charter of which includes amongst the organisation's purposes by Article 2(1)(c) the defence of sovereignty, territorial integrity and independence and to these ends requires by Article 2(2)(f) that member states engage in cooperation for defence and security. The OAU expressed its willingness to undertake peace support operations at the 1997 Chiefs of Staff meeting in Harare, whilst confirming that any such operations would have to be in accordance with the UN Charter. Non-consensual operations would thus, subject possibly to the same questions as arose for NATO in relation to Kosovo in March 1999, require a UN mandate and for this purpose mechanisms for consultation have been established between the OAU and the UN Security Council.

The operational capacity of the OAU is however open to some debate, past OAU peace support operations sending out rather mixed messages. The Inter-African Force sent into Chad at the end of 1981 suffered from a failure by many states to supply promised contingents, defective mission definition and exit strategy and problems of command and control. The force was withdrawn after only six months and must be considered to have been a failure, though valuable lessons may have been learnt. The OAU undoubtedly has operation-ally capable forces at its disposal and the organisation is exploring cooperation with external actors such as NATO, and the WEU, in training and infrastructural development. Such support is rendered the more necessary by the large financial deficit carried by the organisation, but requires politically sensitive handling. There are lessons to be learnt from the US sponsored concept of an African Crisis Management Force which has become effectively moribund largely through failure to consult within Africa. The more recent African Security Studies Institute initiative, also supported by the USA, is thought to have a better chance of success because African powers have been involved from the outset. However, the most effective role for the OAU in the security sector is, in view of the size and diversity of the membership, probably one of peace and confidence building rather than peacekeeping and peace enforcement.

Sub-regional organisations are also of great importance in sub-Saharan Africa, albeit, again, of variable potential and impact. The ECOWAS ceasefire monitoring group ECOMOG, sent into Liberia in 1990, proved problematic from the outset. There were again problems of mission definition and of command and control. There were also serious problems arising from the conduct of elements of the forces on the ground, especially the large Nigerian contingent, which rapidly gained an unenviable reputation in their areas of operation. This again raises the problem of the dangers of regional hegemonism as, implicitly, in the case of the CIS. In any regional or sub-regional approach it has to be borne in mind that major regional actors may in some cases not be the solution to the problem but may themselves be a large part of the problem!

Other sub-regional actors of potential significance include SADC. SADC is a grouping of southern African states of which South Africa itself is the largest and most militarily capable, but which also includes such significant actors as Zimbabwe and Ghana. The organization evidently has genuine military capability, but much will turn upon the attitude adopted by South Africa. The massive tasks of post-*apartheid* reconstruction, including the sensitive task of restructuring the defence forces, seems likely to disincline the country from engagement in external crisis management for some time to come. When and if the SADC does move into a regional peace support role, however, it may be an actor of very considerable potential, with the beneficial effect also of balancing the military strength of Nigeria in African security calculations.

It is improbable that there is any single African solution to Africa's security problems. It does seem probable, however, that the OAU will be active at least in peace and confidence building measures and possibly in more forceful action, although here in particular it seems likely that UN and other external support will continue to be called for. The great question mark for sub-Saharan African and the continent more generally concerns the role of SADC and this, as so much else, turns essentially upon the ultimate development of South Africa. At the time of writing this necessarily remains uncertain, although the 1998 experience of the intervention in Lesotho counsels some degree of caution in the expectations which may be entertained.

In post-colonial Southeast Asia ideas of security are at least as much bound up with questions of internal stabilisation and economic development as with fears of external threat. This stems in part from the troubled past of the region which itself derives in part from the imposition of a 'European' concept of statehood with significant resulting political distortions and social tensions. Defensive alliances tend to be perceived as exclusive and threatening rather than inclusive and protective [11] and also as contrary to the urge towards consensualism which is a significant imperative of regional relations. This is not, however, to say that there is a lack of collective security consciousness and relevant regional organisations or that the dynamics of the Cold War and its ending left the region untouched. [12]

The principal regional organisation is ASEAN, although it is not strictly a regional security organisation, still less a military alliance, and has been concerned primarily with confidence building and transparency as between its members. Nonetheless, despite the continuing emphasis upon 'preventive diplomacy' inherent in the 'ASEAN way', the 1990s have brought about some changes in the direction of regional security thinking. The establishment, in July 1993, of the ASEAN Regional Forum (ARF) was a major indicator of this change. The ARF involves the overwhelming majority of the regional powers, extending well beyond the ASEAN member and its credibility as an actor in the region is underpinned by its acceptance by both the PRC and the USA, neither of which would have been happy to see a Southeast Asian security forum dominated by the other. The ARF may play a highly significant role in regional confidence building and conflict avoidance, if, however, the region were to face a major military crisis it may be questioned whether it could in the short or even medium term function as an effective mechanism of regional collective security.

It is undoubtedly a major advance upon earlier organisations, such as the South East Asia Treaty Organisation (SEATO), founded upon the post-Korean War 1954 South-East Asia Collective Defence Treaty and modelled upon NATO. SEATO was a western dominated anti-Communist alliance which in many ways symbolised external intervention in regional security and its failure emphasised the need for regionally appropriate models rather than the importation of other region's practices. In practice any East Asian regional peace support action is likely to rely upon a coalition of the willing, almost certainly underpinned by one or other of the interested external powers.

There arises also the question of Japan. Japan possesses substantial defence forces but external operations raise difficult questions within Japan by reason of article 9 of the Constitution, and beyond it by reason of the long shadow cast by memories of the Second World War. Article 9 has been taken to preclude Japanese involvement in UN collective security action, although Japanese Maritime Self-Defence Force (JMSDF) minesweepers were sent to the Gulf after the conclusion of hostilities in the 1990-91 Gulf Conflict. Even more pointedly Japanese Self-Defence Force (JSDF) forces were deployed in UN operations in Cambodia and Japan is now playing a major role in ARF security discussions. At the same time the USA has become dissatisfied with the disproportion between Japanese economic power and the level of its contribution to regional security. The reduction of the US military presence in the region, initiated by the 1990 East Asian Strategy Initiative (EASI) and domestic pressure within Japan for early reduction if not removal of the US military presence have all lent point to a significant reorientation of Japanese defence and security planning. The future in this respect, however, remains very uncertain.

As to the PRC, China was historically the dominant power in the region and in the post-Mao era is rapidly becoming so again. However, the present economic restructuring processes within the country render a large scale involvement in peace support rather unlikely in the medium term and, again, the acceptability of action by the People's Liberation Army in many countries of Southeast Asia must seem very doubtful.

The immediate future of peace support in East and Southeast Asia would seem necessarily to rest upon ad hoc foundations. The essential basis of any such operations will almost certainly rest upon bilateral or multilateral coalitions of the willing, subject to the rather unpredictable, future development of the ARF and the continuing presence and interest of, in particular, the USA and the PRC.

The region of the Middle East and Islamic North Africa pose, at both the regional and the UN level, particularly acute problems in terms of peacekeeping. Amongst more radically Islamic regimes such as those in Iran and Sudan, the question of Western dominance of the UN dictates a cautious approach toward the organisation's activities. Similar fears also have a part to play in the policies of those more pro-Western states facing radical Islamic domestic opposition. UN detractors advocating such a stance base their criticisms upon issues of Western bias and domination rather than upon more fundamental opposition to the UN itself. Thus more traditional UN peacekeeping, based upon the consent of the parties to the conflict, remains a feasible option in situations where conflict arises. However, more robust forms of peace support operation, especially where connotations of enforcement action exist, are likely to remain taboo. The UN's response to the Iraqi invasion of Kuwait is instructive insofar as the tensions created within the Arab world were in large part a response to what was perceived as a Western led military intervention in a situation which would have been better handled within a regional forum.

Whatever the wisdom of such a regionalist approach, it is clear that organisations such as the Arab League and the Organization of the Islamic Conference are particularly ill suited to dealing with the most protracted problem in modern day Middle Eastern affairs, namely the relationship between the Arab states and Israel. While regional organisations are often seen as appropriate fora for conflict resolution because of the motivation to act demonstrated by the membership, in the case of the Middle East this clearly does not represent a viable option.

Sub-Continental South Asia poses different, but no less acute problems in terms of regional and UN peacekeeping. Traditionally staunch supporters of UN peacekeeping operations, India, and to a lesser extent Pakistan, have recently seen their relationship with the UN and crucial members therein deteriorate. In the case of India in particular this can for the most part be explained by a reassessment of foreign policy belying a more nationalistic and assertive view of the world. As Alan Bullion explains, the 'altruistic and solidaristic objectives have been superseded by India's wider global ambition for recognition and influence on the world stage' [13] This has inevitably exacerbated existing tensions between India and Pakistan, the decision by both to test their nuclear weapons capabilities serving to further accentuate the situation and introduce a potentially even more dangerous element into Sub-Continental relations. Given the refusal of both states to submit to the will of the international community, or the terms of the CTBT, it is unlikely, at least in the immediate term, that the UN will entrust either with a principal role in a peacekeeping mandate, particularly so given the state of relations between New Delhi and Washington. The absence of a regional institutional framework through which peacekeeping operations could be undertaken exacerbates this already difficult situation. The only recent example of a 'regional' operation was that of the Indian Peace-Keeping Force which operated in Sri Lanka between 1987 and 1990 and which met with ignominious failure. Single nation forces of this type are unusual and in most cases highly undesirable. In any event, the Indian action in Sri Lanka cannot be seen as a useful precedent. The operation failed not only in its basic objectives, but also in the extent to which it accorded with established norms of peacekeeping. Other 'single nation' operations have included the UN instruction to the United Kingdom in relation to the UDI regime in Southern Rhodesia (now Zimbabwe), [14] but this was an all but unique case of an imperial power being required to take measures for the resumption of an illegitimately interrupted process of decolonisation which was seen as a threat to peace and security. [15] In the context of the South Asian sub-continent it must also finally be said that in present circumstances the development of a capable regional organisation seems exceedingly unlikely.

TOWARDS A NEW PARADIGM OF PEACE SUPPORT?

It remains to be considered whether the changes in the global and regional security environment which have occurred since the end of the 1980s are of sufficient significance to justify a discourse of change of paradigms. There can be no doubt that the international security environment has been much changed since the end of the Cold War and both the United Nations and relevant international organisations have found it necessary to adopt processes of radical change in practice and orientation in order to address the challenges of a new era. Although the changes have manifestly been less stark and traumatic than those which followed the First and Second World Wars, they can reasonably be argued to have been no less significant in their actual and potential impact. They in no sense represent a reversion to the intended, but never – not even Korea – truly operative, UN collective system of 1945. The presumptions of that era, both the real and retrospectively attributed, are as much or more a matter of history than former Cold War attitudes. The changes which are now occurring in global and regional security concepts and architecture represent a shift to new methods and assumptions in the face of a changed and more uncertain situation for which both the pre-existing structures and the resources available to them have rapidly proved inadequate. Upon this basis the process of transition which has been in hand since the late 1980s can, indeed, fairly be represented as one involving a change in peace support paradigms. Like any process of transition, this involves large elements of both uncertainty and instability and developing new or revised approaches to the maintenance of international peace and security requires experimentation and a degree *ad hoc* expediency. This can be both controversial and difficult, as the uncertain legal status of the 'emergency' Anglo-US 'Operation Desert Fox', in December 1998 and the NATO air strikes against Serbia-Montenegro in the March 1999 flare-up of the Kosovo crisis painfully demonstrated. These uncertainties seem set to continue into the 21st century and indeed, subject to certain clear stabilising norms, may even come to constitute a basic element of a new and more flexible paradigm of peace support. This may ultimately be the answer in a more diverse and less constrained international general and security order, involving a more extensive use of suitable regional and sub-regional organisations including delegation of enforcement measures, where and if a suitable organisation is available. It also seems highly probable that a key role will be played by 'coalitions of the willing'. The extent and form of these changes in practice will no doubt vary significantly not only from region to region, but from situation to situation within regions. The terminology of flexibility of response is, indeed, becoming commonplace in the discourse of both the UN itself and many of the regional organisations and alliances. Within this rapidly evolving context a variety of political and legal concerns arise which will require urgent and continuing address. The UN will no doubt remain directly involved in smaller scale enforcement measures, but the major question for the organisation will almost certainly be the means by which it will retain political control over 'delegated' peace support action. Again, the Operation Desert Fox and Kosovo air strike questions represent an early surfacing of just this issue. There is, thus, a need to maintain impartiality whilst securing efficacy and to retain ultimate UN oversight whilst affording clear mandates for action and efficient mechanisms of command and control. There are also basic needs, emphasised by the experiences of former-Yugoslavia and Somalia, for clear mission planning and objectives, especially exit strategies founded upon defined end states rather than end dates, and awareness of both the positive and negative potential of so-called 'mission creep'. If these matters can be resolved satisfactorily the end result may be a much improved, more flexible and more effective multipartite peace support paradigm. If they are not, the clear danger is that of a reversion to balances of power and regional hegemonism of the sort which generated both the First and Second World Wars.

As remarked at the outset, the initial adoption of a more activist stance on the part of the UN at the end of the Cold War had initial success in the 1990-91 Gulf Conflict but was followed by disappointments of expectation in former-Yugoslavia and Somalia. These experiences are likely to shape UN perceptions of the role the organisation is capable of playing and hence it is likely to look toward regional organisations as primary actors in peace support. However, as the analysis set out above indicates, there is so great a degree of diversity in both the structure and capabilities of these organisations and in the nature of the states of which they are comprised that no simple or singular global pattern for future development can reasonably be proposed. This diversity of capability calls for an expansion of inter-organisational support and facilitation as well as experience-sharing. This latter is beginning to develop, for example, between NATO, the WEU and the OAU. The OAS is also beginning to consider such an agenda, e.g., between itself and the OSCE and OAU. A commitment by the major powers is also essential if regional organisations which are currently incapable of carrying out major UN mandated peace support operations are to develop the capacity to do so.

The utilisation of more highly developed regional peace support capabilities must take place within the constitutional parameters laid down by the United Nations Charter, with Chapters VII and VIII serving as the foundations of peace support and inter-organisational cooperation. The broader membership of the United Nations must be secure in the confidence that actions carried out on their behalf are not the result of regional power-plays in which the UN serves to do no more than legitimise regional hegemonic ambitions. Impressions of Security Council impropriety were raised, for example, by widespread reports in 1994 that the USA and Russia had agreed a deal whereby the two Permanent Members would provide reciprocal support for proposals on military intervention within their traditional spheres of influence. Moscow had sought a UN mandate authorising deployment of a peacekeeping force in the neighbouring state of Georgia, but this had not been forthcoming. However, subject to the proviso that each carry out its actions under UN supervision, Washington agreed to support the UN plan in return for the latter's support for American proposals for military intervention in Haiti. According to James Bone, the deal,

"reflected the dilemma that great powers face in an era of greater international cooperation when they want to play by the rules while still policing their backyards in the time-honoured fashion." [16]

Similarly, the security agenda which the UN and the regional organisations with which it collaborates pursues, while being sufficiently broad to account for the changing prerogatives of the post-Cold War world, must be based upon the politics of consensus rather than dictation. The lessons of the Concert of Europe should not go unheeded, for that, arguably the first attempt to replace a simple balance of power mechanism with one founded on the principles of collective security, foundered upon a commitment of some of the member states to the political principle of autocracy which could in modern terms be considered a 'broadening of the concept of security'. Quite apart from the possibly divisive effect of such broadening of agendas, the question of capacity arises. Regional organisations are not necessarily well resourced and their capacity to take on ever expanding remits must be doubted. Suggestions of some form of international peace support contingency fund are not without a *prima facie* attraction but in practice they simply restate the problem. The source of such funding is uncertain and there is no reason to imagine that it would be any more forthcoming than that currently available to the organisations. It may also be pointed out that the political suspicions which undermined the concept of stand by forces held in readiness for UN use might well also be an obstacle to the setting up of any such contingency fund.

Despite these caveats, a concept of security suited to the complexities of the 21st Century necessitates an approach to peace support which emphasises the inter-related nature of military, economic and social concerns. Within this context organisations should look to be pro-active rather than reactive, but where a military solution is required, states and organisations need to realise the continuing nature of peace support commitment. It is preferable to remain engaged for a prolonged period than to be forced to return to resurgent and possibly exacerbated troubles in a former area of operations. In short, effective peace and confidence building measures must be seen as part of a seamless spectrum of peace support action with any necessary military action seen as the last and least desirable resort. It is necessary not merely to terminate hostilities but also to attempt to resolve the causes of conflict.

It would be satisfying from an academic, and possibly also a practical, point of view to advance some single theory to underpin peace support action in the post-Cold War era. Such an endeavour must, however, be suggested to be fundamentally misconceived. The diversity of the situations and organisations which are likely to be involved is such that a much more flexible approach involving a multiplicity of conceptual formulations will certainly be necessary in any global, or even regional, appreciation of future patterns of peace support action and developing ideas of security. A holistic concept of security in a new and more complex international relations environment in fact precludes any simple or singular formula for future development in this area. The flexible responses which have been, and will be, demanded of regional organisations and defensive alliances in volatile and rapidly evolving situations mean that patterns of response into the next century will, by their nature, develop pragmatically upon a case by case basis. This does not, however, mean that patterns of future response and action will be devoid of a principled base and theoretical underpinning. The essential imperatives which have here been suggested may at least be argued to define the limits within which the necessary flexibility of response in the evolving global and regional security agenda must be framed. Out of this process of development, it may be suggested, there is likely to emerge not a single new paradigm for the maintenance of international peace and security but rather a paradigm involving a wide variety of modes, better suited to a diverse and volatile international relations context.

NOTES

1. *Supplement to Agenda for Peace*, S/1995/1, 3 January 1995, paragraph 86.
2. For analysis of this see below.
3. For discussion of the forces in former-Yugoslavia, see below.
4. The Western European Union can also make this claim, but in any event the membership of the two organisations largely overlap.
5. See Chapter 2.

6. See Article 53(1) of the UN Charter. See also Chapters 2, 9 and 10.
7. The Organization of the Islamic Conference and the Arab League by definition exclude Israel and are largely disabled in the primary source of regional conflict.
8. *Britain, NATO and European Security* (HMSO, 1994), p.33.
9. For further discussion see Chapter 4.
10. Some of these ideas were considered at the OAS Unit for the Promotion of Democracy Conference upon 'OAS Peace Building Experiences: Progress Achieved, Lessons Learned and Future Possibilities' in Washington DC on 20 October 1998.
11. The mirror image nature of the NATO/Warsaw Pact relationship in the Cold War era illustrates this point.
12. See C. Mackerras, 'From Imperialism to the end of the Cold War' in A. McGrew and C. Brook, *Asia-Pacific in the New World Order* (Routledge, 1998), p.35 at pp.44-5.
13. Alan Bullion,'India and UN Peacekeeping Operations', *International Peacekeeping*, Vol.4, No.1, 1997, p.99.
14. UN SC Resolution 217 of 20 November 1965, referring specifically to the Rhodesian situation as a threat to international peace and security.
15. For discussion of the Rhodesian case see J. Morris, 'The United Nations: Collective Security and Individual Rights' in M. Jane Davis, ed., *Security Issues in the Post-Cold War World*, (Edward Elgar, 1996), pp.116-120.
16. *The Times* (London) 27 September 1994. See also Security Council Resolutions 934, 937 and 940 of 1994.

CHAPTER 4

The European Perspective:
NATO, the WEU, OSCE and the CIS

As a result of the historic Eurocentric focus of the early modern development of international relations and international law, from, in crude terms, the 1648 Peace of Westphalia to the 1918 Treaty of Versailles and even to the end of the Second World War in 1945, the European experience has had an inevitably large role in shaping concepts of security and the law pertaining thereto. [1] In the modern, post-1945, era Europe has again played a central role in the development of security concepts, only this time not so much as the location of Powers which have been the central actors as a focus of the interests of the post-war Superpowers. The Cold War confrontation between the USA and the USSR shaped European concepts of collective security, on both sides of the 'iron curtain', [2] for half a century. In particular it shaped the development of the North Atlantic Treaty Organisation (NATO) and the former Warsaw Pact. The end of the Cold War, with first the reformist Gorbachev administration in the former USSR and later the actual dissolution of the Soviet Union, leading, probably inevitably, to the winding up of the Warsaw Pact alliance, has had a dramatic effect upon defence and security thinking in Europe. The termination of the Cold War dynamic in which the potential security threat was readily, if perhaps a little over simply, identified – from the western view, the USSR and Warsaw Pact, from the eastern view the USA and NATO – rendered necessary a reconsideration of security concepts and concerns in, and in relation to, Europe as a whole. [3] The development of collective security concepts as they are expressed in the UN Charter has been considered above, [4] but a review of the development of the principal security actors in modern Europe is called for here as a preliminary to consideration of their present and potential future roles.

After the Second World War the reconstitution of the security architecture of western Europe was based upon the perceived need to face two quite different potential threats. One, looking back to the experience of the first half of the 20th century, was the possible peril at some future date of a renewal of militarism and expansionism in Germany. The other looked to the increasingly evident danger posed by a newly powerful Soviet Union which, as the war time alliances of necessity dissolved, was increasingly seen as a potential aggressor. The first step in the development of post-1945 western European security structures was undertaken with the conclusion on 17 March 1948 of the Treaty of Brussels, by which Belgium, Britain, France, Luxembourg and the Netherlands agreed upon measures of political, cultural and economic co-operation and also measures intended to ensure containment of any renewal of German aggression. The Treaty was, however, phrased in terms of general collective defence. Specifically article V [5] provides that,

> "If any of the High Contracting Parties should be the object of an armed attack in Europe, the other High Contracting Parties will, in accordance with the provisions of Article 51 of the Charter of the United Nations, afford the Party so attacked all the military and other aid and assistance in their power."

In reality, and not very surprisingly in the historical context, France particularly emphasised the necessity for concern with a possible renewal of German expansionism. The United States in particular took a different view and was concerned to reduce its commitments in Europe and to enable the continent to maintain its own defence and security. From the US perspective that necessarily involved a rehabilitation and rearmament of, by then, West Germany, seen as a 'front line State' [6] in the developing ideological and military confrontation with the Eastern bloc. These, very divisive, differences of opinion and emphasis were manifestly damaging to the development of western security concepts in the immediate post-war era, and, indeed, indicated fault lines which, in slightly different forms, continue to affect European and North Atlantic defence and security debate even at the end of the 20th century. In 1952 a potential resolution of these difficulties emerged with the European Defence Community [7] (EDC), but this failed when France refused to ratify the agreement. Two years later in 1954 the Western European Union (WEU) was established by the Paris Agreement which adopted a Protocol modifying the 1948 Brussels Treaty [8] and brought the original parties, with the addition of [West] Germany and Italy, into the new organisation. The WEU had, however, in practice been rendered functionally redundant as a defence and security structure even at the time when it was established. Its defence and security functions had *ab initio* been taken over by the differently conceived North Atlantic Treaty Organisation (NATO), the importance of which, in terms of the necessity for 'close co-operation' was recognised by the new article IV of the Brussels Treaty inserted by the 1954 Modifying Protocol. These developments took place against the background of the first moves towards more general European integration, signalled by the formation of the European Coal and Steel Community (ECSC). Significantly, however, these moves were also initially linked with US support for European regeneration through the Marshall Aid plan. These events were of direct security relevance in that on the one hand European integration was seen as a means of binding Germany into a new European order and on the other hand also of creating a prosperous western Europe capable of taking responsibility for its own security in relation to any potential Soviet threat.

At later stages in the course of development new actors entered upon the scene, notably the CSCE – born of the 'Helsinki' process, of which at one time high hopes were entertained as a potential new overarching European security organisation possibly replacing both NATO and the Warsaw Pact. This has not happened and does no seem likely to happen, although a lesser but still significant role may yet be played by the organisation. Be that as it may NATO is currently the key to European security structures and its background and capacities therefore remain issues of primary importance in European defence and security calculations.

NATO AND POST-COLD WAR REORIENTATION

NATO was established by the 1949 North Atlantic Treaty and from the beginning combined the European and Atlanticist dimensions of western security and in so doing set an agenda which remains the dominant dynamic in this area to the present time. The role of NATO was shaped by the Cold War, which is taken to have had its origin in the 1948 assault upon, and relief of, Berlin. This symbolised the ideological confrontation in which Europe had become an object of contention between the two post-war Superpowers. Nonetheless, the vital Atlanticist dimension of the NATO alliance remained a focus for controversy especially from the viewpoint of France. It was this issue which led in 1966 to French withdrawal from the NATO unified command structure. The question remains significant, although French relations with NATO are probably better in the later 1990s than at any time since the 1960s. [9] It is, indeed, highly probable that the tension generated by a French perception of an 'Anglo-Saxon' (i.e. US-UK) domination of NATO has been at least one motivation for the revival of the WEU after the 1984 Rome Conference [10] and may generate difficulties in relations between the two organisations. At the same time positive co-operation between the two organisations may lead to processes of further development, not least through the Combined Joint Task Forces initiative. [11]

Although NATO was, and is, primarily a defensive alliance – it does *not* consider itself to be a 'regional organisation', it recognises that that role must be conceived and implemented in a somewhat broader perspective. Thus, Article 2 of the North Atlantic Treaty provides that,

"The Parties will contribute toward the further development of peaceful and friendly international relations by strengthening their free institutions, by bringing about a better understanding of the principles upon which these institutions are founded, and by pro- moting conditions of stability and well being. They will seek to eliminate conflict in their

international economic policies and will encourage economic collaboration between any
or all of them."

Article 3 then goes on to state that maintenance and development of collective
capacity to resist armed attack is a means 'more effectively to achieve [these]
objectives'. This is an interesting statement in the present context, especially
in view of its date, since it suggests already an implicit broadening of the
security agenda to include both democracy and economic stability – both very
much issues in current debates upon the nature of 'security'. [12] Admittedly
the 1949 statements almost certainly took their shape and implication from the
ideological fears of the early years of the Cold War, but are no less interesting
for that.

Be that as it may, the structure of NATO, both in its primary collective
defence role and in broader contexts, was shaped in an international relations
context which has radically changed and the organisation is therefore faced
with the necessity to reorient its objectives and to do so within legal and
constitutional structures devised in earlier and different circumstances. It
might be suggested that with the demise of the anticipated principal enemy,
the Warsaw Pact, NATO had become *functus officio* and without justification
for existence. This seems in principle a rather naive view in so far as the end
of one security threat does not mean an end to all security menaces, even if the
political and economic instability of Russia in the 1990s did not contain the
seeds of potential future concerns. [13] Nonetheless in the circumstance of the
new post-Cold War state of European relations very significant redefinition
of NATO functions and objectives are clearly required. This process has been
in hand since the 1990 Madrid meeting at which policies founded upon the
Cold War structure of opposed blocs was, necessarily, abandoned and, at the
time of writing, is expected to culminate in the 1999 Washington Conference.
Major issues under consideration include involvement in peace support
operations – especially in the light of the IFOR/SFOR and KFOR operations
in former-Yugoslavia, 'out-of-area' operations and the fraught question of
NATO expansion. The first two questions involve major legal issues and are
as such considered below, the latter is a matter of fierce political and strategic
controversy.

The idea of expansion was adopted in earnest at the January 1994 NATO
Summit which also launched the Partnership for Peace (PFP) initiative
designed to 'forge new security relationships' with non-NATO Members. [14]
PFP is not simply or necessarily a part of the process of enlargement [15] and
does not extend either the collective security guarantee of article 5 of the
North Atlantic Treaty or a promise of eventual membership to partner States.
It is, however, clearly a NATO outreach particularly to Eastern Europe. It
builds upon the work done by the North Atlantic Co-operation Council

(NACC), formed in December 1991 to promote dialogue between NATO and its former Warsaw Pact adversaries. PFP, however, goes well beyond the NACC agenda of dialogue and confidence building measures. In particular, it contemplates co-operation and joint action for the maintenance of stability and security. PFP partners are represented at NATO Headquarters and a Partnership Co-ordination Cell has been established at Mons, conveniently close to the Supreme Headquarters Allied Powers Europe (SHAPE). The very practical question of interoperability, not yet perfectly achieved even within NATO, is under active consideration. The PFP may represent a way forward towards a new form of overarching European security architecture and its inclusion of Russia may prove very significant. As the late Joseph Kruzel remarked,

> "One of the most ingenious aspects of the PFP is that it hedges the cosmic bet about the future of Russia. Russia will be a part of the European Security system by dint of its geography and power. It will not go away. It is in the interests of us all, especially Russia, that Russia's role be a constructive and cooperative one. The path of partnership cooperation has the potential to be a powerful tool to help integrate Russia into Europe." [16]

This is indeed an important potential benefit, although the expectation could become no more than another over optimistic vision to add to a number which have arisen in the post-Cold War era. The PFP may also be a stepping stone towards NATO enlargement, especially for those East European States of more 'western' orientation. Eastward expansion is already in hand, with Poland, Hungary and the Czech Republic having become NATO members on 12 March 1999, pursuant to formal offers made at the Madrid Summit in July 1997. Other possible entrants include Slovakia and the Ukraine. All these formerly rather restive members of the Soviet bloc, or in the latter case a constituent republic of the former-USSR itself, have clear motivations for engagement with NATO and in terms of a regional security provision such developments have clear positive dimensions. There are also, however, dangers. Rapid and ill-considered expansion might destabilise the Alliance, it might also, by manifesting an apparent 'threat' in Moscow's view, precipitate the very crisis which is in part intended to avert. Probably neither the extremes of enthusiasm or of pessimism are much to be encouraged. In this as in many matters a more cautious appraisal seems to be demanded. A continuation of considered and staged admissions of new members to NATO in the overall context of European security concerns seems almost inevitable, but this must also be accompanied by continued dialogue and confidence building, above all but not only with Russia, and engagement with other potentially relevant actors such as the OSCE.

Such confidence building measures have been developed, including most significantly the Founding Act on Mutual Relations, Cooperation and Security between NATO and the Russian Federation signed, in advance of the Madrid NATO Summit, on 27 May 1997. [17] Klaus-Peter Klaiber, NATO's Assistant Secretary-General for Political Affairs, remarked of this measure that,

> "NATO and Russia have instituted a new form of consultation on security related issues ... Through our work ... we are seeking, unprecedented, forms of cooperation. ... We want to make the NATO-Russia partnership a permanent fixture of Euro-Atlantic security." [18]

Important as this step undoubtedly was, the Founding Act did not by any means wholly alleviate Russian sensitivities with regard to the expansion of NATO membership in Eastern Europe. By the same token Russian policy makers continued to emphasise the potential role of the OSCE as the dominant European security actor. Marianne Hanson remarks that,

> "There exists a unanimity among Russian political parties – both radical and moderate – that NATO expansion is both unnecessary and provocative. Reflecting this, Moscow had asked [at the December 1996 OSCE Summit] instead that the ... OSCE be strengthened and endowed with the capability to make it into an effective pan-European security organisation." [19]

The Russian proposal to which Hanson refers was abandoned at the 1977 Copenhagen Ministerial Council [20] but Russian doubts remain as is made clear by the statement made by the Minister of Defence, Marshal Igor Sergeyev, to the effect that,

> "Russia cannot remain passive in response to NATO's eastward expansion ... The implementation of these plans, ... could be a destabilising factor in contemporary international relations ... In our view NATO must be transformed into a political organisation which would comprise one of the components of European security in the 21st century. This security architecture should be based on ... the OSCE, the only international organisation on the continent that fully reflects the interests of all participating states ... and ensures that all have equal rights ... ." [21]

Notwithstanding this severe caveat the Marshal did nonetheless view the Founding Act as a positive move for the improvement of NATO-Russian relations and this at least qualifies it as a genuine confidence building measure. The delicacy of relations between NATO and Russia were, however, illustrated by the 1999 Kosovo crisis [22] in which Russia, led by its historic support for Serbia going back at least to the reign of Tsar Alexander II (1856-81) and the agitation of far-right wing Russian nationalists, withdrew its ambassador from NATO and attempted unsuccessfully to persuade the UN Security Council to denounce NATO action for the ending of 'ethnic cleansing' in the territory as 'aggression'.

The question of enlargement is also of great functional significance and will clearly to some degree shape NATO's continuing defence and security roles into the 21st century. At this stage it is at least clear that NATO does not anticipate becoming a major actor in the field of humanitarian relief operations, for which as a combat organisation it is not well suited, but sees its core defence role as expanding into regional peacekeeping and associated functions. Admittedly, the definition of these roles is not always entirely clear cut and, for example, the NATO intervention in Kosovo in March 1999 was in much public discussion characterised as a humanitarian intervention. Thus George Robertson, UK Secretary of State for Defence, stated that,

> "We are confronting a regime which is intent on genocide. These air strikes have one purpose only: to stop the genocidal violence. We are going to hit heavily his [Milosevic's] ability to wage his murderous campaign." [23]

Notwithstanding such statements, the security basis for the operation was also obvious in that, as remarked above, there was, and at the time of writing still is, a real potential for general south east European war. That NATO has the military resources and infrastructure available to it to perform these roles can hardly be doubted, but there also arise other highly significant questions, not least in the context of the organisation's legal structures and abilities.

INTERNATIONAL LAW AND THE RETHINKING OF NATO'S ROLES

NATO is a collective defence organisation [24] operating within the collective self-defence provisions of the UN Charter with its primary function founded upon the provision made by article 51 of the Charter for collective self-defence. The alliance was not, and is not, intended in any sense to be an alternative to the United Nations, a point made explicitly by article 7 of the North Atlantic Treaty which provides that,

> "This Treaty does not affect, and shall not be interpreted as ,affecting in any way the right and obligations under the Charter of the ... United Nations, or the primary responsibility of the Security Council for the maintenance of international peace and security."

The key provisions for the understanding of the legal capacity of the alliance are articles 5 and 6 of the North Atlantic Treaty. Article 5 provides that,

> "The Parties agree that an armed attack against one or more of them in Europe or North America shall be considered an attack against them all and consequently they agree that, if such an armed attack occurs each of them, in exercise of the right of individual or collective self-defence recognised by Article 51 of the Charter of the United Nations, will assist the Party or Parties so attacked by taking forthwith, individually and in concert with the other Parties, such action as it deems necessary, including the use of armed force, to restore and maintain the security of the North Atlantic area.
>
> Any such armed attack and all measures taken as a result thereof shall immediately be reported to the Security Council. Such measures shall be terminated when the Security Council has taken the measures necessary to restore and maintain international peace and security."

Article 6 then defines the geographical parameters of NATO action more specifically and provides that,

> "For the purpose of article 5, an attack on one or more of the Parties is deemed to include an attack:
>
> – on the territory of any of the parties in Europe or North America, ... on the territory of Turkey or on the Islands under the jurisdiction of any of the Parties in the North Atlantic area north of the Tropic of Cancer; ..."

The omitted sections refer to the former Algerian territories of France and to territories under Allied occupation after the Second World War and no longer have application. It will be noticed that the remit is strictly European, North Atlantic and North American, so that crises such as the 1982 Falklands Conflict, involving attack upon a British *South Atlantic* territory fall clearly outwith NATO concerns.

The legal foundation for NATO action is thus, article 5 of the Treaty, founded upon the 'inherent' right of individual and collective self-defence preserved by article 51 of the UN Charter. This provision is notoriously ambiguous, having in the practical exigencies of the Cold War been called upon to perform a much broader role than seems originally to have been intended. [25] In the case of NATO, however, the resulting problems, such as the interpretation of when, for this purpose, an armed attack is deemed to have "occurred" [26] have been of slight, if any, practical significance. In the circumstances actually envisaged by article 5 of the North Atlantic Treaty it is unlikely that there would be much doubt over the applicability of article 51. The further requirements of article 5 of the North Atlantic Treaty that action taken be reported to the UN Security Council and that it be ended when the Council has taken necessary "measures" also accord precisely with article 51. The question of what would amount to "measures necessary to maintain international peace and security" for the purposes of article 51 is in itself a matter open to some doubt. Do such "measures" have to be effective, and if so how is this to be judged? [27] What indeed happens where such "measures" have been implemented and have proved clearly ineffective – does the right of individual and collective self-defence, if superseded in the given circumstances, become reactivated? These are important general questions but not, historically, issues of great practical importance in a NATO context. In the practical politics of the Cold War era, and especially in the light of veto powers in the Security Council, it can hardly be imagined that the Security Council could have determined upon or implemented such "measures" in any actual or potential conflict between NATO and the former Warsaw Pact. This, in part, is what is meant by the view of the Cold War UN system as at most one of qualified collective security, at least in relation to the major Powers.

The collective self-defence function defined by article 51 of the UN Charter remains, pursuant to article 5 of the North Atlantic Treaty, the core NATO concern and, whilst the immediate focus of security concern may be less certain following the demise of the Warsaw Pact and the potential entry into NATO of some of its former members, [28] there is little reason to imagine that this will change. The point is put strongly by Colin S. Gray in remarking that,

> "NATO should not change its character as the collective defence organisation that works. Suggestions that NATO should greatly dilute its military character and become more politically correct for the 1990s, by dropping or otherwise downgrading the Article [5] guarantee of mutual military assistance should be dismissed as folly. ... The key mission of NATO is that of handling the truly difficult, large-scale cases of international insecurity which could arise in Europe." [29]

This does not, of course, deny that there are other actual and potential roles for the Alliance in the post-Cold War situation and these clearly require clarification of legal capacity.

The possible demands placed upon NATO as a regional peace support actor and enforcement agency in the post-Cold War context are prominent amongst these issues. An expanded role of this type would not occasion any legal difficulty from the UN perspective. [30] Article 52(1) of the UN Charter provides that,

> "Nothing in the present Charter precludes the existence of regional arrangements or agencies for dealing with such matters relating to the maintenance of international peace and security as are appropriate for regional action provided that such arrangements or agencies and their activities are consistent with the Purposes and Principles of the United Nations."

No definition of "regional arrangements or agencies" is provided by the UN Charter and in fact NATO does not consider itself a "regional organisation", essentially because, as N.D. White remarks,

> "organisations such as ... NATO and the former Warsaw Pact are not, *prima facie* regional arrangements under Chapter VIII [of the UN Charter]. Indeed the treaties establishing these bodies seem to be clear that they are based on Article 51." [31]

In practice this is, however, a technicality rather than a point of substance and in historical practice the United Nations has always accepted that organisations which meet regional needs in given circumstances fall within the meaning of article 52.

From NATO's viewpoint there may be greater complications. It is clear, for example, that the role of the NATO-led IFOR, SFOR and KFOR Forces in former-Yugoslavia involved a rather generous interpretation of the remit set out by articles 5 and 6 of the North Atlantic Treaty. The former Federal Republic of Yugoslavia was not a NATO Member nor did the conflicts which accompanied its dissolution constitute an attack upon any Member of the Alliance. The deployment of these forces was, of course, undertaken with UN Security Council authorisation [32] and, as forces tasked with supporting the implementation of the Dayton Peace Accords, was, at least in principle, founded upon the consent of the host States. There is some disagreement within NATO as to whether a UN, or maybe OSCE, mandate is required for operations falling outside the remit of article 5 of the North Atlantic Treaty. It is probably safe to say that if the operations in question are consensual in nature then no mandate would be necessary, but to proceed with a non-consensual operation without a mandate would, at the very least, be very unwise. The difficulties which might arise in this context were made abundantly clear in the 1999 Kosovo crisis. Kosovo, with its majority Albanian population, had been a reasonably settled province of the former multi-ethnic [33] Yugoslavia but which, like the non-Serb constituent republics, had become increasingly restless under the hard-line greater-Serbian nationalist rule of the post-Tito Milosevic regime. In this context a separatist movement developed led by the Kosovo Liberation Army (KLA) which engendered violent confrontation and a quasi-genocidal response by the Serbian police and security forces. Internationally sponsored negotiations between the KLA and the Milosevic regime at Rambouillet collapsed in early March 1999 when Serbia-Montenegro refused to countenance the international supervision or monitoring of any 'agreement' reached which previous experience indicated was a prerequisite for meaningful application.

At this point NATO, already playing through SFOR a major peace support role in former-Yugoslavia, took it upon itself to undertake air strikes with a view to ending the 'ethnic cleansing' in Kosovo. The NATO, and principally US and UK, argument that earlier Security Council resolutions implicitly authorised a use of force in the Kosovo situation must be doubted. Indeed UN Security Council Resolution 1199 of 23 September 1998 concluded that the Security Council,

"(16) Decides, should the concrete measures demanded in this resolution and resolution 1160 (1998) not be taken, to consider further action and additional measures to maintain or restore peace and stability in the region;

(17) Decides to remain seized of the matter."

This position was in no way altered by the subsequent Security Council Resolution 1203 of 24 October 1998 and it must be concluded that authorisation for NATO action was demanded under the provision of article 53(1) of the UN Charter.

This said, the situation in Kosovo in March 1999 was manifestly both a humanitarian emergency and an immediate threat to international peace and security – threatening, as at the time of writing it may still do, a general south east European war dragging in Albania, FYROM, [34] Greece, and Turkey. Russian support for Serbia and its policies rendered it highly unlikely that the UN Security Council would have been able to undertake action beyond counselling the continuation of the stalled negotiations – whilst Serbian repression and 'ethnic cleansing' continued unhindered in the territory. However, on 26 March 1999 Russia raised the question of the NATO air strikes before the Security Council, denouncing them as an illegal act of military aggression. The motion gained the predictable support of the PRC, which shares with Russia an extreme sensitivity to any suggestion that repression of subject peoples can be a matter of international security concern and a rather outdated interpretation of the 'domestic jurisdiction' caveat in article 2(7) of the UN Charter, [35] and Namibia. The motion was, however, defeated by the majority vote of five NATO member states, Canada, France, Holland, the UK and the USA, and seven non-NATO members, Argentina, Bahrain, Brazil, Gabon, Gambia, Malaysia and Slovenia. Andrew Lloyd, speaking for the UK Mission to the UN, was reported as stating that,

"When the Council was asked to confirm Russia's interpretation of international law, it refused to do so. Effectively, the Security Council is not prepared to ask NATO to stop." [36]

This is essentially correct, although had the Security Council accepted the Russian motion it would have done rather more than 'ask NATO to stop'. The subsequent decision of the Security Council to deploy the NATO-led KFOR Force, [37] with a Russian contingent, can to some extent be seen as condoning the earlier NATO action. It must also, however, be said that whilst robust action may in any event have been necessary, the end result, the KFOR ground commitment, might have been more easily achieved with Russian involvement under formal aegis of the OSCE, although it would no doubt still have been largely a NATO operation. One of the general lessons from this episode may be thought to be, again, the early and appropriate selection of agencies and mechanisms which in turn reflects the need for a continuing decisive Security Council in crisis management which was dangerously lacking in the case. There also arises the question of management of the initial NATO action in which, arguably, the problem of micro-management commonly associated with "Blue Helmet" Forces arose. Concerns with political presentation seem to some extent to have overridden tactical decision making in the conduct of an air campaign which, arguably, could not ultimately succeed in the absence of a ground commitment and which may have exacerbated casualties beyond the numbers which were "necessary". Although public comment beyond a minimal level is unlikely, all the available indications suggest that professional military opinion was disquieted by aspects of this management, for the same reasons that NATO is known to be uneasy with "double key" approaches to command and control in UN operations *stricto sensu*.

The difficulties for both the UN and regional organisations in the development of post-Cold War peace support are obvious. As in many other matters concerning both the UN Charter and the North Atlantic Charter a careful reading of both the letter and the implications of the texts in a flexible interpretation may in most cases be hoped to supply an acceptable answer, but the prerequisite for this is the establishment of a clear doctrine within which the limits of that necessary flexibility can be constrained. The Kosovo crisis is evidence of the distance to be travelled before this can be achieved and the establishment of such a 'doctrine' will form a large part of the redefinition of NATO's role and that of the UN itself well into the 21st century. It may, in parenthesis, be added that the NATO response in Kosovo also opens more general questions in a peace support context, notably those of definition of mission and exit strategy, neither of which in March 1999 seemed very clear. [38]

RETHINKING EUROPEAN SECURITY: THE WEU

One factor in the rethinking of NATO's post-Cold War European role has been the revival in the 1980s of the Western European Union (WEU). This may be seen as having resulted from the combination of a number of influences. The end of the Cold War and an associated sense in US domestic politics that the time had come for the European Powers to rely less upon the United States for their security and to a much greater degree to shoulder the burdens of their own defence was certainly one consideration. This coincided with the development of much more ambitious political, as compared with economic, agendas by the European Union (EU) including concern with the security sector and a concomitant desire for a 'European' security organisation in contrast, or in combination, with the existing 'Atlanticist' NATO structure. This latter aspect was an important question especially for France with its traditional suspicions of 'Anglo-Saxon' orientations within NATO.

The post-war origins of the WEU have been considered above, but after a period from the late 1940s to the 1980s during which the organisation became effectively moribund except as an occasional forum for European security consultation (and even in that role no ministerial level meetings occurred between 1973 and 1984) [39] it was revived at the 1984 Rome Conference upon the bases expressed in the Rome Declaration of 27 October 1984.

The broad objectives of the revived organisation were set out in 1987 in the policy document, *Platform on European Security*, and in 1991 the WEU became, through the Maastricht Treaty on European Union, formally the security mechanism of the EU [40] whilst yet retaining its separate identity. This was part of the development of a European Union Common Foreign and Security Policy (CFSP) but there are continuing and wide differences of view within both the EU and WEU upon the present and future significance of these moves.

The future of the WEU depends crucially upon the development of its relationship with the EU on the one hand and with NATO on the other. [41] Within Europe there is a considerable degree of ambivalence upon both these issues, notwithstanding the originally stated position found in the 1984 Rome Declaration, the most significant parts of which for this purpose are paragraphs 3, 4 and 5. Paragraph 3 draws attention to the need to enhance co-operation upon security within Europe, but article 4 then adds that,

> "the Atlantic Alliance ... remains the foundation of Western Security ... [and the] Ministers are convinced that a better utilisation of the WEU would not only contribute to the security of Western Europe but also to an improvement in the common defence of all countries of the Atlantic Alliance and to greater solidarity among its members".

Paragraph 5 underlines this by affirming 'the indivisibility of security within the North Atlantic Treaty Area. The current ambivalence is reflected in the Maastricht Treaty with its references to the WEU as the security arm of the EU, whilst also recognising it as the European pillar of NATO. In principle there is no reason why these visions should necessarily be in conflict, but in practice they are so. The 'debate' is informed by strongly divided opinions upon both the future development of the EU [42] itself and by the divergence, in particular, between the United Kingdom and France upon the real importance of the North Atlantic link in European defence, although the French position upon this has somewhat moderated in the 1990s. [43] Despite the Maastricht commitment to develop the WEU in its role as the EU security arm, the treaty itself recognises that the NATO commitments of some Member States, not least the United Kingdom, will not readily, or at all, be overtaken by the WEU. Article J.4.2 expressly provides that,

> " [EU security development] shall not prejudice the specific character of the security and defence policy of certain Member States and shall respect the obligations of certain Member States under the North Atlantic Treaty ..."

The United Kingdom has it made it clear that from its perspective the WEU is, at most, a parallel organisation with NATO and in no sense a potential replacement for it. Specifically a booklet published under the aegis of the Central Office of Information states that,

> "The WEU was reactivated in 1984 when its members agreed in Rome that it should play an important role in ensuring the security of Western Europe and improving the common defence of all NATO countries. ... [I]n 1987, WEU ministers [agreed] ... that a more

united Europe would make a stronger contribution to NATO and help to ensure the basis for a balanced partnership across the Atlantic. The WEU offers a means of strengthening the European pillar of the Alliance and of giving concrete form to Europe's security and defence." [43]

This statement actually reflects the relevant substance of the 1992 *Declaration on the Western European Union* which, in effect, recognised the importance of the USA in the continuing and long term architecture of European security. There is, nonetheless, a diverse range of visions of the organisation's potential future both amongst and beyond the membership.

Prevailing opinion within the WEU tends to emphasise the continuing independent existence of the organisation and to resist any tendency to make it simply the security organ of the EU. An ambitious agenda was set out for the organisation at a meeting held at Petersberg Castle near Bonn on 19 June 1992 to consider the WEU's operational role in the post-Maastricht context. The resulting Petersberg Declaration [44] set out an ambitious action agenda comprising categories of operations now known as the 'Petersberg Tasks'. These are humanitarian and rescue missions, peacekeeping actions, peace enforcement and combat task roles and general crisis management. These tasks do not include collective self-defence, which is recognised as NATO's principal function, but they still represent an ambitious agenda. No less ambitious is the geographical remit considered by the organisation. The WEU Council has designated S.E. Europe, the Mediterranean basin and Africa as areas of special concern to the organisation.. The inclusion of Africa in general in this list seems to have resulted from concerns with Francophone Africa arising particularly from the experience of the Great Lakes crisis. There must be some doubt over the wisdom of this. It must seriously be questioned whether European forces, in many cases coming from former Imperial Powers, would be well received in a peace support role in Sub-Saharan Africa in the light of colonial legacies and the modern imperative of Africanisation of operations in the continent. It has been argued that a 'WEU' force might, as compared to one actually led by one of the former colonial Powers, avoid that problem, [45] but this seems unlikely since the force would still significantly involve the forces of the ex-Imperial Powers. The unfortunate experience of European involvement in the Great Lakes may be thought to suggest extreme caution so far as this type of action might be concerned.

Behind all these issues there lurks also the fundamental question of the material capacity of the organisation. Since 1992 the WEU has undoubtedly expanded its capabilities, albeit not from a high starting point. It has a Defence Planing Cell comprising, in 1998, 55 personnel from 12 countries, which, amongst other tasks, will screen applications for assistance and function as a database for decision-making upon actual and potential action. If the WEU were to become involved in any major non-consensual operations it would, like any other regional organisation, seek a United Nations, or possibly an OSCE, mandate, bearing in mind that it does not consider itself to have a role in collective self-defence within the meaning of article 51 of the UN Charter. It would, of course, undertake humanitarian relief or evacuation operations without an external mandate.

Possible advantages of the WEU organisation include the fact that it is not subject to NATO's geographical limitations and has in some respects a different approach to peace support questions from that of the North Atlantic Alliance. It is developing strategic mobility in co-ordination with NATO but tends to focus upon micro-management rather than the macro-management. The WEU Mobility Working Group in particular focuses upon the minutiae of tactical mobility which may be vital in the management of small multi-national operations. These developments are, so far as they go, encouraging, but, as Dominic McGoldrick remarks,

"The operational, institutional and administrative capability of the WEU needs to be significantly expanded in line with the new aspects of defence [in Europe] ... Much of the attention will be focused on the development of the WEU's operational capability in the fields of crisis management, crisis prevention and peacekeeping." [46]

At present, and for the foreseeable future, the military assets which are available to the WEU are to a large extent also those available to NATO, the operational experience of which is much greater. In this context it has been suggested that the WEU might be used as an umbrella organisation for operations which are out-of-area from a NATO viewpoint but using forces which would normally operate under NATO's aegis. One way forward in this area has been sought in NATO's development from January 1994 of the Combined Joint Task Force (CJTF) command and control concept which was, at least in part, predicated upon the possible need to develop a capacity for 'out of area' operations in the post-Cold War era. Whilst conceding that there is some political difficulty in defining precisely the nature of a CJTF, Charles Barry offers the following useful description,

" [I]n the light of the 1994 Summit language and related US doctrine, a CJTF can be described as: a multinational, multiservice, task-tailored force consisting of NATO and possibly non-NATO forces capable of rapid deployment to conduct limited duration peace operations beyond Alliance borders, under the control of either NATO's integrated military structure or the Western European Union (WEU)." [47]

There is obvious potential from the viewpoint of both NATO and the WEU in this form of arrangement and as Trine Flockhart and G. Wyn Rees remark,

"At the 1994 NATO Brussels summit, the United States agreed that NATO assets could be made available to European operations under the mantle of the WEU. ... The WEU was saved [by this agreement] from the prospect of having to duplicate the provision of military capabilities ... that would have necessitated considerable new spending. In return, the US was granted an effective veto over European operations. The CJTF [Combined

Joint Task Forces] arrangement has, on the one hand, made small scale European-only military operations more credible, while at the same time [it] symbolised the subordination of the WEU to NATO." [48]

It must nonetheless be wondered just how far this type of joint activity will develop or will need to develop. In grave cases it seems highly probably that the problem of 'out of area' operations from a NATO perspective could just as well, and possibly more conveniently, be performed by 'coalitions of the NATO willing'. An example of an operation which very largely took this form can be seen in the Coalition action in the 1990-91 Gulf Conflict. In the light of this it is indeed possible to argue that the reorientation of NATO and the continuing engagement of the USA with general western defence and security suggest that the WEU has no real function other than as a pawn in the internal politics of the EU and should be disbanded. It is certainly the case that the agenda set out by the Petersberg tasks is over- ambitions and the geographical remit which has been adopted by the organisation, especially as regards Africa, must be considered exaggerated. Nonetheless the organisation may have a valuable role to play. It may perform a useful continuing function as a forum for European security discussion and co-operation and also as a mechanism for the performance of limited peace support tasks in areas in which the presence of 'labelled' NATO forces and/or, in particular, US forces might be unhelpful or unacceptable. In this connection, some areas of the former Soviet bloc would be a possibility. These roles are potentially significant but, it is suggested, they must at the present time be viewed as peripheral to the continuing core role of NATO in European regional security and defence from, at least, a western perspective.

At present the pointed remark of Philip H. Gordon that,

"Of all the organisations currently existing in the world the Western European Union ... must be one of those whose length of existence is the most inversely proportional to the actual functions it has fulfilled. WEU never developed the sort of organisation, forces, reputation, or credibility normally required of a defence institution. Despite many revivals ... WEU has remained in the shadow of NATO, fulfilling a symbolic and potential role, but no real function." [49]

remains a possibly harsh but largely accurate judgment. The WEU may well in fact develop a real, if somewhat marginal, function in European security, specifically as a means of strengthening and co-ordinating its European arm, [50] but that it will remain 'in the shadow' of NATO seems certain and the likelihood of its taking over the role of principal European security actor may in any presently foreseeable circumstances be considered very slight indeed.

RETHINKING EUROPEAN SECURITY: THE OSCE

Rather different and broader considerations arise in relation to the possible future impact of the Organisation for Peace and Security in Europe (OSCE). The end of the Cold War in the late 1980s, followed by the dissolution of both the former Soviet Union and the Warsaw Pact, fundamentally changed the European security environment, having indeed a more dramatic impact upon this region than in any other part of the world. In the context of international co-operation during the 1990-91 Gulf Conflict President Bush was moved to proclaim a "new world order" in the maintenance of peace and security, although the subsequent debacles in Somalia, the Great Lakes, former-Yugoslavia and, indeed, the recurrent crises over post-conflict weapon inspections in Iraq serve, sadly, to relegate this pronouncement to the realms of hyperbole. If there is no new "world order" in quite the sense meant by President Bush, there is, however, clearly a new and somewhat uncertain European security order.

The order is not, even in Europe, quite so "new" as many expected in the immediate aftermath of the end of the Cold War. It was anticipated in many quarters, not least by the Russian government, that with the termination of their *raison d'être* of the preceding half century both NATO and the Warsaw Pact would be dissolved and replaced by some new and more broadly based regional security organisation, a role which, if the organisation was considered at all, was certainly beyond the WEU.

One candidate for this overarching replacement role was seen in the Conference on Security and Co-operation in Europe (CSCE) which became the OSCE from January 1995. The CSCE had its origins in discussions held in 1973 and played something of the role of a bridging institution keeping lines of communication open across the ideological divide in Europe. With the Helsinki Final Act of 1 August 1975 the institution became an important element of the "Helsinki" process, in particular as the medium for the conduct of meetings for the oversight of the implementation of the agreements embodied in the Final Act which included, in addition to human rights and economic issues, discussion of confidence building which are today seen as part of the broader peace support agenda. In this sense the CSCE was born of and operated within the Cold War context and, in common with NATO and other organisations, the end of that era demanded a significant reorientation of its roles and functions.

Part of the OSCE's new post-Cold War direction was found in an attempt to develop a new European security architecture. Tentative beginnings were made at the 1990 Paris Summit which produced *The Paris Charter for a New Europe*. Amongst a number of other institutions this led to the establishment in Vienna of the OSCE Conflict Prevention Centre. Despite this and the reference of the Paris Charter to "common efforts in the field of military security" there was little practical attention devoted to such issues in the euphoria of the immediate post-Cold War era. [51] Subsequently, however, and especially from the Helsinki Meeting in July 1992, which produced the document *The Challenges of Change*, onwards, the OSCE has developed much more direct concerns with regional security. Institutionally the Conflict Prevention Centre was reorganised and renamed the Forum for Security Co-operation with tasks including disarmament negotiations and continuing confidence-building measures as well as the regulation and amelioration of civil-military relations – this latter being again a part of the modern broadening of the security agenda which is also of much concern, e.g., to the Organization of American States (OAS). In relation to these and other developments J.M. Nowak comments that,

> "Of all the international bodies the CSCE [OSCE] has changed most in the post-Cold War period in response to the pressures of the new era. It has ceased to be the "Helsinki process", a discussion club or nascent international organization and has been transformed into a regional security arrangement ... based on well-defined common values and political obligations. By declaring itself a regional arrangement, the CSCE established a link not only with the UN as an institution but also between the European and global security systems." [52]

The agenda of the post-Cold War OSCE undoubtedly represents, *inter alia*, an ambitious plan for the restructuring of European security mechanisms, however, the expectations which it reflects have, so far, proved over optimistic. In the immediate aftermath of the end of the Cold War there were, as Adrian Hyde-Price points out, both 'maximalist' and 'miminalist' expectations of the organisation. He comments that,

> " [The maximalists] would like to see the [OSCE] absorb the responsibilities of the remaining military alliances, eventually replacing them by a pan-European collective security arrangement. ... The deployment of [OSCE] ... forces would be the prerogative of a ... "Security Council", modelled on the UN Security Council, with some permanent members and a system of weighted majority voting.
>   The minimalists would also like to see a new pan-European security system, but recognise an enduring – albeit limited – role for both NATO and the EC/EPC/WEU. NATO, they suggest, will continue as a framework for transatlantic defence cooperation ... but with no wider security role for the rest of Europe. The Community, along with the WEU, ... will not assume responsibility for military security issues ... [and the OSCE] will provide a framework for pan-European security dialogue and consultation ... and the deployment of peacekeeping forces if necessary; ..." [53]

The OSCE, including both NATO and former Warsaw Pact States amongst its membership, might in principle have developed into an overarching European security mechanism but this has not in practice happened. The diverse political agendas within and beyond post-Cold War Europe have effectively precluded the development of the unified agenda and will which would have enabled the OSCE to become a major regional peace support actor though it has played minor roles in former-Yugoslavia, Nagorno-Karabakh, South Ossetia and Abkhazia, and in Moldova. A Russian plan under which NATO and the Western European Union would both become legally subordinate to the OSCE was abandoned at the 1997 Copenhagen Ministerial Council when it became clear that NATO would not accept such a diminution of its position. Whether the continuing role of NATO is the product or a major cause of the disappointment of expectations for the role of the OSCE must be considered debatable but the future of the OSCE remains uncertain. As Adrian Hyde-Price remarks,

> "the majority of western political leaders had no desire to give up the proven advantages of an existing collective defence alliance (namely NATO) for the dubious promises of an untested collective security system. Nevertheless, western countries did agree that the CSCE [OSCE] could provide a key forum for broad-ranging co-operation in a Europe no longer divided in hostile blocs. The goal in other words, was to be *cooperative* -not collective – security." [54]

However this may be, the present likelihood of the OSCE supplanting NATO as the principal European security actor must appear to be vanishingly small. Moreover any consideration of the future of the OSCE must be conditioned by the very uncertain future roles of Russia and the CIS. Writing in 1998 it is difficult to predict what the future of the Russian Republic might be. Clearly it will remain, as it was under both the Tsars and the Communists, a centrally important if physically marginal, actor in the European security agenda, but with what purposes and consequences must remain a matter for speculation. [55]

RUSSIA, THE CIS AND EUROPEAN SECURITY

From the time of the post-Napoleonic Holy Alliance onwards Russia has played a significant, if often highly equivocal, role in the development of European security concepts. In the early 20th century the Russian Empire underwent some degree of military eclipse, with defeat in the 1904-5 Russo-Japanese War and collapse and revolution in the First World War leading to the imposition by Germany of the humiliating Treaty of Brest-Litovsk on 15 December 1917. The revolution and the ensuing period of civil war greatly weakened the new Soviet Union militarily and recovery was further delayed by the effect of the Stalinist purges in the 1930s. Dogged Soviet resistance to the Nazi invasion and the massive development of the Soviet armed forces that went with it caused the USSR to emerge in 1945 not only as the rival Superpower to the USA but also as the effective suzerain of the Eastern part of Europe, behind the division known in the Churchillian phrase as the Iron Curtain. Within this Soviet-dominated bloc the Warsaw Pact was created in May 1955 and included provision for mutual military assistance in the event of armed aggression in Europe against any of the Member States. Its original 20 year term was extended by as further 10 years in 1975 and another 20 years in 1985. The Pact was dissolved in July 1991 following the collapse of communism in the former-Soviet Union.

In the Cold War era the USSR played only a very limited peacekeeping role. This disinterest can be seen as the result of a number of interconnected factors. In the first place few conflicts arose which the Soviet Union saw as posing any direct threats to its security, with the notable exception of the conflict in Afghanistan in which Soviet forces became heavily, and disastrously, involved – inspiring perceptions that the conflict was in some ways 'Russia's Vietnam'. During this period the USSR was frequently more concerned with the suppression of ideological 'deviance' amongst the dependent East European countries, including notably the suppression of the Hungarian Revolution in 1956 and the subsequent elimination of the Dubcek reform movement in former-Czechoslovakia. Further, the Soviet Union, as a permanent Member of the UN Security Council was precluded by accepted general UN practice from actually deploying its forces in a singular peacekeeping role. Finally the actual and potential expense of peace support commitments was a demand which the USSR was unwilling, and perhaps unable, to undertake, notwithstanding, or possibly because of, its vast national military budget and its willingness in some cases to underwrite its client states. The Soviet Union in fact took part only in eight out of twenty-two UN peacekeeping operations during the Cold War period.

The dissolution of the former USSR led, inevitably to a variety of radical policy changes on the part of its principal successor State, the Russian Federation. This included, at least initially, a much more positive attitude to the involvement of Russian forces in peace support operations. As part of this new and more 'liberal' foreign policy direction Russia undertook no less than eight new peacekeeping missions in the period between 1992 and 1997, commencing with operations in Croatia and Angola. The extent of this change can be seen in the remarkable statistic that in the period 1996-1997 Russia made the third largest contribution to UN peacekeeping operations and became a significant element in the UN-mandated, NATO-led, IFOR/SFOR forces in former Yugoslavia. This latter was of considerable political importance in the light of the close historical ties between Russia and Serbia stretching well back into the Tsarist era. For a variety of reasons, however, this phase of activity proved to be short-lived. Principal amongst these has been the very troubled economic and political situation within Russia which has in practice rendered such levels of external involvement unsustainable. From the early part of 1998 Russia has effected an 80% reduction in its contribution to peacekeeping forces and has moved from third to sixteenth in its level of involvement in UN peacekeeping operations. The Russian Federation remains involved in the SFOR and KFOR operations in former-Yugoslavia and, for the political reasons suggested above, this seems likely to continue with some beneficial effect. Whilst, however, the developing situation in the former Soviet Union, including the occurrence of crises such as that in Chechnya, remains highly unpredictable, an early resumption of large-scale involvement in peace support action seems very unlikely.

If direct participation in UN and/or UN-sanctioned operations on the part of Russia may for the time being be dismissed from consideration, other forms of involvement remain open and possibly distinctly less desirable. In the late 1990s Russia entered upon a period of political and economic instability which, without seeking to overstate the analogy, had some parallels with the condition of the Weimar Republic. There was no catastrophic military defeat, but the collapse of the ruling ideology, the dissolution of the USSR and the loss of Superpower status were all in their ways grave national humiliations, in no way mitigated by the tendency to western triumphalism, and these factors when accompanied by massive economic dislocation, including unpaid armed forces, created a situation of considerable national and international danger. It is possible that out of these troubles a stable democracy will emerge, it is, sadly, at the very least equally possible that there will be either a return to Stalinism or an adoption of neo-Fascist nationalism. Either of these, even in the significantly weakened military state of post-Soviet Russia, would be a serious menace to European security. For the present, in the period since the collapse of Soviet communism Russia has undertaken a number of missions, unilateral and multilateral, frequently under the apparent aegis of the Commonwealth of Independent States (CIS). These 'CIS' operations have during this period actually engaged some three to five times as many Russian military personnel as extra-CIS UN and/or UN sanctioned operations. Many of these operations have been profoundly problematic and, rightly or wrongly, are seen as carrying more than a slight taint of the practices of former-Soviet hegemonism and this represents a continuing and serious concern for other CIS Member States. Amongst other issues, the premature deployment of Russian troops before cease-fires are in place and a frequent willingness to employ force at levels normally considered excessive for peacekeeping, and possibly even for peace enforcement, actions have all generated doubts about the suitability of Russia as a major peace support actor. If at some future time the UN or, indeed the OSCE, were to embrace Russian initiatives to any great degree they would risk becoming complicit in Moscow's perceived hegemonistic aspirations. If the UN chooses to engage more closely with Russian peacekeeping initiatives, it runs the risk of appearing to legitimise Moscow's regional ambitions, much as it was seen to do in Abkhazia. Yet if the UN adopts a more distant stance, this may similarly be perceived by Moscow as amounting to a green light to intervene. [56]

The serious questions which continue to surround Russia, and by the same token the CIS, as peace support actors clearly raises difficult questions for at least the short and medium term roles of the OSCE. Whilst the OSCE is clearly not a mere Russian dependency or *alter ego*, its particular potential value as an overarching European security organisation lies precisely in the fact of its inclusion of the Russian Federation and other former-Eastern bloc States amongst its members along with NATO and WEU Members. The uncertainties over the future and policy direction of, in particular, Russia, must therefore, as suggested above, remain a source of uncertainty also for the future role and functions of the OSCE.

SECURITY ARCHITECTURE IN THE NEW EUROPE

It is clear that more than ten years after the end of the Cold War the reshaping of the security architecture of Europe shows few, if any, signs of developing in the ways which were at first, by many anticipated. Organisations such as, in particular, the WEU and the OSCE, of which much was originally expected in the context of a new post-Cold War Europe have, so far, in many ways disappointed the expectations originally held of them. Whilst both may yet perform significant functions as European security actors, the former in particular in cases where 'NATO' and/or US forces might be unwelcome or inappropriate or in certain out-of-NATO-area operations and the latter as a means of bridging security divisions with the former Eastern bloc, these will be relatively limited remits. It must also be said that contention within and without the EU upon the nature and future of the WEU and the unstable condition of the Russian Federation and the CIS suggest that in each case the unified political will requisite for further major development is, and is likely to remain, lacking. In this context it seems certain that NATO will remain the principal European security actor, both by reason of its experience and institutional stability as well as the fact that no very credible alternative exists or seems likely to come into existence in prevailing circumstances. That said, NATO, like the former Warsaw Pact, was essentially a product of, or at least largely moulded by, the Cold War and in the new post-Cold War era it has been called upon to find new roles and expressions of function. In this context its legal structures and capacities. like those of many other security and defence organisations, will continue to demand radical re-interpretation in a pattern of international relations quite different from that which existed at the time when the organisation was called into being. Amongst the issues urgently arising are those of potential out-of-area operations, co-operation with other regional organisations [57] and possibly extended roles under UN mandates as, for example, in the NATO-led IFOR/SFOR forces in former-Yugoslavia. This will undoubtedly demand a new, and possibly more flexible, interpretation of the 1949 North Atlantic Treaty although, as remarked above, for a variety of political and practical reasons, it would not be appropriate in present, or any foreseeably likely, circumstances to attempt to redraft the Treaty. [58] The considerable risks involved might, in the extreme case, actually bring about the collapse of the Alliance with incalculable consequences. Counsel against any such redrafting endeavour may be advanced with the greater confidence granted that there seems to be no good reason for thinking that the existing provision could not sustain the probably future demands upon NATO and its Members.

Articles 5 and 6 of the 1949 Treaty, in conjunction with article 51 of the UN Charter, will thus continue to provide the fundamental legal underpinning for military operations conducted by NATO in its strictly 'defence' role. The new situation in Europe, and the world, post-Cold War does not materially affect this dimension of the Alliance, even if the identity of the potential enemy may be less clear, but not necessarily less threatening, in the fraught exigencies of modern international relations. Thus, if an armed attack were now to occur against the territory of a NATO member state within the geographical area defined by article 6 of the North Atlantic Treaty, the legal basis for military response remains exactly as it was during the Cold War and rests ultimately upon the preservation of the inherent right of individual and collective self-defence by article 51 of the UN Charter. [59] It is the possibility of action beyond that core remit which raised the most interesting current legal and political questions in relation to NATO and European security.

The possibility of attack upon the territory of a NATO member state beyond the area defined by article 6 of the North Atlantic Treaty is a declining likelihood in the post-Colonial era although it happened in the 1982 Falklands Conflict. That conflict provides a useful hypothetical illustration in that although NATO was not, and by reference to the terms of articles 5 and 6 legally could not have been, involved, the right of collective self-defence preserved by article 51 of the UN Charter would obviously have empowered NATO Member States to come to the aid of the United Kingdom in exercise of their own sovereign capacities, had such assistance been sought – which it was not. Any such action would not have been a NATO action and it may be assumed, in the context, that it would not have involved the USA for a variety of hemispheric political reasons. It would, however, have involved use of assets generally available to NATO and would have represented, as in a different way did the Coalition action in the 1990-91 Gulf Conflict, an operation by a 'Coalition of the NATO Willing'. It is of course the case that the commitment of NATO Members under articles 5 and 6 of the North Atlantic Treaty is a particular obligation and not a limitation upon general sovereign capacity, except in so far as it involves an undertaking not to act in ways contrary to the Alliance agreement. The North Atlantic Treaty does not preclude Member States from undertaking action outwith the Treaty for which provision is made by the UN Charter and, in a statement of the legally obvious, Article 7 of the Treaty provides that it confirms that their 'rights and obligations under the Charter ... of the United Nations' are not affected by membership. As suggested above, this reasoning may underpin legal analysis of the involvement of the largely, but not entirely, NATO Coalition in the 1990-91 Gulf Conflict. A State which is not, and could not be, a Member of NATO was subjected to external aggression and sought military support from friendly States, many of which were NATO members. This clearly fell outside the North Atlantic Treaty, but was a classic instance of collective self defence within the meaning of article 51 of the UN Charter. Subsequently, the operation was mandated by the UN Security Council [60] at which point it must be concluded that 'measures' had been taken by the Council and article 51 ceased to be applicable. Be that as it may, the operation continued for the most part to be an exercise by a coalition of the NATO willing. In any such case the operation will, *ex hypothesi*, involve to a very substantial degree the use of NATO infrastructure and national assets which would, under normal circumstances, be earmarked for NATO use. The distinction between this and a 'NATO' operation *stricto sensu* may for most purposes reasonably be suggested to be technical rather than real.

In time, broader arguments might also be advanced. Since the end of the Cold War there has been a broadening of the concept of security, with varying effects, both globally and regionally. [61] To take just one significant example, the Organization of American States (OAS) has in this period come to include the maintenance of democratic governance in the region as a major plank of its concept of security. [62] Whether this broadening of the agenda is wholly desirable may be open to debate. [63] These developments in the concept of security are admittedly much more limited than that here hypo-thetically envisaged, but it might conceivably be argued that, granted the economic significance of the Gulf oil supplies, an attack upon Kuwait which was at least in part aimed at western economic stability could be considered a genuine threat to the more widely conceived 'security' of NATO Member States. In the particular context of the 1990-91 Gulf Conflict such an argument would be otiose in that the situation was in any event well covered by the article 51 collective right of self-defence and, subsequently, by UN Security Council mandate. Its possibility points out, however, both the possibilities and the dangers of the present security debate. It shows the possibilities in that it underlines the value of flexible response in a dynamically evolving environment and the dangers in that it shows the way in which maintenance of broadly conceived security might all too easily shade into action not clearly differentiated from aggression – in a manner not far removed from a reversion to a form of Palmerstonian 'gunboat diplomacy'. This prospect is at present remote, and certainly forms no part of the reformulation of NATO concerns. It is, however, an indicator of the legal limitation set to flexibility of response in the new security era, in this case by the imperatives for peaceful dispute resolution and avoidance of resort to international armed force as an instrument of policy set out in article 2(3)(4) of the UN Charter. In practice it seems probable that the core element of European security for the foreseeable future will be a combination of the North Atlantic Alliance within the remit of articles 5 and 6 of the North Atlantic Treaty so far as non-consensual action is concerned with a somewhat broader remit in cases of consensual action and, more arguably, specific UN mandates. Beyond this coalitions of the willing, here as elsewhere, will no doubt continue to be a significant factor as, in greater or lesser degrees in appropriate circumstances, may organisations like the OSCE and WEU which, if they have not withered on the vine, have certainly disappointed the more ambitious expectations once entertained of them.

Ultimately, therefore, NATO seems certain to remain the linchpin of European security and defence. The expanded role demanded of the organisation and its Members may in some regards demand a new and more flexible interpretation of the 1949 North Atlantic Treaty, but there is no reason to think that these requirements will strain their terms and intentions beyond endurance. In the present general context, however, one concluding warning note requires to be sounded. In the debates upon future regional security mechanisms it is sometimes implied that NATO offers a model for general imitation. It does not. Far from being a paradigmatic defence alliance or security organisation NATO is, as the rest of this book demonstrates, markedly atypical in its experience, cohesion and capacities. It is a very particular example of a security and defence organisation which owes much to its specific origins; to take it as a more general model would dangerously distort the debate. As this book argues, a usefully holistic appreciation of the realities and prospects of peace support action the post-Cold War era requires, above all, an appreciation of the diversity of both regional requirements and the capacities of the organisations operating within them. In this respect Europe,

North America and NATO are important examples, but not in any sense global paradigms.

NOTES

1. For detailed discussion of this see Chapter 1. For analysis of the end of the Eurocentric focus see P. Foot, 'The end of Eurocentricism and its consequences' in C. McInnes, ed., *Security and Strategy in the New Europe* (Routledge, 1992), pp.82-92.
2. A phrase coined by Sir Winston Churchill in a speech drawing attention to the potential Soviet threat delivered on 11 March 1946.
3. The term is here used in its geographical rather than its 'EU' political sense.
4. See Chapter 1.
5. Originally article IV but renumbered as a result of insertions by the 1954 modifying Protocol.
6. This term is borrowed from the context of the former *Apartheid* State in South Africa.
7. Comprising Belgium, Federal Republic of Germany, France, Italy, Luxembourg and the Netherlands.
8. It also adopted three other Protocols, the second of which dealt the provision of Forces to be used by the WEU.
9. For discussion of the modern French view see F. Bozo, 'French security policy and the new European order' in C. McInnes, ed., op.cit.mi pp.197-216
10. See below,
11. For discussion see below.
12. See Chapter 1.
13. See below.
14. NATO Summit Declaration, Press Communique M-1(94)3, 11 January 1994.
15. For discussion see N. Williams, 'Partnership for Peace: Permanent Fixture or Declining Asset?' in P.H. Gordon, *NATO's Transformation: The Changing Shape of the Atlantic Alliance*(Rowman and Littlefield, 1997), pp.221-233.
16. J. Kruzel, 'Partnership for Peace and the Transformation of North Atlantic Security' in S.V. Papacosma and M.A. Heiss, eds., *NATO in the Post-Cold War Era: Does it have a Future?* (St. Martin's Press, 1995), p.339 at p.344.
17. For text see *NATO Review*, Summer, 1997.
18. K-P Klaiber, 'The NATO-Russia relationship a year after Paris', *NATO Review*, Autumn 1998, p.16.
19. M. Hanson, 'Russia and NATO Expansion: The Uneasy Basis of the Founding Act', *European Security* Vol. 7, No.2, (1998), pp.13-29 at p.15.
20. For discussion see below.
21. I. Sergeyev, ' We are not adversaries, we are partners', *NATO Review*, Spring 1998, pp.15-18 at p.17.
22. See below.
23. *The Guardian* (London) 29 March 1999.
24. The difference between collective security and collective defence is crucial to understanding the roles of the various organisations here discussed. In both forms of organisation member state agree to respond collectively to acts of aggression. However, in a collective defence organisation it is presumed that the act of aggression will be carried out by a state which is not a member of the organisation, a presumption which is not inherent in the concept of collective security.
25. For discussion see Chapter 1.
26. See D. W. Greig, 'Self-Defence and the Security Council: What does Article 51 Require?' (1991) 40 *International and Comparative Law Quarterly*, 366. Also R. Higgins, *Problems and Process: International Law and How We Use It* (1994), pp.248-251.
27. See N.D. White, *Keeping the Peace* 2 ed., (1997) pp.53 ff.
28. In the late 1990s notably Poland and the Ukraine.
29. C.S. Gray, *NATO and the Evolving Structure of Order in Europe: Changing Terms of the TransAtlantic Bargain?* in the Hull Strategy Papers (University of Hull Centre for Security Studies, 1997), p.48.

30. See Chapter 2.

31. N.D. White, op.cit., p.21.

32. See in particular SC Resolution 1031 of 15 December 1995, UN Doc. SC/6155, authorising the establishment of IFOR.

33. The term 'ethnic' in relation to former-Yugoslavia is actually inaccurate but has become a conventional usage which cannot easily be avoided.

34. The former-Yugoslav Republic of Macedonia.

35. Both the Preamble and article 1 of the charter suggest clearly that actions such as those of the Belgrade regime in Kosovo fall well outwith any such legitimate 'domestic jurisdiction'.

36. *The Daily Telegraph* (London), 27 March 1999

37. UN Security Council Resolution 1244 of 10 June 1999, passed nem con, with one abstention (PRC).

38. For general discussion see Chapter 2.

39. A. Cahen, *The Western European Union and NATO* (Brassey's, 1989), p.5.

40. See article J.4.

41. For discussion see A.J.K. Bailes, 'European Defence and Security: The Role of NATO, WEU and EU' (1996) 27 *Security Dialogue*, p.55, especially at p.59.

42. See above.

43. *Britain, NATO and European Security* (HMSO, 1994), p.33.

44. In no wise to be confused with the 1868 Declaration of St. Petersburg, an arms control treaty which also sets out the fundamental *jus in bello* doctrine of 'unnecessary suffering'.

45. See P.H. Gordon, 'The Western European Union and NATO's "Europeanisation"' in P.H. Gordon, ed., *NATO's Transformation: The Changing Shape of the Atlantic Alliance* (Rowman and Liitlefield, 1997). p.257 at p.260

46. D. McGoldrick, *International Relations of the European Union* Longman, 1997), p.171.

47. C. Barry, 'Combined Joint Task Forces in Theory and Practice' in P.H. Gordon, op.cit., p.203 at p.206

48. T. Flockhart and G.W. Rees "A core Europe? The EU and the WEU" in W. Park and G.W. Rees, eds., *Rethinking Security in Post-Cold War Europe* (1998), p.61 at p.71.

49. P.H. Gordon, "Does Western European Union Have A Role?" in A. Deighton, ed., *Western European Union 1954-1997: Defence, Security Integration* (1997), 103

50. For discussion see D. Greenwood, 'Constructing the European Pillar: Issues and Institutions'*NATO Review* No.3, June 1988, p.13.

51. See J.M. Nowak, "The Organization for Security and Co-operation in Europe, in T. Findlay, ed., *Challenges for the New Peacekeepers*, SIPRI Research Report No. 12 (Oxford University Press,1996). p.121 at p.128-9

52. J.M. Nowak, op.cit., p.121 at p.122

53. A. Hyde-Price, "Future Security Systems for Europe" in C. McInnes, ed., *Security and Strategy in the New Europe* (1992), p.37 at pp.50-51.

54. A. Hyde-Price, 'The OSCE and European Security' in W. Park and G. Wyn Rees, eds., *Rethinking Security in Post-Cold War Europe* (Longman, 1998), p.23 at p.26.

55. See generally W. Park, "A New Russia in a New Europe: still back to the future?" in W. Park and G.Wyn Rees, eds.,op.cit., pp.96-114.

56. T. McNeill, 'Humanitarian Intervention and Peacekeeping in the Former Soviet Union and Eastern Europe', International Political Science Review, Vol.18, No.1, 1997, p.98.

57. The term is here used generally as a geographical description, NATO doers not of course consider itself a 'regional organisation' *stricto sensu*.

58. It may be added that the improbability of securing a political consensus upon any such redrafting also counsels strongly against any such endeavours.

59. The right of collective defence under Article 51 of the UN Charter of course ceases once the Security Council has taken 'measures' necessary to restore international peace and security. The precise nature of the 'measures' technically required to trigger termination of the inherent right exercised under Article 51 remains open some debate. See D.W. Greig, op.cit, ante. So too may the definition of what may constitute a restoration of 'international peace and security'.

60. Specifically by UN SC Resolution 678 of 29 November 1990 (UN Doc S/INF/46) authorising use of 'all necessary means' to secure Iraqi compliance. For discussion see N.D. White and H. McCoubrey 'International Law and the Use of Force in the Gulf' (1991) X *International Relations*, pp.347-373.

61. This debate has been particularly associated with the work of Barry Buzan and the 'Copenhagen School'. The seminal text is B. Buzan, *People, States and Fear* (1991); for an excellent overview of contemporary international relations literature see S. Burchill and A. Linklater, *Theories of International Relations* (1996).

62. See J.I. Dominguez, 'Security, Peace, and Democracy in Latin America and the Caribbean: Challenges for the Post-Cold War Era' and M. Hirst, 'Security Policies, Democratization and Regional Integration in the Southern Cone' in J.I. Domiguez, ed., *International Security and Democracy: Latin America and the Caribbean in the Post-Cold War Era* (1998), pp.3-29 and 102-118. For further discussion see Chapter 5.

63. See Chapter 1.

CHAPTER 5

The Organization of American States
and the Security of the Western Hemisphere [1]

The Organization of American States (OAS) boasts the longest continuous history of any major regional organisation, tracing a direct lineage back into the nineteenth century to the first Congress of American States held in Panama in 1826 and, through a further five Congresses, to the first International Conference of American States held in Washington in 1889-90. In his letter of invitation to the Panama Congress Simón Bolívar predicted that: 'The day that our plenipotentiaries exchange their powers, an immortal era will be established in the diplomatic history of the Americas" [2] and it was in this spirit, and premised upon a separation of New World from Old under the so-called 'Doctrine of the Two Spheres', that the Inter-American system was built. At the Washington Conference a US proposal to establish a Pan-American customs union was rejected, but the conference nevertheless inaugurated the International Union of American States which, operating primarily as an economic rather than a political institution, was developed through the course of a series of meetings held prior to the outbreak of the Second World War. Following various changes to the organisation's official title – the International Conference of American States became the Union of American Republics in 1910 which in turn became the Union of American States in 1928 – the Organization of American States was officially institu-tionalised in 1948 with the signing of the Charter of Bogota. [3] The latter years of the 1940s also saw significant developments in hemispheric security provision, for while on the verge of European war in 1938 the Union of American States had taken tentative steps toward the creation of a pan-American security apparatus, this did not take more concrete form until the signing of the Inter-American Treaty of Reciprocal Assistance (The 'Rio Treaty') in 1947 and the following year of the American Treaty on Pacific Settlement (the 'Pact of Bogota'). [4]

In addition to its pedigree, the OAS is also notable for the fact that it counts the United States of America amongst its membership. This factor is one the significance of which must be stressed from the outset for, unlike NATO, a regional organisation of which the US is also a member, in the OAS the economic and military power disparities are such that the US enjoys a position of unassailable hegemony. This is not to suggest that the US is not, by far, the

most powerful and therefore dominant player within NATO, but rather that in
the case of the Western Hemisphere historical, political, strategic and to some
extent geographical factors have led to the development of a series of intra-
regional relations the likes of which are not present within the Euro-Atlantic
context. In particular with respect to Central America and the Caribbean, the
relationship between the United States and Latin America is one which can
most clearly be categorised as being between hegemon and subordinates in
nature. This fact is reflected in the differing experiences, in both economic and
military terms, of the Americas and Europe and itself reflects the differing
rationales behind the creation of the organisations in which the US participates
on the two continents. While NATO was established primarily as a defensive
alliance designed to counter perceived Soviet expansionist designs, the OAS
and its predecessors were created in significant part to assist Latin American
states in dealing with their giant northern neighbour. Too weak to successfully
interact on a bilateral basis, collective, multilateral action provided a means
by which inequalities could at least be mitigated and thus the OAS serves as
a means and a mechanism of communication and diplomatic intercourse.
While it would be inaccurate to suggest that in its contemporary role within
the OAS the US always acts as a dominant member, it is nevertheless the case
that structural factors within the organisation encumber both the other
members and the Secretariat in their dealings with the US and beyond. Of not
least significance here is the fact that Washington, through a 60% contribution
to the assessed budget and additional voluntary contributions, pays approximately 70% of the organisation's running costs, while the next largest
contributor, Canada, pays approximately 11%. It is against this position of
hyper-dominance on the part of the United States that the activities and future
potential of the OAS must be judged. [5]

THE INTER-AMERICAN SYSTEM AND THE PURPOSES AND PRINCIPLES OF THE ORGANIZATION OF AMERICAN STATES [6]

The Charter of the OAS, the Rio Treaty and the Pact of Bogota (the latter two
themselves being a codification of a complex series of bilateral and multilateral treaties) provide the constitutional basis upon which regional organisation
in the Western Hemisphere is conducted. Chapters I and II of the OAS Charter
enunciate a number of purposes and principles to guide the operations of the
organisation and these can be considered under five generic groupings,
namely; non-intervention and sovereign equality, representative democracy
and human rights, mutual security, peaceful settlement of disputes and
economic co-operation and development. [7] These cannot, of course, be

viewed as separate areas of concern; an examination of intra-regional relations clearly demonstrates the manner in which the USA, as the dominant hemispheric actor, has sought through the initiation and implementation of policies relating to human rights, democratisation and social and economic development, to promote its own security both within and beyond the Americas. The principles of sovereign equality and non-intervention have been most threatened by the activities of the USA which for over a century predicated its regional policies upon the infamous Monroe Doctrine. [8] Even after its formal denunciation, the spectre of intervention, be it overt or covert, was far from banished and throughout the Cold War – and therefore throughout the vast majority of the OAS' existence – Washington sought to manipulate the principles laid out in the Charter and to exercise its hegemonic advantage through a utilisation of the organisation as an 'anti-communist alliance'. That the most blatant examples of such action were undertaken in Central America and the Caribbean does not negate the fact that throughout Latin America the US stretched the organisation's guiding principles to breaking point.

The principle of non-intervention now enshrined in article 19 of the OAS Charter is itself the product of a tortuous debate between the United States and its southern neighbours. The articulation of the Calvo Doctrine in 1868 emphasised the absolute nature of sovereign equality and inviolability, as did the Drago Doctrine which was to follow (and in certain minor respects amend it) some thirty-four years later. Both precepts were cited in defence against first European and later US incursions into the southern Americas, though in practice they provided little protection. During inter-American conferences held between 1906 and 1928 the US sought to keep the issue of intervention off the agenda, while Latin American states castigated the US for unjustly and illegally violating the principle of non-intervention and eventually made continued inter-American co-operation conditional upon the acceptance of formal restrictions upon Washington's activities. The US, eager to extend its continental links and seeing no real European threat to the Western Hemisphere, accepted the concept and renounced – or at least changed its perception of – the Monroe Doctrine. While some debate continued regarding exactly what constituted 'intervention', with the US restricting the term to military activities, in opposition to the insistence of Latin American states that a broad definition including diplomatic, economic and military actions be adopted, the dispute was eventually resolved in 1936 with the adoption of the 'Additional Protocol Relative to Non-Intervention' which prohibited intervention 'directly or indirectly, and for whatever reason, in the internal or external affairs of the parties'. This prohibition of intervention can now be seen in articles 19 to 21 of the OAS Charter:

"Article 19

No state or group of states has the right to intervene, directly or indirectly, for any reason whatsoever in the internal or external affairs of any other state. The foregoing principle prohibits not only armed force but also any other form of interference or attempted threat against the personality of the state or against its political, economic, and cultural elements.

Article 20

No state may use or encourage the use of coercive measures of an economic or political character in order to force the sovereign will of another State and to obtain from it advantages of any kind.

Article 21

The territory of a state is inviolable; it may not be the object, even temporarily, of military occupation or of other measures of force taken by another State, directly or indirectly, on any grounds whatever... ."

What appears to be a relatively straightforward and unequivocal legal position is, however, confused by Charter references to human rights and democratic governance and even more so by the fact that, in practice, the USA has adopted policies in almost total contradiction to this element of the Charter framework, whilst in so doing citing the principles of the inter-American system as justification for its actions. A brief examination of the apparent contradictions within the Charter of Bogota is thus here required. A more extensive discussion of US policies pertaining to the Western Hemisphere will be undertaken later in the chapter.

The question of the extent to which the Inter-American system should seek to promote representative democracy and human rights has troubled the OAS throughout it history, in part because of principled concerns over intervention, but also because of more pragmatic worries over the hegemonic aspirations of the USA. At first glance the OAS Charter, in conjunction with other treaties integral to the inter-American system, would suggest considerable institutional commitment to democracy and human rights. The preamble of the Charter states that:

"The true significance of American solidarity and good neighbourliness can only mean the consolidation on this continent, within the framework of democratic institutions, of a system of individual liberty and social justice based on respect for the essential rights of man."

while article 3 of the Charter, which is devoted to the principles of the organisation, states:

"d) The solidarity of the American states and the high aims which are sought through it require the political organisation of those states on the basis of the effective exercise of representative democracy.

h)   Social justice and social security are bases of lasting peace."

The Charter thus appears to encapsulate a contradiction, not unfamiliar to other international organisations; how can democracy and human rights be promoted and enforced while simultaneously observing and respecting the principle of non-intervention? One possible solution presents itself in the words of article 23 according to which:

"Measures adopted for the maintenance of peace and security in accordance with existing treaties do not constitute a violation of the principles set forth in Articles 19 and 21"

It follows that, under the terms of the Charter, where the practices of a non-democratic regime and/or abuses of human rights constitute a threat to region security, the principle of non-intervention is not applicable. But as with other institution which have adopted this approach, most notably the UN, member states have proven less than willing to avail themselves of this procedural 'get-out' clause. Indeed, in the case of the OAS, the membership addressed the issue directly at a Council meeting held in 1950 at which it declared:

" [Considering] that both the principle of representative democracy and that of non-intervention are established in many inter-American pronouncements, and that both are basic principles of harmonious relations among the countries of America ; and that there exists some confusion of ideas as to the means of harmonising the effective execution and application of the basic principle of non-intervention and that of the exercise of democracy ; [be it resolved] to reaffirm the principles of representative democracy [but] to declare that the aforementioned principles do not in any way and under any concept authorise any governments to violate inter-American commitments relative to the principles of non-intervention." [9]

It would appear therefore that the prioritisation of the two principles had been determined. It should however be noted that members of the Inter-American system were not left totally free to determine the form of internal political system which they were to adopt, since both regional treaty and state practice developed which negated recourse to the principle of non-intervention in defence against action taken to prevent the establishment of a communist government. This idea of the OAS functioning as an 'Anti-Communist Alliance' reflected the US Cold War pre-occupation with the potential for communist infiltration of the Western Hemisphere and was facilitated by a constitutional slight of hand performed at the Tenth Inter-American Conference held in Caracas in March 1954. The *Declaration of Solidarity for the Political Integrity of the American States Against the Intervention of International Communism* passed at the conference posits *inter alia* that:

"The domination or control of the political institution of any American State by the international communist movement extending to this Hemisphere the political system of an extra-continental power, would constitute a threat to the sovereignty and political independence of the American States, endangering the peace of America, and would call for a Meeting of Consultation to consider the adoption of appropriate action in accordance with existing treaties." [10]

While the Caracas Declaration provides only for consideration by the OAS of action to be taken when faced with the establishment of a communist government, in practice the US succeeded in circumnavigating this, as it did the proviso that the Declaration was only applicable where the establishment of a communist government was the result of 'domination or control of the political institution of any American State by the *international communist movement*'. (emphasis added) In constitutional terms the significance of the Declaration lay in the fact that, as a threat to regional security, communist government no longer fell within the remit of the principle of non-intervention since, as noted above, under article 23 of the OAS Charter:

> "Measures adopted for the maintenance of peace and security in accordance with existing treaties do not constitute a violation of the principles [of non-intervention] set forth in Articles 19 and 21."

What had been created, therefore, was a regional system which prioritised otherwise contradictory principles. Hemispheric security, now understood to include the prevention of communist government, had precedence over non-intervention, which in turn had priority over the promotion of democratic government and human rights. The US was thus able to utilise the inter-American framework in an attempt to provide legal legitimacy for its actions in preventing the spread of communism to the Western Hemisphere. Given the USA's ability to block UN consideration of interventionary action by means of its Security Council veto, Washington was able to pursue this crucial part of its Cold War strategy cloaked in the legitimacy of OAS sanction. We shall return to this point in due course, but first it is necessary to consider more recent developments in the relationship between non-intervention and the promotion and protection of democratic government.

In June 1991 the OAS passed Resolution 1080 by which it committed itself to respond to interruptions of constitutional government in the Americas by holding, within a period of 10 days, a meeting of foreign ministers to decide upon a collective response. [11] As Richard Bloomfield comments:

> "The 1991 decision by the members of the OAS actually to do something about threats to democracy was the culmination of the wave of democratization which swept over Latin America in the 1980s when the dictatorships which had dominated the region for the previous two decades proved themselves incompetent to deal with the grave problems facing their societies. Large numbers of citizens in the newly restored democracies had suffered brutal persecution during the years of dictatorial rule. The atmosphere at the Santiago meeting reflected the slogan "never again," which had become a watchword in many Latin American countries. The end of the Cold War had removed what had been the principal motive for US intervention in Latin America and thus made collective action through the OAS seem less problematic." [12]

The Santiago Declaration, as Resolution 1080 came to be known, was further strengthened when, in 1997, member states ratified the Washington Protocol which, through an amendment to the OAS Charter, [13] allows for the suspension from the organisation of member states whose democratically elected governments have been overthrown by force. [14] In combination, the Santiago Declaration and the newly amended OAS Charter constitute a significant change in emphasis within the OAS. For deep-seated historical reasons many member states are reluctant in the extreme to disregard the principle on non-intervention, but in the contemporary post-Cold War political and strategic environment this is no longer seen as a necessity which must be privileged at the expense of democracy and human rights. While in its utilisation of the Santiago mechanism the organisation has met with mixed results, there can be little doubt that the development of machinery, the objective of which is to promote democracy, represents a major step forward, especially judged against the years of brutal military dictatorship which blighted the history of much of the Western Hemisphere. It may also be hoped that, in the longer term, improvements in the governance of the Americas will produce dividends in terms of both hemispheric and national security.

The issue of inter-state security within the Western Hemisphere is dealt with by Chapter VI, specifically articles 28 and 29 of the OAS Charter, and in far greater detail by the provisions of the Rio Treaty. Articles 28 and 29 state:

"Article 28

Every act of aggression against the territorial integrity or the inviolability of the territory or against the sovereignty or political independence of an American State shall be considered an act of aggression against the other American States.

Article 29

If the inviolability or integrity of the territory or the sovereignty or political independence of any American State should be affected by an armed attack or by an act of aggression that is not an armed attack, or by an extracontinental conflict, or by a conflict between two or more American States, or by any other fact or situation that might endanger the peace of America, the American States, in furtherance of the principle of continental solidarity or collective self-defence, shall apply the measures and procedures established in the special treaties on the subject."

The treaties to which article 29 refers are principally the Rio Treaty and the Pact of Bogota. The former, which through the provisions of articles 2, 3(4) and 5 pays full regard to the provisions of the UN Charter, reaffirms the collective security commitment contained in article 28 of the OAS Charter. [15] Article 3(1) of the Treaty states that an attack against an American state by any other state, including another American state, is deemed to be an attack against all states within the Inter-American system and consequently will result in the exercise, by the Contracting Parties, of the right of individual and collective self-defence recognised by article 51 of the UN Charter. Where an act of aggression occurs, and upon the request of any member of the OAS, a 'Meeting of Consultation of Ministers of Foreign Affairs' will be held and, in accordance with article 3(2) of the Rio Treaty and Chapter X of the OAS Charter, this will act as a 'Organ of Consultation' to decide upon the collective measures to be undertaken. The Treaty differentiates between an attack by an American state and an attack of extra-hemispheric origin primarily under the terms of article 7, by which it places American states under an obligation to suspend hostilities, to restore matters to the *status quo ante bellum* and to resolve the conflict through peaceful means. Failure to abide by these obligations will be taken into consideration in determining which party is the aggressor and what further actions, if any, are to be taken.

The pacific settlement of disputes is cited in article 2(b) of the OAS Charter as a purpose of the organisation and through the provisions of Chapter V (articles 24-27) member states are placed under an obligation to settle their disputes by peaceful means. Additional provisions regarding pacific settlement are contained in a somewhat impenetrable web of treaties and accords which have been built up by members of the Inter-American system. An attempt to co-ordinate these agreements was made in 1945 at the Mexico City Conference, the product of which was the 1948 Inter American Treaty of Pacific Settlement, but whilst this places ratifying states under an obligation to seek a peaceful settlement to their disputes, it has not been universally ratified by all American states and thus in a limited number of cases in which one or both parties have not ratified the treaty, earlier instruments remain in force.

SECURITY IN THE AMERICAS: FROM COERCION TO CO-OPERATION

Differing emphases upon economic and security issues, along with divergent views of what constitutes 'security' within a Western Hemispheric context have, throughout the history of the inter-American system, given rise to considerable tension among member states as to the objectives of hemispheric co-operation and how these can best be realised. Principally this has taken the form of disagreement between the Southern and Central American states on the one hand and the United States on the other, as the latter has sought to impose its political will and pursue its perceived national interests, often at the expense of its southern neighbours. In this regard US policy has been somewhat mutable as intra and extra-regional concerns have dictated changes in Washington's approach. However, notwithstanding what have often been abrupt changes in US policy, two inter-related long-term policy objectives have, as G. Pope Atkins observes, remained dominant.

"The United States has sought to minimize foreign intrusions and to promote Latin American stability as essential to its strategic, political, economic, military and ideological interests (as specifically defined at different times). Thus the degree of US concern with Latin America and the level of its activities there have fluctuated with US perceptions of foreign threats in the region and its views about Latin American political instability. ... Geographic distinctions and capability estimates have been factored into the security calculations shaping US actions in the region. The United States has adopted differentiated views of the sub-regions within Latin America, and different capability considerations have been applied to these different policy arenas." [16]

Given the United States' hegemonic status within the region, a brief discussion of the historical development of the Inter-American system outlining the divergent views of Washington and its neighbours and of the adaptations of US policies is crucial to an understanding of current American attitudes to security within the Western Hemisphere.

The development of the principle of hemispheric mutual security enshrined within the inter-American system centred around the changing nature of the Monroe Doctrine. Initially viewed by the US as a unilateral concept providing for intervention throughout Latin America but excluding any form of reciprocal element, it was, during the 1930s, accepted by the United States as a multi-lateral principle of hemispheric security and defence. The 1947 Rio Treaty, and the summarised version of its commitments contained in articles 28 and 29 of the OAS Charter, are a reaffirmation of the process of multi-lateralisation of the Monroe Doctrine which took place throughout the 1930s and during the Second World War. The Monroe Doctrine was enunciated by President James Monroe in 1823 and was predicated upon the idea that the 'Old World' and the 'New World' had different political systems and should remain distinct spheres. This 'Doctrine of the Two Spheres' had four central themes, firstly that the US would not interfere in the internal affairs of European states or in wars between them; secondly that the US recognised and would not interfere in existing colonies in the Western Hemisphere; thirdly that the Western Hemisphere was closed to future colonisation and finally that any attempt by a European power to oppress or control any nation in the Western Hemisphere would be viewed as a hostile act against the US.

Initially promulgated in response to fears that Russia aspired to the acquisition of territory in the north-west of the continent and that Spain coveted the re-establishment of imperial possessions in the south, the policy was intended as a temporary and specific statement based upon the United State's perception of Euro-American relations. Over a period of time, however, the presidential utterance acquired the more elevated status of a foreign policy doctrine which for over a century defined the relationship between the USA and the rest of the Americas. This relationship, while often portrayed in paternalistic terms, in practice came to be characterised by an aggressive interventionism on the part of the US, motivated by a complex combination of security, economic and ideological concerns. That the relationship was one conditioned by a thinly veiled – and sometimes open – self-perception of superiority is apparent from President Taft's declaration that:

> "The day is not far distant when three Stars and Stripes at three equidistant points will mark our territory: one at the North Pole, another at the Panama Canal, and the third at the South Pole. The whole hemisphere will be ours in fact as, by virtue of our superiority of race, it already is ours morally" [17]

Taft's use of language must, of course, be judged against the standards of the day, but while the presentation may have changed over the decades, the substance remained fundamentally unaltered and thus it is hard to disagree with Kenneth Coleman when he comments that the Monroe Doctrine was 'an attempt to reconcile the contradiction between the professed values of US culture and the actual behaviour of the US government' [18] This behaviour, vacillating as it has been, has rarely constituted the basis for harmonious inter-American relations.

During the period in which the American states met under the guise of the International Conference of American States (i.e. 1889-1928) the US had two inter-connected aims, firstly, to expand commercial relations with Latin America and secondly to establish procedures for the peaceful settlement of Latin American disputes. The latter was primarily motivated by a desire to bring political stability to the region, thus facilitating trade and preempting extra-Hemispheric influences. Latin American states generally shared the USA's enthusiasm for promoting trade and pacific settlement of disputes, but they perceived Pan-Americanism primarily as a means by which to ensure security from outside intervention, firstly fearing European incursion, but subsequently coming to fear the USA itself. Latin American appeals that the doctrine be invoked in defence against extra-hemispheric incursions fell on deaf ears in Washington where policy makers instead concentrated their efforts upon developing it as a means by which US intervention throughout the continent could be validated, from the 'Big Stick' of Theodore Roosevelt to the 'Dollar Diplomacy' of William Taft and its embrace by subsequent Presidents Wilson, Harding and Coolidge.

The most significant and wide-ranging addition to the doctrine came in President Theodore Roosevelt's annual message to Congress in 1904 in which he declared that:

> "If a nation shows that it knows how to act with reasonable efficiency and decency in social and political matters; if it keeps order and pays its obligations, it need fear no interference from the United States. Chronic wrongdoing or an impotence which results in a general loosening of the ties of civilized society, may in America, as elsewhere, ultimately require intervention by some civilized nation, and in the Western Hemisphere the adherence of the United States to the Monroe Doctrine may force the United States, how-

ever reluctantly, in flagrant cases of such wrong doing or impotence, to the exercise of an international police power. ... It is a mere truism to say that every nation, whether in America or anywhere else, which desires to maintain its freedom, its independence, must ultimately realize that the right of such independence cannot be separated from the responsibility of making good use of it." [19]

Roosevelt's statement amounted to no less that a redefinition of the Monroe Doctrine bestowing upon the US the role of hemispheric policeman in an attempt to ensure the avoidance of situations in which European powers would intervene against Latin American states, particularly in order to reclaim monies owed. Earlier in the year the Hague Court of Arbitration had ruled that such intervention by creditor states was legally justifiable and thus financial impropriety or mismanagement on the part of Southern or Central American states threatened to jeopardise hemispheric security. [20] The Roosevelt Corollary, as it became known, was followed by a supplementation of a threatening military posture by capital penetration – so-called Dollar diplomacy – with the never distant possibility of the exercise of the former to safeguard the latter. These developments saw the attitude of Southern and Central American states toward the USA's abuse of the Inter-American system develop from restrained hostility at the turn of the century to bitter public condemnation by the late 1920s, but geographic proximity to a burgeoning global great power brought with it an inescapable strategic and economic logic which dictated that Latin America could do nothing but seek to engage the US on a constructive basis and thus the system, while replete with imperfections, could not be wholly abandoned.

The advent of the Union of American States in 1928 coincided with a more harmonious period of inter-American relations and a general coincidence of interests which was, for the most part, to prevail until the end of the Second World War. Chronically weakened by the First World War, the US rightly saw the European powers as constituting little, if any, threat in terms of Western Hemispheric intervention and accordingly Washington was able to reduce its own 'protective' interventionary stance. Moreover, political instability within Central and Southern America was such that it posed only a minimal threat to US interests and thus little was to be gained from opposing demands that coercive intervention cease in order that intra-regional co-operation could continue. The USA was able, therefore, to progressively accept the definition of non-intervention advocated by its neighbours to the south and to participate in the building of regional security arrangements premised upon the multi-lateralisation of the Monroe Doctrine. The 'Good Neighbour Policy', the seeds of which were planted by President Hoover but which was brought to fruition under the presidency of Franklin D. Roosevelt, was centred upon this multi-lateralisation, though the US also continued to pursue policy objectives on a bi-lateral basis, thus maximising its negotiating advantage. In his Pan-American Day speech the President proclaimed:

> "The essential qualities of true Pan Americanism must be the same as those which constitute a good neighbour, namely, mutual understanding, a sympathetic understanding of the other's point of view. It is only in this manner that we can hope to build a system of which confidence, friendship, and good will are the cornerstones." [21]

The new approach to regional affairs manifested itself most clearly in the withdrawal of the US from its Caribbean protectorates and in the fact that potential conflict situations were resolved through diplomatic means.

One negative consequence of the United States' renunciation of intervention was the proliferation, particularly in Central America, of non-democratic regimes pre-disposed to brutal suppression of political dissent. Washington's professed policy of refusing to recognise non-constitutional governments was abandoned along with coercive intervention, but intervention had allowed the US to protect the interests of its commercial enterprises, and with this option no longer available, the alternative policy of tacitly supporting (and on occasion installing) dictatorial regimes in return for the security of such activities was adopted. Less parochial concerns could also be cited in favour of such co-operation, for with the rise of Fascism in Europe, the prospect of Central and Southern American states which readily identified with such credos coming under more direct extra-hemispheric influence could not be discounted. Consequently, from the late 1930s and throughout the course of the war, the United States invested heavily, financially, politically and militarily, in the development of a Western Hemispheric security architecture.

The institutional co-operation and development which the Western Hemisphere had enjoyed prior to and during the Second World War culminated in the creation of the Organization of American States and the signing of the Rio Treaty and the Pact of Bogota. Yet as at the end of war the US emerged as the world's greatest power, so it looked beyond the Western Hemisphere to the assumption of a global role commensurate with its status. With the Western European imperial dynasties effectively destroyed or in terminal decline, the Soviet Union came to represent the most direct challenge to the US, and in the ideological confrontation of the Cold War Latin America was a less pressing priority. The Doctrine of the Two Spheres stood abandoned; faced with the Cold War threat of international communism, Latin America appeared relatively secure and thus US energy and resources were primarily invested elsewhere as Washington pledged itself to the defence of Europe, and then to that of Asia. Guatemala provided the only notable exception to US perceptions of a secure continent, but with a friendly regime ensconced in Guatemala City and the Caracas Declaration established as the foundation of the 'Anti-Communist Alliance' Washington could turn once more to more pressing concerns. Efforts on the part of Latin American states to further develop the OAS system and to elicit US assistance in promoting their economic interests met with strictly limited success and where aid was forthcoming it was so on the basis of Cold War security prerogatives.

Fidel Castro's seizure of power in Cuba demonstrated to the US that the Western Hemisphere was not as secure against communist incursion as had been presumed and thus served as a catalyst in changing regional policy. [22] The 'Alliance for Progress', announced by President Kennedy in March 1961 as 'a plan to transform the 1960s into a historic decade of democratic progress' [23] and adopted as OAS policy in the form of the Charter of Punta del Este [24] later that year, centred around the provision of economic and military assistance with the express aim of promoting social reform and democratisation. Underlying the policy was a powerful security rationale, in that events in Cuba had been interpreted as suggesting that social and economic deprivation provided the conditions conducive to communist insurgency. According to Jerome Slater:

> "The new policy ... still had political stability in Latin America as its *ultimate* objective, but it was based on the assumption that the preservation of the status quo was a chimerical as well as an unworthy goal and that the wisest course for the United States would be to help guide Latin American revolutionary forces into reasonably moderate, non-Communist channels. Thus, as the keystone to its anti-Communist strategy the United States became a powerful force for Latin American change." [25]

Both Eisenhower and Truman before had authorised assistance to Central and Southern American states, including defence assistance, on a basis which paid scant regard to internal political credentials and this was now viewed as potentially destabilising. Accordingly, Kennedy advocated a policy of democratisation and opposition to military coups and governments, but his assassination and the assumption of power by Lyndon Johnson heralded a return to policies more accommodating of military regimes as the US sought to preclude further communist inroads into the Western Hemisphere. The massive US intervention in the Dominican Republic in 1965 constituted the most dramatic measure taken in this regard, though as conflict in Vietnam came to evermore dominate the concerns of Washington policy makers, this action proved to be an exception to the norm and Latin America was once more relegated to the lower echelons of security thinking with the resultant scaling down of financial and military assistance to the region.

With the notable exception of US collusion in the ousting from power of Chile's President Allende in 1973 and despite the announcement of policy initiatives to the contrary, the US continued to pay little heed to Western Hemispheric concerns throughout the presidencies of both Nixon and Ford. Superpower détente provided respite during which the extra-hemispheric threats to the region were minimal and the proliferation of authoritarian right wing governments, many of which received covert, if not large scale overt support from Washington provided a Cold War arena in which the US could feel relatively secure. However, upon President Carter's assumption of power in 1977 he declared his intention to develop a foreign policy premised upon reduced militarism, non-proliferation of nuclear and conventional weaponry and the promotion of human rights. In his famous address at Notre Dame University in 1977, the new President declared, in words that would later be turned against him by his Republican opponents, that:

> "We are now free of that inordinate fear of communism which once led us to embrace any dictator in that fear ... For too many years we've been willing to adopt the flawed and erroneous principles and tactics of our adversaries, sometimes abandoning our values for theirs." [26]

On this basis relations with many countries in Southern American deteriorated as the US, though implicated in establishing or securing many of the regimes in question, castigated states such as Argentina, Brazil, Chile, Paraguay and Uruguay for their poor human rights records, ceased arms transfers and significantly curtailed economic assistance. Initial attempts to improve US-Caribbean relations, and in particular those with Havana, also foundered as Soviet backed Cuban activities, both sub-region and farther afield, served to undermine the very foundations of the Administration's foreign policy.

A change in US presidential incumbent was accompanied by a radical change in policy toward Central, if not the whole of Latin America. While never explicitly defined by its eponym or any of those who served under him, the central theme of the so-called Reagan Doctrine is well captured by Gaddis Smith:

> "President Reagan, before the American Legion in February 1983, declared that the United States must abandon a policy of merely reacting to 'the offensive actions of those hostile to freedom and democracy' and go on the offensive itself – above all in Central America. 'The spectre of Marxist-Leninist controlled governments in Central America with ideological and political loyalties to Cuba and the Soviet Union poses a direct challenge to which we must respond.'" [27]

Smith continues:

> "Administration spokesmen from the outset reasserted the principles of the [Monroe] doctrine with a stridency not heard since the days of John Foster Dulles, perhaps even Richard Olney and Theodore Roosevelt. An alien threat of international Communism carried by Soviet power and applied through proxies was depicted by the White House and State Department in rhetoric more alarmist, even apocalyptic, than at any time since the brief and very real crisis of 1962 over the nuclear missiles in Cuba." [28]

On the grounds that, in the words of the National Bipartisan Commission on Central America 'the triumph of hostile forces in what the Soviet Union calls the "strategic rear" of the United States would be read as a sign of US impotence', [29] the new doctrine was centred on the Caribbean. The geographic proximity, the presence of Cuba, the precarious position of many governments in the sub-region and the strategic importance of the Panama Canal and vital lanes of shipping were all cited as factors necessitating the new, more robust approach. However, the nature of the problem itself, namely Soviet expansionism, whether perceived or genuine, was not particularly amenable to the rather simplistic analysis and approach which under-pinned the application of the Reagan Doctrine in the Caribbean, while the 'alarmist, even apocalyptic' style and content of the doctrine attracted reprobation both at home and abroad, including formal censure by the International Court of Justice [30] and the eventual embarrassment of the Iran-Contra scandal.

The Reagan Administration also attempted to adapt policy in Southern America to better suit its peculiar world view and in particular sought to resume arms transfers to states to which they were precluded by legislation introduced by the Carter Administration in accordance with its stance on human rights. Progress towards a legislative framework more conducive to the accommodation of this new policy was temporarily interrupted by the 1982 Falkland Conflict which also served to complicate US-South America relations more generally, as did the issue of narcotics in certain cases (primarily Bolivia, Columbia and Peru) and the burgeoning debt which virtually all states in the Southern Cone had accumulated. However, domestic legal hurdles were rendered otiose by the wave of democratisation which swept Southern America during the 1980s as first Argentina and then Uruguay, Brazil and Bolivia adopted democratically accountable forms of government. Prohibition on arms transfers remained in force with respect to Chile and Paraguay, but by the close of the decade these states too had taken the first tentative steps on the road to democracy. [31] Sadly for much of Central America the wait for democracy was somewhat more prolonged, but by the close of the 1990s all governments within the Western Hemisphere, with the exception of Cuba, could claim democratic credentials. Civil-military relations have often remained problematic and democratic ideals have had to be tempered in the face of these and other problems, particularly those engendered by social and economic deprivation and organised crime, but significant though such problems are, the Western Hemisphere looks set to emerge from the twentieth century in better shape politically than at any time in its past. Perhaps most crucially it appears to have relatively little to fear form either extra-hemispheric influences or from its great American cousin to the north.

THE AMERICAS IN THE POST-COLD WAR ERA

Writing in 1991 Peter Hakin and Abraham Lowenthal commented of the Western Hemisphere that:

> "... democracy in Latin America is far from robust. It is nowhere fully achieved, and is perhaps most firmly established in those few countries where it was already deeply rooted and vibrant a generation ago. In most other nations, democracy is endangered by political and criminal violence, conflicts between civilian and military authorities, prolonged economic decline and gross social and economic inequalities. Democratic institutions in much of Latin America remain weak – plagued by rampant corruption , political polarization, and growing public scepticism about government and politics. In some countries, democratic forms are still a facade; in others they are precarious and vulnerable. Latin American democracy today needs reinforcement, not premature celebration."
> [32]

That much of what Hakim and Lowenthal wrote still holds true today, almost a decade later, should not be seen so much as an indictment of those in and beyond the continent who seek to promote democratic values and institutions, but rather as lasting evidence of the political, economic and social deterioration suffered during the Cold War and, indeed, before. Cautious celebration may, now, be warranted, but the need for reinforcement remains. For its – very significant – part the OAS has taken steps to promote and protect this democratisation process, in particular through the Santiago Declaration and Charter amendment discussed above and this is indicative of a broadened security agenda which is now understood to include intra and trans-state issues rather than those of an exclusively inter-state nature. The maintenance of democracy is just one such issue; it stands alongside and is intimately connected with others, such as drugs trafficking and the violence and corruptive influences associated with the drugs trade, ecological degradation, political and economic refugees, the collapse of state infrastructure and institutions and gross social and economic disparity. The radically altered political and strategic environment of the post-Cold War world, of which the Western Hemisphere is but a part, is one which irresistibly suggests concern with such a wider array of issues.

International collaboration is a key element in dealing with such problems, and the OAS membership, recognising the nature of the challenge facing them and their responsibilities in this regard, agreed a wide-ranging set of objectives at the Summit of the Americas held in Miami in December 1994. [33] Indeed, the scope of the agenda set at Miami is such that questions must be asked as to whether the organisation is in danger of over-stretching its capacity to act. As Andrew Hurrell comments, regional responses to this new security agenda are likely to prove problematic

"... for three reasons. First, because, below the level of rhetoric, there is very little consensus as to what the new security agenda means or implies. ... Second, because unlike traditional threats which press allies together, problems such as drug related criminality, migration and terrorism tend to undermine regional consensus because of the enormous difficulties of defining state interests and, especially, for deciding upon the appropriate role for the use of military force. And third, because of the two factors which together condition the politics of security in the Americas. On the one hand, deeper and denser interdependence across the region is increasing levels of mutual vulnerability, and any effective regional order will consequently impinge very deeply on how societies are organised domestically. But on the other hand, the region is still marked politically by inequalities of power – between Brazil and its neighbours in South America, but, much more importantly, between the United States and the rest of the hemisphere. It is this combination of interdependence and inequality that makes regional security management so difficult." [34]

The problems which Hurrell identifies – difficulties in consensus building, the role of military force, issues of sovereignty and intervention, and power disparities and the role of the USA – are not new to the OAS, but they must now be addressed within the new, post-Cold War environment.

It is, perhaps surprisingly, in relation to the issue of sovereignty and non-intervention, and with specific regard to the promotion and protection of democratic government, that the OAS has made some of the most notable progress. To date the Santiago Declaration has been employed on four occasions; in Haiti in 1991, in Peru the following year, in Guatemala in 1993, and in Paraguay in 1996. In Haiti the OAS acted decisively and its participation in and support for sanctions against the Cedras regime which overthrew the democratically elected government of Jean Bertrand Aristide was decisive in soliciting and maintaining the broad international support which eventually led to the return of democratic civilian rule. [35] With the situation in Haiti ongoing, the OAS was called upon to respond to the introduction of anti-democratic powers by Peru's President Fujimori. In an attempt to remedy the guerrilla threat posed by the *Sendero Luminoso* (Shinning Path) movement and the country's worsening economic problems, Fujimori carried out an *autogolpe* when he closed Congress, sacked key members of the judiciary and established a new government of 'national emergency and reconstruction'. Fears that the president had succumbed to the influence of the military proved ill-founded as the armed forces demonstrated their loyalty to the president through the exercise of constraint. For its part the OAS, rather than attempting to restore the *status quo ante* as it was doing in Haiti, accepted the need for political reform but sought to ensure that this was achieved within a broadly democratic framework and with the involvement of all political parties. [36] However, in Peru the organisation proved less decisive, and with greatly inflated presidential powers and a compliant Congress, its aims were only realised to a limited degree as key actors both within the organisation and without pursued agendas which were not wholly in accord with that of hemispheric democratisation. Neighbouring states such as Brazil and Chile feared the destabilising repercussions which would have inevitably resulted from a continuation or intensification of the conflict in Peru; the US sought co-operation in its anti-drugs strategy and Japan, a major Peruvian benefactor, desired a continuation of aid to a state the head of which was himself of Japanese descent. Within the context of a discussion of democratisation it is also worthy of note that, despite the unequivocally non-democratic nature of the Fujimori reforms, they enjoyed widespread popular support. The new constitution was approved in a national plebiscite and Fujimori secured a resounding electoral victory in April 1995. Moreover, while the President's style of government remains no less autocratic, limited progress in achieving his earlier stated goals is apparent.

The OAS was also called upon to act in Guatemala, a state which had for more than 35 years endured civil war before a degree of civilian rule was re-established in 1986. [37] Continuing guerrilla activity by the Unidad Revolucionaria Nacional Guatemalteca (URNG), whilst not directly challenging government control, ensured continued military involvement in Guatemalan politics and repression at the hands of the army, most particularly in rural areas. The democratic process had to attempt to accommodate bitter ethnic and social cleavages which also served to exacerbate civil conflict and to endure attempted military coups in 1988 and 1989. Elections in 1990-91 were marred by political violence and produced little, if any, alleviation of guerrilla activity. The new government of Jorge Serrano Elías initiated talks with the guerrillas and sought to bolster the country's democratic credentials through attempts to ensure military subservience to civilian authority, but both initiatives met with limited success and in the light of this, widespread human rights abuses and continuing economic decline, the President suspended the constitution in May 1993. Pursuant to Resolution 1080 the OAS was at the forefront of international efforts to restore constitutional rule [38] and, acting in combination with domestic political opposition parties, business representatives and the army, this objective was secured in a matter of only three days. Despite continuing guerrilla activity, human rights abuses and economic turmoil, Guatemala's fragile democratic system saw presidential elections in 1995 undertaken with the assistance of the OAS' Unit for the Promotion of Democracy (UDP). In September 1996 the new president, Alvaro Arzú Irigoyen, acting with the support of the military, secured a peace agreement with the URNG so bringing an end to Americas longest running conflict. This breakthrough, accompanied by progress in combating corruption and military repression, prodived the basis upon which Guatemala continues to build its democratic institutions and a political culture which rejects authoritarian military rule.

In Paraguay the population had toiled for decades under repressive military regimes, the last of which, that of General Alfredo Stroessner, endured for 35 years. In February 1989 the country began its precarious move toward democratic rule when the army itself forced Stroessner from power and, having done so, delivered on its promise of democratic elections. [39] That this was the product of an intense need to secure domestic and international support rather than of a dedication to the principles of democracy, and that they failed to live up to the highest of electoral standards, is of lesser importance than the fact that, by May of 1989, Paraguay had experienced its first democratic elections. A Constituent Assembly was convened in 1992 to adopt a new democratic constitution and new general elections were set for the following year. The victor was Juan Carlos Wasmosy, the country's first freely elected civilian president, but his tenure in office was to be threatened by elements within a military which had grown accustomed to controlling Paraguay's political destiny. Wasmosy's attempt to sack the army chief, General Lino César Oviedo, was resisted by Oviedo and key elements within the military loyal to him, but faced with a possible reversion to military rule, the domestic and international forces which had initially combined to assist in the deliverance of Paraguayan democracy united once more to ensure its survival. Oviedo's grip on the military – especially the air force – was far from complete and significant components remained loyal to the President. In combination with Paraguayan political parties, social and business elites and large segments of the general population, these amounted to a domestic opposition to Oviedo the importance of which should not be overlooked. International support for the democratic office and process was also swift and decisive. The Permanent Council of the OAS met immediately under the Resolution 1080 mechanism with key members of the organisation, including the USA, Brazil and Argentina, pledging their support for Wasmosy and their willingness, if necessary, to take robust measures within the OAS framework. As events unfolded the need for such action was negated by Oviedo's acceptance of the President's decision, a reversal prompted by the combined domestic and international forced outlined above. That at the time of writing Oviedo continues to play a prominent role in Paraguayan politics, and indeed may well emerge as a future presidential candidate is evidence of the problems which emerging democratic regimes are likely to encounter, but is should not be understood as being destructive of the democratisation process *per se*.

Against the historical backdrop of American politics, in particular the Cold War years during which military dictatorship was allowed to flourish, the Santiago Declaration constitutes a significant development in the OAS' ability to contribute toward the Western Hemisphere's progress toward continent-wide democratic governance. Indeed, in that it has the potential to play a significant role in safeguarding the development and entrenchment of democratic processes and ideals within the Western Hemisphere, it may well prove to be the organisation's most significant contribution the people of the Americas. The limitations of the current Resolution 1080 mechanism must, however, be acknowledged. As Artori Valenzuela comments:

> "Resolution 1080 is clearly a valuable mechanism for bringing members of the international community together to consider possible responses to the interruption of the democratic process in any country of the hemisphere. It can also serve to deter those who may be tempted to launch a coup. The resolution does not however provide an effective mechanism for rapid mobilization of the international community to protect the legitimacy of popularly constituted authority. ... if the OAS is to be truly effective in defending democracy in the region, it must move beyond its reactive stance; in consultation with elected leaders in member states, it must actively monitor situations in which democracy is vulnerable. It should also help devise mechanisms and procedures for early consultations before the onset of a regime-threatening crisis and provide resources for a coordinated response should such a crisis develop." [40]

To the extent that such progress has been possible, member-states have moved beyond their traditional interpretation of what constitutes domestic jurisdiction and external intervention. In addition to Resolution 1080, UDP and the Inter-American Commission of Human Rights provide the OAS with the ability to assist member states in the organisation and running of elections and with the monitoring of human rights. There is still further progress to be made, but momentum appears to be building and the co-operative framework which the OAS embodies is crucial to maintaining this. There are, however, roles which the OAS is, at present, unable to assume and of particular relevance here is its inability to function as a coercive enforcement mechanism in situations in which pacific and co-operative frameworks are unavailable or inapplicable.

The role of military force within the Western Hemisphere is a subject which gives rise to considerable unease amongst OAS member states. In part this is due to what are often precarious relations between the military and civilian authorities within member states, as the latter struggle to establish and maintain control over the former. There is also, as Andrew Hurrell notes, the question of disparate military capability and with it associated fears of regional hegemonism. Brazil, as the most powerful actor within Southern America, may cast such a shadow, but this fear is overwhelmed when the thoughts of member states are focused upon the United States of America. Not only is the US by far the most powerful state in continental America, but as the preceding discussion has demonstrated, Washington policy makers have been far from reluctant to exercise this power in situations in which they have perceived it as being in the national interest to do so. In the post-World War Two era the US sought to use is position within the OAS to provide institutional legitimisation for actions motivated by Cold War concerns while at the same time preventing UN censure through the exercise of the Security Council veto. It is against this background of abuse of regional apparatus that attitudes toward the future potential of military action within an OAS framework must be judged and elaboration of past ventures thus requires further scrutiny.

In June 1954 the government of Jacobo Arbenz was overthrown by Guatemalan opposition forces, led by Castillo Armas, which crossed over the border from Honduras. [41] The USA was strongly implicated in the over-throw, having been an opponent of the Arbenz regime which it claimed was pro-communist. In fact there was little if any evidence to support the assertion that the euphemistically termed International Communist Movement supported Arbenz, a CIA report of the time noted that 'direct connections between Guatemala and Moscow are difficult to prove .... no proof of direct control has yet been established' [42] That the Eisenhower Administration was fully aware that communist influence over Arbenz was limited appears irrefutable, but nevertheless it viewed him – and particularly his programme of land reform – as adverse to US interests and in this sense portraying him as a communist served a purpose both domestically and regionally. As the US Ambassador to Guatemala reported back to his government immediately prior to the coup 'Arbenz thought like a communist and talked like a communist and if not actually one would do until one came along.' [43] At the regional level US determination to portray Arbenz as a communist backed by Moscow is to be explained by reference to wider developments in Western Hemisphere politics. The Guatemalan leader had few friends in the region, and with neighbouring states, backed by the US allied against him, the recently passed Caracas Declaration provided the mechanism by which US actions could receive the stamp of regional approval.

Guatemala's appeal for assistance to the United Nations Security Council (UNSC) proved fruitless, as representatives of Honduras and Nicaragua, denying that their countries had been involved in any military invasion, argued that the Guatemalan issue should be considered by the OAS rather than in New York. Brazil and Columbia also argued in favour of OAS action, claiming that the regional organisation was, in accordance with article 33 of Chapter VI and 52(2) of Chapter VIII, the appropriate forum for discussion. The Guatemalan representative rejected the applicability of articles 33 and 52(2) on the grounds that the situation did not constitute a 'dispute', but rather 'an act of aggression' and thus the Security Council should take action under article 39 of the UN Charter. A draft resolution, submitted by Columbia and Brazil, proposing that the issue be considered by the OAS received majority support, but its passage was blocked by a negative vote by the USSR, though a resolution introduced by France calling for the cessation of hostilities and requesting that members of the UN refrain from giving assistance to the parties to the conflict, but making no mention of the OAS and apportioning no blame, was passed unanimously. [44] A further attempt by Guatemala and the Soviet Union to have the issue discussed by the Security Council was blocked by a US veto, the representative, supported by those from Brazil and Columbia, arguing that the UN should not hamper the efforts of the OAS. In early July 1954, Armas having secured his grip on power, the President of the Security Council received a message from the new Guatemalan government stating that order and peace had been restored and therefore there was no grounds for the question to remain on the Council's agenda.

Perceived by the United States as the most significant intra-regional threat to Western Hemispheric security, Fidel Castro's seizure of power in Cuba in 1959 prompted the imposition of stringent economic sanctions by the OAS. Despite overwhelming popular support and the wholly discredited nature of the Batista regime which he forced from power, the organisation, often acting under considerable US influence, suspended Cuban membership and instituted what was to be an increasingly severe sanctions regime in January 1962. As Cuban alienation within the region deepened, and with the 1962 Missile Crisis serving to further increase tensions, the ninth OAS Foreign Ministers' Meeting in July 1964, at which Cuba was found guilty of aggression against Venezuela, decided upon the suspension by all OAS members of diplomatic and economic relations with Cuba. [45] That the Castro regime came to adopt policies the pursuit of which were likely to cause regional destabilisation is in little doubt, but questions remain over whether the Cuban leader initially held such intentions. In this regard US policy appears to have been hugely influential, as Washington chose to support US business interests at the expense of much needed social and economic reform. As Jenny Pearce comments:

"Clearly the United States was not exclusively responsible for the radicalization of the revolution; there were many internal factors involved. But it certainly helped force Cuba into a closer relationship with the Soviet Union, and the [disastrous] Bay of Pigs invasion consolidated that trend still further." [46]

The accuracy of Pearce's comment and the illegality of the Bay of Pigs operation notwithstanding, OAS sanctions continued in place for over a decade, until, at the Meeting of Foreign Ministers held in July 1974, the OAS enacted, with US support, the 'Freedom of Action Resolution' which effectively brought an end to the sanctions regime. Throughout the Cold War Cuba posed successive US presidential administrations a common problem, the danger, noted by Jerome Slater:

"... of on the one hand proceeding so vigorously as to alienate large numbers of Latin Americans and the risk of confrontation with the Soviet Union, or on the other hand, so cautiously as to risk repudiation at home and the spread of Communist movements in the rest of the hemisphere." [47]

This problem remained largely unresolved, and it was the end of Superpower conflict rather than its solution which eventually served to mitigate Washington's concerns – if not its paranoia – over its tiny Caribbean neighbour.

In late May 1965, following a series of non-constitutional changes of government – in many of which the CIA and other US agencies were implicated – the US dispatched a force of over 20,000 marines to secure the establishment of a government favourable to its interests. [48] Washington sought to defend its actions, *inter alia*, on the grounds that it was preventing the establishment of a communist government in accordance with the Caracas Declaration. President Johnson, in a nationwide address, stated:

> "There are times in the affairs of nations when great principles are tested in an ordeal of conflict and danger. This is such a time for the American nations ... What began as a popular democratic revolution that was committed to democracy and social justice moved into the hands of a band of communist conspirators ... The American nations cannot, must not, and will not permit the establishment of another communist government in the Western Hemisphere..." [49]

Despite the Santiago Declaration's stipulation that OAS involvement be conditional upon extra-hemispheric influences in the establishment of a communist government, and the limitation that it only allows for the calling of a Meeting of Consultation, the US proceeded in dispatching a 'peacekeeping' force for which it subsequently sought retrospective OAS authorisation. OAS sanction was only partially forthcoming in the form of the "Resolution Establishing the Inter-American Armed Force in the Dominican Republic", but the resolution sufficed as diplomatic camouflage in the Cold War diplomatic confrontation which ensued.

The issue of intervention in the Dominican Republic was raised in the Security Council by the USSR on 1 May, and was to be discussed on no less than 30 occasions between then and late July. The Soviet and Cuban representatives argued throughout the debates that US intervention was a flagrant and unjustifiable violation of state sovereignty. Both contended that the UNSC rather that the OAS was the appropriate body to consider the issue, and rejected arguments that consideration of the question by the regional organisation should exclude involvement by the Security Council which had primary jurisdiction in all matters relating to threats to international peace and security. OAS action, rather than conforming with Chapter VIII of the UN Charter, was in fact a violation of article 53(1) which prohibits enforcement action by regional organisations without prior Security Council authorisation. Despite the apparently sound *legal* logic of the Soviet position, its draft resolution condemning US aggression and calling for the withdrawal of all foreign troops failed to attract the requisite number of affirmative votes.

The majority of Security Council members expressed an understanding of the action taken by the US and welcomed the involvement of the OAS. The most notable exception to this position was Uruguay, whose representative argued that civil unrest within the Dominican Republic was a wholly domestic concern and therefore that the US intervention was an illegal breach of state sovereignty which could not be justified under the auspices of the OAS. A draft resolution calling on the UNSC to exercise its competence in the field of international security failed to gain sufficient support within the chamber, as did a revised Soviet version of the resolution which was more overtly critical of the US. The Security Council in fact did little to exercise its competence, achieving no more than the passage of resolutions calling for a ceasefire, the dispatch of a special representative under the auspices of the Secretary General's office and a request that a ceasefire be made permanent. In the meantime the situation in the Dominican Republic was moving toward a resolution. A "Government of National Reconciliation" was established in September 1965, and in elections the following year a candidate supported by the US secured the presidency.

Grenada, a tiny south-eastern Caribbean state which had experienced considerable civil unrest, was the target of a US dominated – over 95% of the force's 8300 personnel were US servicemen – military operation in October 1983. [50] In defence of its actions the US claimed, *inter alia*, that the intervention had been undertaken in conformity with the Treaty of the Organization of Eastern Caribbean States (OECS) which had called on the US and other Caribbean states to provide military assistance. However, the OECS treaty only provides for collective defence against external aggression, specifically it provides no mechanism by which the organisation can invite non-members to take action against a member state and neither the US, Jamaica or Barbados are parties to the treaty. Moreover, the treaty requires unanimous support for decisions pertaining to defence and security, yet in the Grenadan case several members failed to lend such support. Finally, these issues apart, it is questionable as to whether OECS sanctioned action would accord with the provisions of the Charters of either the UN or the OAS.

The US dominated intervention was heavily criticised within the United Nations following a request by Nicaragua that the UNSC consider the issue. The passage of a resolution proposed by Nicaragua which condemned US action as a violation of international law and of the sovereign independence of Grenada and also calling for the immediate withdrawal of all foreign troops was prevented by a negative vote by the US. The resolution had overwhelming support, however, among the totality of states which addressed the Council. In addition to the somewhat predictable accusations from states such as the USSR, Cuba, Yemen and Nicaragua, considerable opposition was voiced from other quarters. France voted in favour of the Nicaraguan resolution and even the United Kingdom representative was critical, though he chose to abstain on the vote. Brazil and Venezuela argued that US action violated the principle of non-intervention enshrined in the Charters of both the UN and the OAS, and that US pretexts for intervening were totally unacceptable. The passage of its Security Council resolution having been blocked, Nicaragua requested that the issue be considered under the Uniting for Peace Resolution in the General Assembly where a resolution condemning the intervention was passed overwhelmingly. Voting on the operative paragraph which ' [D]eplore [d] the armed intervention in Grenada, which constitutes a flagrant violation of international law and the independence, sovereignty and territorial integrity of Grenada...', 106 affirmative votes were cast, with only 8 votes against (those of the states which participated in the intervention) and 25 abstentions.

In December 1989 over ten thousand United States troops entered Panama in 'Operation Just Cause', which culminated in the seizure of the Panamanian leader Manuel Noriega, and the installation of Guillermo Andera, whose democratic election had earlier been annulled, as head of government. The US government cited four objectives; firstly the protection of American lives; secondly the assistance of the lawful and democratically elected government of Panama; thirdly the seizure and arrest of General Noriega, an indicted drugs trafficker; and finally the defence of United States rights under the Panama Canal treaties. [51] While it remains a matter of political debate as to the legitimacy of these objectives, and though their legal standing is, at best, dubious, of more direct significance to the current discussion is the fact that in the case of Panama the US did not attempt to elicit the support of the OAS or any sub-regional organisation. Indeed, the OAS, in stark contrast with past practice, passed a resolution which was highly critical of the US action and in so doing signalled the organisation's continuing emergence from the Cold War politico-strategic environment which throughout its existence had compelled compliance with US actions. The wider international response to the intervention was also overwhelmingly hostile. The passing of a Security Council resolution which: ' [S]trongly deplored the intervention in Panama by the armed forces of the United States of America [and] demanded their immediate withdrawal' was blocked only by negative votes from the US, the UK and France. A number of Latin American states – including Argentina, Brazil, Mexico, Peru and Venezuela – were overtly critical of the US' actions.

Panama proved to be the last example of Cold War US intervention within the Americas. However, in 1991 the prospect of interventionary action within the region was again raised when the democratically elected Haitian government of Jean Bertrand Aristide was ousted by a military *coup*. [52] The Haitian case, though primarily debated within the UN Security Council, tells us much about post-Cold War OAS attitudes toward the use of military force. The *coup* received a mixed response from the international community. The

Permanent Council of the OAS issued an immediate condemnation, and on 3 October 1991 the organisation's Ministers for Foreign Affairs, having heard a statement from President Aristide, adopted a resolution demanding his immediate reinstatement, and recommending the economic, financial and diplomatic isolation of the military regime, and the cessation of all non-humanitarian aid. [53] Following the swearing in of Joseph Nerette as 'Acting President' and the naming of Jean-Jacques Honorat as Haiti's new Prime Minister, the OAS Ministers of Foreign Affairs passed a further resolution condemning the replacement of President Aristide and declaring the new regime unacceptable. When, in June 1993, the UNSC finally came to take action over Haiti with the passing of Resolution 841, several states emphasised that their support for economic sanctions was motivated by the fact that they were to be imposed as part of an on-going process aimed at the restoration of democracy in Haiti involving the UN Secretary General and General Assembly and the OAS.

This institutional coalition served as the foundation for what was to prove a somewhat fragile international consensus, and while the UNSC voted to impose a military blockade and more comprehensive economic sanctions it was clear that this represented the co-operative zenith on the matter. [54] When a draft resolution proposing the sanctioning of military intervention was placed before the Council, despite President Aristide's backing for the resolution, the diplomatic consensus collapsed. [55] While the twelve votes cast in its favour were easily sufficient to ensure the resolution's adoption, speeches made by a number of states, prominent amongst which were those from Latin American, demonstrate the unease with which the plan was viewed. The Brazilian representative suggested that the draft resolution was:

> "not felicitous in the invocation of the criteria and the choice of means for attaining the goal of restoring democracy and reinstating the legitimately elected government of Haiti.....the defence of democracy should always be consistent with principles governing relations between states and does not entail recourse to force under the terms now being considered." [56]

Similarly Mexico, Cuba, Uruguay and Venezuela argued that the Council should not mandate the use of force in order to bring about the restoration of the Aristide government. Venezuela argued that the economic sanctions and other peaceful solutions of which it had been a staunch advocate had been given insufficient time to bring about the desired end. Mexico and Uruguay both declared their support for economic sanctions, but rejected recourse to the use of force on the grounds that the situation in Haiti did not constitute a threat to international peace and security within the meaning of Chapter VII of the UN Charter. As the Uruguayan representative explained:

"...although – with a view to the restoration of law , order and democracy – we have unswervingly supported the imposition of economic sanctions in accordance with Article 41 of the Charter, we do not support the application of military action provided for in Article 42. We do not believe that the internal political situation in Haiti projects externally in such a way as to represent a threat to international peace and security." [57]

At the constitutional level this line of argument is not sustainable, since, under the Security Council's enforcement powers laid out in Chapter VII of the Charter, no distinction is made between situations in which economic and military sanctions may be employed; once it has been determined by the Council that a 'threat to international peace and security' exists, either or both articles 41 and 42 may be utilised. Nevertheless, this line of argument clearly demonstrates the fears of Latin American states regarding the exercise of military force within the hemisphere by the US and reflectes more generally concerns over its historical relationship with Haiti, the Caribbean and the wider Western Hemisphere. As Paul Sutton remarks, the Caribbean stands as 'proof of American power', the significance of the region lying in:

"what it represents to the people of the US and to the outside world .... a belief that if the US cannot deal effectively with events in its own sphere of influence it will not deal effectively with events elsewhere." [58]

Echoing this observation and the anxieties to which it gives rise, the Mexican representative commented during the debate that 'history...has shown that military intervention in our hemisphere has invariably been traumatic', while the Cuban delegate went further in claiming that ' [t]he de facto military regime is an expression of a dictatorship created, supported and financed for decades by the United States. The coup was the result of the same policy'. While such Cuban rhetoric is often dismissed lightly, history, accompanied by revelations from US officials that key members of the Haitian military junta were on the CIA payroll as late as 1991, suggests that Washington may not have come to the chamber with totally clean hands. Impressions of political and diplomatic impropriety were further enhanced by reports that the US and Russia had agreed a deal whereby the two permanent members would provide reciprocal support for proposals on military action within their traditional spheres of influence. Moscow had long sought a UN mandate authorising deployment of a peace-keeping force in the neighbouring state of Georgia and Washington, subject to the proviso that each carry out its actions under UN supervision, agreed to support the Russian plan in return for a vote in favour of Resolution 940. [59] According to James Bone the deal:

"reflected the dilemma that great powers face in an era of greater international co-operation when they want to play by the rule, while still policing their backyards in the time honoured fashion." [60]

An appreciation of the fact that the end of the Cold War does not signal the end of a hegemonic regional role for the USA is crucial to understanding the future potential and role of the OAS. The Cold War was but a passing phase in a regional relationship which is likely to prove far more enduring. Hence the end of Superpower confrontation does not dispel factors which will continue to shape intra-regional affairs, nor does it dispose of a history of regional relations during which the United States has proven little restrained in exerting its overwhelming economic and military strength. That such disparities will almost inevitably be reflected in the composition and operation of any OAS peacekeeping or peace-enforcement action only serves to accentuate fears regarding the employment of military means. Though Canadian expertise in the area of peacekeeping should not here be disregarded, the variability in both strength and capacity of military forces from Central and Southern American states is a significant impediment, while the delicate nature of civil-military relations throughout much of the hemisphere raises further complications. Moreover, for many Latin American states a vicious circularity here prevails, for as economic and social conditions deteriorate so civil order may be endangered and the military look once more to exert its influence domestically. In so doing they are likely to further destabilise the county's economic and social conditions, hence exacerbating the initial problem.

It is for these reasons that OAS member states are liable to continue to demonstrate extreme reluctance in their approach to the use of military force. Only in the most extreme of cases will the organisation countenance such action and where it seeks to deploy a force in the absence of agreement by all the parties to a conflict it is most probable that UN oversight will be sought. The area of OAS-UN relations in one in which there remains considerable scope for improvement, for while the organisations are in no way ill-disposed toward one another, and indeed in the post-Cold War era they share essentially common aspirations and goals – albeit operating within differing geographical remits – inter-organisational cooperation remains *ad hoc* in nature. Collaborative ventures have been undertaken with regard to specific cases, such as in Haiti, and over specific issues, such as landmines, but no institutionalised cooperative framwork exists. In the case of Haiti the OAS' desire to elicit UN assistance was borne of a realisation that the former was unable, both legally and practically, to police the sanctions which it sought to impose and yet even here cooperation did not emerge through institutional means, but rather through the involvement and initiative of ministries in certain OAS member states, namely the US, Canada, Argentina and Venezuela. The OAS Secretariat would welcome closer and more formal links with the UN, but to date progress in this area has been slow and has tended to be dependant upon and to revolve around the origin of conflicts and the personalities involved. A significant obstacle to closer collaboration is the sheer difference in size, which means that in practice where the UN and the OAS seek to work together the result is the envelopment of the latter by the former. It should also be acknowledged, however, that many OAS member states do not share their Secretariat's enthusiasm for closer ties with the UN, a view which in part reflects the premier status which members attach to the OAS and fear is threatened by the UN, and in remainder their desire to maintain a decision making process in which they are intricately engaged at the expense of Secretariat autonomy. The ability of the UN Secretary General to exercise political initiative, in contemporary practice beyond that envisaged by the UN Charter, stands in sharp contrast to the role of his OAS counterpart. The fact that UN-OAS cooperation would inevitably involve Secterariat to Secretariat cooperation is not lost on those within the inter-American system who seek to perpetuate the current internal OAS competencies, and as a result the full potential for inter-organisational projects and initiatives may yet remain unfulfilled.

For the above reasons the OAS would appear, at least in the short to medium term, ill suited to a role involving the use of military force, but in other regards the prospects of it assisting in the development of post-Cold War inter and intra-American relations are more promising. At the Miami Summit the organisation undertook an ambitious agenda including, *inter alia*, promoting of hemispheric democracy and human rights, combating corruption, illegal drugs and related crime, fighting terrorism and promoting education and health issues, economic development and free trade. In virtually all these areas the problems facing Latin America are intense and the profundity of the OAS' likely impact may be questionable. However that this agenda exists, and more so that the organisation and its membership are developing a realisation of the relationship between it and region security, stability and prosperity in the broadest sense, is a significant step in the right direction. In large part the OAS was created so as to facilitate dialogue and diplomatic intercourse between the states of Central and Southern America and the USA, but today its role must be to address the broad array of security issues facing the Americas and integral to this it must facilitate the active engagement of the United States in the development of the Western Hemisphere. As a narrowly defined security actor concerned with inter-state and even intra state military issues its present role is, at best, limited, but in this broader sense, it has considerable potential.

NOTES

1. Throughout this chapter the term 'America' will be used to refer to the whole of the Western Hemisphere and the term 'American' to refer to the sovereign states which comprise the Western Hemisphere (rather than to the United States of America). For reasons of convenience, the term 'Latin America' will be used to refer collectively to Southern and Central America, including the Caribbean.

2. Quoted in Inter-American Institute of International Legal Studies, *The Inter-American System: Its Development and Strengthening*, (New York: Oceana Publications, 1966), p. xv.

3. Chapter III, and specifically Article 4 of the Charter of the Organization of American States, provides that "all American States that ratify the present Charter are members of the Organization". This procedure has remained unchanged since the OAS Charter was drawn up, at the Ninth International Conference of American States (Bogota, Colombia, March 20-May 2, 1948). Twenty-one American States participated in that conference. They were: Argentina, Bolivia, Brazil, Chile, Colombia, Costa Rica, Cuba (By resolution of the Eight Meeting of Consultation of Ministers of Foreign Affairs, 1962, the current Government of Cuba is excluded from participation in the OAS), Dominican Republic, Ecuador, El Salvador, Guatemala, Haiti, Honduras, Mexico, Nicaragua, Panama, Paraguay, Peru, United States of America, Uruguay and Venezuela. Subsequently, 14 other American States joined the Organization by signing and ratifying the Charter, as follows: Barbados and Trinidad and Tobago (1967), Jamaica (1969), Grenada (1975), Surinam (1977), Dominica and Saint Lucia (1979), Antigua and Barbuda and Saint Vincent and the Grenadines (1981), Bahamas (1982), St. Kitts and Nevis (1984), Canada (1990), and Belize and Guyana (1991), bringing to 35 the number of Member States. At this time, all the American States have ratified the Charter and are Member States of the OAS.

4. For further discussion of the development of the Inter-American system see Inter-American Institute of International Legal Studies, *The Inter-American System: Its Development and Strengthening* (New York: Oceana Publications, 1966); G. P. Atkins, *Latin America in the International Political System* (Boulder: Westview Press, 1989); and P. Calvert, *The International Politics of Latin America* (Manchester: Manchester University Press, 1994).

5. For further discussion of U.S.-Latin American relations see J. L. Mecham, *A Survey of United States Latin American Relations* (Boston: Houghton Mifflin, 1965); J. Slater, *The OAS and United States Foreign Policy* (Cleveland: Ohio State University Press, 1967); G. P. Atkins, *Latin America in the International Political System*, pp. 108-34; J. Pearce, *Under the Eagle: U.S. Intervention in Central America and the Caribbean* (Boston: South End Press, 1982); G. Smith, *The Last Years of the Monroe Doctrine, 1945-1993* (New York: Hill and Wang, 1994) and J. I. Domínguez, International Security and Democracy: Latin America and the Caribbean in the Post-Cold War Era (Pittsburgh PA: University of Pittsburgh Press, 1998).

6. Unless otherwise stated, all references to the Charter of the OAS refer to the document as amended by the ratification of the 1992 'Protocol of Washington' in 1997.

7. The issue of economic co-operation and development will not be discussed in detail in this chapter, although reference to the subject will be made in relation to economic and social programmes undertaken as part of a broader security policy.

8. For further discussion of the Monroe Doctrine see below.

9. Quoted in G. P. Atkins, *Latin America in the International Political System*, p. 230.

10. For full text see *American Journal of International Law*, 1955, Vol. 49, pp. 123-32.

11. For discussion of the cases in which Resolution 1080 has been employed, Haiti 1991), Peru (1992), Guatemala (1993) and Paraguay (1996) see below.

12. R. J. Bloomfield, "Making the Western Hemisphere Safe for Democracy? The OAS Defence of Democracy Regime", *Washington Quarterly*, 1994, Vol. 17 No. 2, pp. 161.

13. The amendment takes the form of a newly inserted article 9, with subsequent articles being renumbered accordingly.

14. For further discussion of the organisation's utilisation of the Santiago mechanism and other steps taken to promote and secure democracy see below.

15. For a discussion of the conceptual and practical differences between collective security and collective defence organisations see Chapter One.

16. G. P. Atkins, *Latin America in the International Political System*, p. 108-9.

17. Quoted in J. Pearce, *Under the Eagle: U.S. Intervention in Central America and the Caribbean* , p. 17.

18. 'The Political Mythology of the Monroe Doctrine: Reflections on the Social Psychology of Hegemony', in *Latin America, the United States, and the Inter-American System*, J. D. Martz and L. Schoultz (eds.) (Boulder: Westview Press, 1980) p. 97.

19. Quoted in , J. L. Mecham, *A Survey of United States Latin American Relations* , p. 68.

20. For a detailed discussion of this and other extensions to the Monroe Doctrine see J. L. Mecham, *A Survey of United States Latin American Relations* , p. 54-83.

21. Quoted in G. P. Atkins, *Latin America in the International Political System*, p. 120.

22. For further discussion of the Cuban case see below.

23. Quoted in G. Smith, *The Last Years of the Monroe Doctrine, 1945-1993* , p. 17.

24. For the text of the Declaration and Charter of Punta del Este see Inter-American Institute of International Legal Studies, *The Inter-American System: Its Development and Strengthening*, pp. 443-58.

25. J. Slater, *The OAS and United States Foreign Policy* , pp. 11-12.

26. Quoted *ibid.*, p. 139.

27. G. Smith, *The Last Years of the Monroe Doctrine, 1945-1993* , p. 165.

28. *ibid.*, p. 187.

29. Quoted in G. P. Atkins, *Latin America in the International Political System*, p. 131.

30. See Case Concerning Military and Paramilitary Activities in and Against Nicaragua, *International Court of Justice Reports*, 1986, p.14.

31. For further discussion of the process of democratisation see below. See also P. Hakim and A. F. Lowenthal, "Latin America;'s Fragile Democracies", *Journal of Democracy*, 1991, Vol. 2 No. 3, pp. 293-306; L. Whitehead, "The Alternatives to 'Liberal Democracy': a Latin American Perspective", *Political Studies*, 1992 Vol. XL (Special Issue), pp. 146-59; and R. J. Bloomfield, "Making the Western Hemisphere Safe for Democracy? The OAS Defence of Democracy Regime", pp. 157-69.

32. P. Hakim and A. F. Lowenthal, "Latin America's Fragile Democracies", *Journal of Democracy*, 1991, Vol. 2(3), p.293.

33. For a discussion of the decisions reached at Miami and progress in implementing them, see "Words into Deeds: Progress Since the Miami Summit", OAS Report on Implementation of the Decisions Reached at the 1994 Miami Summit of the Americas, 1998.

34. A. Hurrell, "Security in Latin America", *International Affairs*, 1998, Vol. 74(3), p.546.

35. For a discussion of this case see below.

36. See OAS Res. 579 of 8 April, 1992.

37. See V. Perera, *Unfinished Conquest: The Guatemalan Tragedy*, (Berkley: University of California Press, 1993) and R. Trudeau, *Guatemalan Politics: The Popular Struggle for Democracy*, (Boulder: Lynne Rienner, 1994).

38. See OAS Res. 605 of 14 May, 1993.

39. See A. Valenzuela, "Paraguay: The Coup That Didn't Happen", *Journal of Democracy*, 1997, Vol. 8(1), pp. 43-55; and Diego Abente-Brun, "'People Power' in Paraguay", *Journal of Democracy*, 1999, Vol. 10(3), pp. 91-100.

40. See A. Valenzuela, "Paraguay: The Coup That Didn't Happen", *Journal of Democracy*, 1997, Vol. 8(1), p. 54.

41. See S. Jonas, *The Battle for Guatemala: Rebels, Death Squads, and U.S. Power*, (Boulder: Westview Press, 1991); G. L. Bowen, " U.S. Foreign Policy Toward Radical Change: Covert Operations in Guatemala, 1950-1954", *Latin American Perspectives*, 1983, Issue 36, Vol. 10(1), pp 88-102.

42. Quoted in G. L. Bowen, " U.S. Foreign Policy Toward Radical Change: Covert Operations in Guatemala, 1950-1954", p. 90

43. Quoted in J. Pearce, *Under the Eagle*, p. 29.

44. Security Council Res. 104, 11 SCOR (1954).

45. The sanctions regime specifically excluded food and medical supplies.

46. J. Pearce, *Under the Eagle*, p. 33.

47. J. Slater, *The OAS and United States Foreign Policy* , pp. 135.

48. See A. F. Lowenthal, *The Dominican Intervention*, (Cambridge, Ma: Harvard University Press, 1972); P. Gleijeses, *The Dominican Crisis* (Baltimore: Johns Hopkins Press, 1978); J. Slater, *Intervention and*

Negotiation: The United States and the Dominican Revolution, (New York: Harper & Row, 1967) ;W. Friedmann, "United States Policy and the Crisis of International Law", *American Journal of International Law*, 1965, Vol. 59, pp. 857-71.

49. Quoted in P. Gleijeses, *The Dominican Crisis* , p.289.

50. See R. J. Beck, *The Grenada Invasion: Politics, Law and Foreign Policy Decision Making*, (Boulder: Westview Press, 1993); G. Sandford and R. Vigilante, *Grenada: The Untold Story* (Lanham: Madison Books, 1984); "The United States Action in Grenada: Reflections on the Lawfulness of Invasion", *American Journal of International Law*, 1984, Vol. 78, pp. 131-75.

51. See B. W. Watson and P. G. Tsouras (eds.), *Operation Just Cause: The U.S. Intervention in Panama*, (Boulder: Westview Press, 1991); M. L. Conniff, *Panama and the United States: The Forced Alliance*, (Athens GA: University of Georgia Press, 1992); "Agora: U.S. Forces in Panama: Defenders, Aggressors or Human Rights Activists?", *American Journal of International Law*, 1990, Vol. 84, pp. 494-524.

52. For further discussion see J. Morris, "Force and Democracy: UN/US Intervention in Haiti", *International Peacekeeping*, 1995, Vol. 2(3), pp. 391-412.

53. OAS Res. 567 of 3 October, 1991.

54. See UN Doc. S/PV 3293 of 16 October 1993 and UN Doc. S/PV. 3376 of 6 May 1994.

55. See UN Doc. S/PV. 3413 of 31 July 1994.

56. Ibid.

57. Ibid.

58. P. Sutton, quoted in A. Payne, 'US Hegemony and the Reconfiguration of the Caribbean', *Review of International Studies*, Vol. 20, 1994, p.158.

59. 'See UNSC Res. 934, 49 UN SCOR (1994) of 30 June 1994 and UNSC Res. 937, 49 UN SCOR (1994) of 21 July 1994.

60. J. Bone, 'US and Russia carve out "spheres of influence"', *The Times*, 27 September 1994.

CHAPTER 6

The African Perspective: OAU, ECOMOG and SADC

Africa and especially sub-Saharan Africa was by no means free from the surrogate conflicts generated by the Cold War superpower rivalry, but the regional security environment has been rendered especially problematic in the 20th century by the effects of both colonialism and the management of decolonisation. It was especially, although not uniquely, the case in Africa that the unitary state concepts imported and imposed by European colonial powers in the 19th and 20th centuries bore little relation to the established political structures and traditions of sub-Saharan African peoples and communities. When, after 1945, the process of decolonisation commenced it was governed by the *uti possidetis* principle, that is to say that it took place within colonial boundaries which were by no means necessarily those which had been generated by the communities within the region. The end result was in all too many cases not so much a process of decolonisation as one of repatriation of colonisation in which essentially colonial structures were handed over to national authorities whilst retaining many of the defects of their origins. This creation and perpetuation of, in some cases, highly artificial states in which diverse and sometimes actually hostile peoples were forced to participate in unitary political institutions within arbitrarily defined frontiers has, inevitably, brought about a very unstable regional structure and security environment. To this, over much of the second half of the 20th century, was added the further destabilising effect in the southern part of the continent of the racist *apartheid* regime in South Africa, the existence and regional impact of which was declared by the UN Security Council in 1977 to be a threat to international peace and security. [1] These various factors have, both during and after the Cold War, generated a predominance of intra-state conflicts and also the, in modern times, 'new' phenomenon of governmental collapse and consequent chaotic conflict in a power vacuum, as in Somalia and Sierra Leone. Interestingly when provision for such situations in international humanitarian law was proposed by the International Committee of the Red Cross (ICRC) in the drafting process which led to 1977 Protocol II Additional to the 1949 Geneva Conventions the problem was dismissed as 'academic'. [2] The destructive impact of these diverse factors in post-Second World War Africa have been seen in a wide range of conflicts, including, *inter alia*, those in Congo/Zaire, Chad, Southern Rhodesia (Zimbabwe), Angola, Ethiopia-Eritrea, Liberia, Sierra Leone, Somalia, Ogaden and Lesotho.

The end of the Cold War and, in 1994, of the *apartheid* regime in South Africa had dramatic implications for the African regional security environment but these, sadly, were by no means entirely pacificatory in effect. In Africa, as elsewhere, the removal of one global superpower and significant retrenchment on the part of the other deprived their, in some cases highly artificial, client states of political, financial and, in some instances, military underpinning, just as in the southern part of the continent the solidarity generated by the spectacle and threat of *apartheid* South Africa began to dissolve. Thus, political fault lines which had to some degree formerly been constrained began to open up as a new post-Cold War, post-*apartheid* security environment emerged with both beneficial and deleterious consequences.

Not surprisingly in view of the disastrous African historical experience of external interventions, African powers have placed an emphasis both in the Cold War era and afterwards, upon the need for African solutions to African problems. The dynamic of a post-Cold War regionalisation of peace support endeavours has thus in principle much to commend it and the global responses in the 1990s to the crises in the Great Lakes region and in Zaire (the Democratic Republic of Congo) has done little to build confidence in the merits of external intervention. Enthusiasm for regionalism must also, however, be conditioned by a number of cautionary factors.

In the first place African governments and peoples neither are nor would wish to be in some sense separated from the world community as some sort of 'special case'. The requirement is not actually for an isolated and isolationist regional Africa but for approaches and solutions which are appropriately conceived and implemented for African needs. As Jean Herskovits remarks in reporting upon a conference held by the International Peace Academy (IPA) in Abuja upon a sub-Saharan Security Project in December 1977,

> "The call for African solutions to African problems, argued for during the Cold War years by African leaders and other students of Africa looking beyond superpower oversimplifications, has, ironically, been turned upside down outside the continent. Yes, Africans still want to solve their problems without interference based on goals that have little to do with them. But at the same time, as an experienced peacekeeper from Southern Africa put it, 'We must not ghettoise peacekeeping or peace support operations.'"[3]

Indeed African regional and sub-regional organisations emphasise that any peace-support or peace enforcement action must, as international law requires, be undertaken in accordance with UN norms and specifically within the legal framework of Chapters VII and VIII of the UN Charter. [4]

Beyond this general consideration, the post-Cold War, post-*apartheid* era in Africa has considerably affected both the nature, modes of operation and diversity of regional and sub-regional security actors. There are a considerable number of regional and sub-regional organisations in the region, few, if any, of which have a primary focus upon security issues. It is also the case that the focus, forces and infrastructure available to the principal relevant organisations for the present purpose, the OAU, ECOWAS and SADC, are highly diverse in character. Africa, in short, faces the same issues of political control, mandating and potential hegemonic threats as other regions, but does so against a particularly fraught post-Cold War and post-colonial background.

This said, a considerable body of experience, positive and negative, of external and regional peace support action has been built up since the 1960s, from Chad to Zaire and Lesotho, and the issue is increasingly prominent upon the African political agenda. An understanding of future African peace support action necessarily rests upon an analysis of the different regional and sub-regional organisations, their capacities and their inter-relationships. This must also involve an acceptance of the diversity of their origins, character and purposes if probable future potential and limitations are to be accurately assessed. In this respect the question of the future patterns of peace support in Africa may be considered a microcosm of that of regional peace support in general. First, however, the Cold War and later experience of UN intervention in the region requires examination as a vital factor in the subsequent development of African regional security architecture.

UN PEACE SUPPORT IN AFRICA

UN peacekeeping commenced early in Africa [5] with the placement of UNEF I to supervise the peace process in the 1956 Suez crisis, following an unsuccessful Anglo-French attempt to frustrate President Nasser's nationalisation of the Suez canal. Interestingly, the UNEF I operation was authorised not by the UN Security Council but by the General Assembly through the 1950 Uniting for Peace Resolution [6] in the face of Cold War impediments in the Security Council. UNEF's limited but important functions were performed successfully, but a more severe test was faced in Congo. [7] As a Belgian colony Congo had initially been run more or less as a private commercial fiefdom by King Leopold and even after more 'normal' colonisation little was done by way of infrastructural or political development. After Belgian withdrawal in 1960 factional conflict broke out accompanied by competition for dominance by the Cold War superpowers and a secessionist movement in the province of Katanga encouraged by Belgium. By Security Council Resolution 143 of 1960 military support was promised to the Congolese government and the ONUC Force was therefore created and sent into the country with a mandate to restore order whilst stabilisation was achieved. As the OAU was to experience in Chad 20 years later, there was immediately dispute with the government as to the extent of ONUC's remit which the UN, contrary to expectations of the Congolese leader, Patrice Lumumba, did not initially consider to extend to the suppression of the Katangese secessionist movement. Lumumba consequently sought assistance from the USSR which did supply some logistical support but not actual fighting forces, although even this significantly heightened Cold War tensions. Superpower suspicions and rivalry led to stalemate in the Security Council upon the role and governance of ONUC and in September 1960 the USA succeeded in persuading the Council, in a procedural vote to which the Soviet veto could not functionally be applied, [8] to remit the matter to the General Assembly [9] by reference to the Uniting for Peace Resolution. The General Assembly, once seized of the issue, passed a resolution on 20 September 1960 which recommended the continued presence of ONUC in Congo and requested the Secretary-General to take 'vigorous action' to preserve the territorial integrity and political independence of the country. This phrasing merits consideration. There is a clear comparison with the later use of the phrase 'all necessary means' used by the Security Council in authorising the use of force in the 1990-91 Gulf Conflict, [10] although the International Court of Justice, in the *Expenses case*, [11] later opined that the ONUC operations had not strictly been an enforcement action. The General Assembly then itself fell prey to factional discord and in February 1961, after the deposition and assassination of Lumumba – who was commemorated in the name of the University in Moscow dedicated to the use of 'foreign friends', the Security Council formally recognised the Congo situation as a threat to international peace and security. [12] Finally, on 29 November 1961, the Council strengthened ONUC's mandate,

> "(a) To maintain the territorial integrity and political independence of the Republic of Congo; ...
>
> (d) To secure the immediate withdrawal and evacuation from the Congo of all foreign military, para-military and advisory personnel not under United Nations command, and mercenaries; ..." [13]

Upon this basis ONUC proceeded to suppress the Katangese secession and finally withdrew in June 1964, having established the territorial integrity and independence of the country but hardly its political stability. [14] Whether this can be viewed as 'enforcement action', notwithstanding the view of the International Court of Justice, must be open to some debate. D.W. Bowett suggests that it falls short of action under article 42 of the UN Charter and rested rather upon article 39 and was therefore not so much enforcement action as robust peacekeeping action. [15] This, for reasons considered above, [16] may be thought an over technical analysis of actual Security Council practice during the Cold War and N.D. White's view that,

"It would be best to summarize ONUC's actions having as their constitutional basis the enforcement of provisional measures under article 40, but since these measures were increasingly widely drawn so as to cope with an ever-deteriorating crisis, they ... amounted to *de facto* enforcement action." [17]

is to be preferred.

The ONUC action in Congo was the UN's first major intervention in intra-State conflict and its most significant military operation since the US-led action in the Korean War. As such it tested UN political and legal resources in the Cold War to the limit and very nearly ended in disaster from the viewpoint of UN order. The experience largely dissuaded the UN from large scale quasi-enforcement action for the duration of the Cold War and indeed afterwards, even where such operations would have been possible in the context of the ideological confrontation. Thereafter UN operations in Africa tended to small in scale and fell more into the category of peace building than of peace enforcement. Examples were seen in the monitoring of the Eritrean referendum leading to the independence of Eritrea by UNOVER in 1993 and the monitoring of elections in Mozambique by UNOMOZ in 1994. Successful as these limited post-Cold War operations were, they occurred in situations in which the parties in conflict had effectively agreed upon peace. A sad contrast is found in the disaster of the UN response to the crises in Somalia and Rwanda.

The situation in Somalia was ultimately one of the most stark products of colonial interference, by both European and African powers, in Africa. The situation as it developed was, as suggested above, in its essence unexampled and involved not civil war or non-international armed conflict in the 'normal' sense but rather a governmental collapse so absolute that the status of Somalia as a state was potentially called into question. [18] Somalia, a territory originally inhabited by tribal clans without a unitary state structure, was divided in the colonial era between Britain, Ethiopia, France and Italy. A revolt in 1899 led by Imam Mohammed ibn Abdullah Hasan drove the British from much of the desert interior but also generated vicious inter-clan warfare which reflected the tradition of feud and vendetta but also looked forward to the situation of the 1980s and 90s. In the 1930s Mussolini used frontier incidents between Italian Somaliland and Ethiopia as an excuse to launch his invasion and occupation of Ethiopia. [19] The post-war settlement in the area was brokered between the Allies with particular reference to the spheres of influence of the USA and the USSR but little concern for the interests of the Somalis themselves. Finally in July 1960 independent Somalia, comprising Italian Somaliland and most of British Somaliland, [20] was created and the new state immediately began to assert irredentist claims against neighbouring states, notably Ethiopia with respect to Ogaden and Kenya with respect to the Northern Frontier District.

The post-independence regime collapsed in 1969 and was replaced by the Soviet-leaning regime of Siad Barre. When Emperor Haile Selassie of Ethiopia was overthrown and replaced by the Mengistu regime in 1974 President Siad Barre proposed a referendum to determine the future of Ogaden hoping to take advantage of the revolutionary dislocation within Ethiopia to press the irredentist claim. When this was refused he provided financial and material support to anti-Ethiopian guerrillas within Ogaden. In 1977 Somalia actually invaded the Ogaden and rapidly conquered most of the territory, but the USSR, of which the Mengistu regime had become a client, decided to back Ethiopian rather than Somalia leading to a terminal break in its relations with the Siad Barre government. By March 1978 Somalia had been defeated and driven from the territory, but thereafter skirmishes and guerrilla warfare continued, whilst Ethiopia was distracted by the Eritrean conflict, until final Somali withdrawal was compelled in 1980. Diplomatic relations between Mogadishu and Addis Ababa were resumed in 1982 but Ethiopia now pursued a policy of setting the Somali clans against each other and from 1982 exiled Issak clansmen began to flow back across the frontier and to mount armed opposition to the increasingly tyrannical Siad Barre regime which largely depended upon the Marehan clan. From 1988 to 1991 outright civil war raged in the country, to which the government responded with mass executions of its actual and supposed enemies. Foreign aid and gradually almost all foreign contact ceased. In early 1991 Siad Barre fled to his home territory on the Kenyan border and in May the former territory of British Somaliland seceded and proclaimed itself the independent Republic of Somaliland. In the remainder of the country there was no longer any discernible government, merely warring clans and factions some of which aspired to authority over some or all of the territory and others of which were quite simply bandits – with many combining elements of both these qualities.

At this rather late stage the UN became actively involved, brokered a cease-fire between two of the principal factions and imposed an arms embargo. [21] A monitoring force, UNOSOM, was emplaced to observe the cease-fire and render humanitarian assistance in the famine which had been brought about by the conflict. The cease-fire rapidly broke down, to the extent that it was ever implemented at all, and in the continuing internecine warfare UNOSOM became virtually helpless. The Security Council then authorised the USA under the Bush administration to lead a mission using 'all necessary means' – a synonym for armed force, here as in Bosnia – to secure humanitarian relief supplies to the disintegrating state. [22] The US-led and initially almost exclusively US-comprised Force was named the United Task Force (UNITAF) but has become better known by its American designation as "Operation Restore Hope".

This operation became itself mired in the factional fighting as it identified one of the principal warlords, General Aideed, as a major obstacle to its mission. This problem continued when UNITAF was replaced by UNOSOM II. [23] The Force sustained heavy casualties in confrontations with Aideed's Somalia National Alliance (SNA), the actions of which were condemned by the UN Security Council on 6 June 1993 in Resolution 837. The situation was exacerbated by the use of crowds at food relief centres as 'human shields' by some of the factions attacking UN Forces. The mission in all its phases suffered from unclear mandating and mission concepts and was also prey to more than its share of operational difficulties and misconduct by members of the forces themselves. [24] When UNOSOM finally withdrew from Somalia in 1995 it had, as the UN Secretary-General pointed out, [25] achieved very significant humanitarian relief work, it had also almost entirely failed to secure a long term stable future for the country. Indeed the Somalia experience was to be one of the driving forces from a UN viewpoint of the urge to develop a policy of regionalisation of peace support action.

A yet greater disaster was seen in the genocidal conflicts in Rwanda and Burundi. The background to these conflicts is complex. Both states have for more than four hundred years been inhabited by two distinct ethnic/cultural populations, the Tutsis and the Hutus, the former having historically been a politically dominant minority and the latter the majority. From 1899 to 1916 both countries, then known as Ruanda-Urundi, were incorporated in the colony of German East Africa, although little affected by German rule which tended to focus attention upon Tanganyika. After the First World War they were handed over to Belgium which by and large preserved the traditional political system and the Tutsi monarchies in both countries. The Tutsi dominated political system was oppressive of and much resented by the Hutu majority population and when the additional distorting element of colonial domination was removed the impetus to political change tragically resulted not in a measured constitutional reform but in episodic genocide. In 1959 the King of Rwanda died and the Hutus rose in rebellion against his successor, a large number of Tutsis were massacred and many more fled into neighbouring Burundi and Uganda. The Belgian colonial authorities were both unable and unwilling to moderate the situation and in 1962 withdrew leaving a Hutu government under President Kayibanda in power.

In Burundi Tutsi rule under the monarchy of the Mwami continued, although prey to many difficulties. During the preparations for independence in late 1961 the Crown Prince was assassinated and the Mwami then assumed autocratic powers which continued into the post-colonial era. Legislative Assembly elections were eventually held in 1965 and returned a large Hutu majority, the Mwami then rejected the election and appointed his own Tutsi government. Rebellion followed and the Mwami was deposed and driven into exile to be replaced by his son, Ntare V, who was himself deposed in an internal Tutsi coup within a year and replaced by a Republic under President Micombero. Major Hutu opposition to the Micombero regime erupted in 1969 and developed into a full scale uprising in 1971-2. This was suppressed with the aid of troops sent by President Mobutu of Zaire and at the same time the regime eliminated another potential source of opposition by persuading President Amin of Uganda to hand over the exiled Ntare V and murdered him upon arrival. There then followed a mass slaughter of Hutus which must be considered to have come close to genocide. Micombero was ousted in a coup in 1976 by President Bagaza, who was himself ousted by President Buyoya in 1987, but cycles of repression and inter-communitarian killings continued and were much exacerbated by the eventual explosion of neighbouring Rwanda, although the Buyoya regime attempted initially to facilitate greater Hutu involvement in national politics.

The outbreak of conflict in Rwanda between government forces and the Tutsi Rwandan Patriotic Front (RPF) in 1993 finally led to UN involvement in the long running crisis. A UN Observer mission, UNOMOR was established in 1993 to monitor the flow of military supplies into the troubled region. [26] Negotiations between the warring parties led to the 1993 Arusha Accords which contained agreement upon a cease fire and preparations for elections and inter-communal integration of the armed forces. A call was also made for a neutral international force to supervise the implementation of this process. In response to this a UN Assistance Mission, UNAMIR, was established [27] to monitor the implementation of the Arusha Accords and the cease fire. Despite some setbacks progress seemed to be being made and UNAMIR's mandate was renewed in 1994. [28] Tragically this relatively hopeful prospect was destroyed by the deaths of the Presidents of Burundi and Rwanda when the plane in which they were travelling was shot down on 6 April 1994 leading to an outbreak of civil war in Rwanda involving the genocidal mass slaughters with which the name of the country has become synonymous at the end of the 20th century.

The response of the UN and its member states to this situation is flattered by a description as merely inadequate. UNAMIR having by this stage been virtually wound down, the Security Council on 17 May 1994 authorised the creation of a new force, UNAMIR II, with a mandate broadly limited to humanitarian relief, although with powers to use force in self-defence or for the actual securing of humanitarian relief. [29] The response of the international community to the call for resources for UNAMIR II was so slight that the deployment of the force was clearly going to be long delayed if possible at all. [30] In these circumstances France offered to lead a humanitarian mission in Rwanda with others states invited to join if they were willing to do so. The neo-colonialist appearance of this proposal caused great concern to many Security Council members and it was eventually authorised with only the narrowest of margins, with no less than five abstentions – including that of Nigeria. [31] In fact French motives for what became "Operation Turquoise" were almost certainly very mixed, including both genuine humanitarianism and a desire to protect a threatened French sphere of influence in West Africa, including concern for possible destabilisation of the Mobutu dictatorship in Zaire. As N.J. Wheeler and J. Morris have commented elsewhere,

"When, in the immediate aftermath of [President of Rwanda] Habyarimana's death, decisive military action might have stopped the killing, France along with others voted to cut back the UNAMIR force. An unnamed Paris source is quoted as saying that '... we voted for the UN force in Rwanda to be reduced when the killing started but now that the killing is mostly over, we suddenly find a burning desire to save lives.' ... [H]ad Paris responded positively to Resolution 918 and provided the support necessary for a rapid deployment of UNAMIR II, the question of unilateral intervention would not have arisen." [32]

"Operation Turquoise" succeeded in establishing a humanitarian protection zone in South Western Rwanda with some success, but with French withdrawal beginning on 31 July 1994 after approximately one month, UNAMIR II still remained undeployed and was not emplaced, and even then massively under-resourced, until after the final RPF victory in August accompanied by further scenes of mass slaughter and one of the greatest refugee crises in African history. The problems spread into neighbouring states in which large refugee camps continued to be troubled by episodic inter-communal massacres with security and eventual repatriation (much of it hardly voluntary) supervised by Tanzanian and Zairean forces. Apart form its rather unimportant and ineffective humanitarian endeavours, the record of the UN in Rwanda must be reckoned one not only of unmitigated failure but of scandalous unconcern. The only positive result was the subsequent establishment of the International Criminal Tribunal for Rwanda by UN Security Council Resolution 955 of 1994 which, along with the equivalent Tribunal for former-Yugoslavia, has made a significant contribution both to dealing with the aftermath of actually or virtually genocidal conflict and to the possible development of a permanent international criminal jurisdiction from the agreement reached at the 1998 Rome Conference. It must at the same time be added that the interest shown in the proceedings of the Tribunal for former-Yugoslavia has greatly exceeded that of the Tribunal for Rwanda, despite the fact that the tragedy investigated by the latter exceeds even that being considered by the former. The political context of the failure of UNAMIR sadly but clearly remains extant.

Although not strictly a UN action, the military response to the 1965 unlawful Unilateral Declaration of Independence (UDI) by the racist Smith regime in former Southern Rhodesia, now Zimbabwe, is of some interest in the present context. The declaration of UDI was an attempt to frustrate the transition to independence with majority rule by seizing independence under what amounted to a quasi-*apartheid* regime. The UN Security Council by Resolution 217 of 20 November 1965 stated that it,

"(4) Calls upon the Government of the United Kingdom to quell this rebellion of the racist minority;

(5) Further calls upon the Government of the United Kingdom to take all other appropriate measures which would prove effective in eliminating the authority of the usurpers and in bringing the minority regime in Southern Rhodesia to an immediate end."

In response to this the United Kingdom mounted the Beira Patrol by which the Royal Navy sought to prevent the illegal regime from importing crude oil via a pipeline from, then Portuguese controlled Beira to the Umtali refinery. In the early days tankers, notably the *Joanna V* and the *Manuela* were prevented from making such supplies but, as the Umtali refinery seized up through non-use, the patrol swiftly lost its point. It was continued until all possibility of sanctions breaking through this route was eliminated by the independence of Mozambique in 1975, but by this time it was in any event little more than a public relations exercise as the illegal regime had for a long time been receiving all the refined oil it needed via the Beits Bridge land route from South Africa. [33] The British Government was to some degree fearful of offending a domestic political constituency which, under a guise of 'patriotism', argued vociferously in favour of the Smith regime, ignoring the fact that this led them with considerable *prima facie* inconsistency to urge support for rebellion. The British response to the UDI was thus less than robust. The Smith regime was ultimately driven from power not by UN sanctions, and still less by the United Kingdom, but by armed resistance which led ultimately to the Lancaster House Agreement and the independence of Zimbabwe. The lesson from the viewpoint of regional or local peace support action to be derived from the Southern Rhodesian debacle is that of effective UN mandating and control, including some sense of the actual willingness of a delegated agency to take the requisite action and of any divergence between its political and diplomatic agendas and those of the UN.

The UN experience in Africa does not as such reveal any lessons greatly different from those to be learnt in other regions, except perhaps as regards the very particular continental issues of self-determination and intra-state conflict. The experience of Somalia was however one of the major indicators of UN incapacity to sustain the post-Cold War demands placed upon its peace support resources and in this respect the African experience and African prospects are a key issue in consideration of the possible development of regional peace support capacities.

THE OAU

The Organisation of African Unity (OAU) is the oldest and largest regional organisation in Africa. Its political origins were complex and, as the name of the organisation implies, some at least of its founders had the original intention of creating in some form a united Africa with pan-continental governing authorities. Not surprisingly there was a wide divergence of opinion between African governments upon the desirability of such a project, ranging from those who advocated what would have amounted to a federal pan-African state, especially associated with President Nkrumah of Ghana, [34] to those who argued for a continental association of sovereign states. The more radical proposals generated the same concerns over independence and sovereignty which arise in any context which carries a potential for regional political unification, as for example in debates upon the possible future developments of the EU and ASEAN. It must also be pointed out that Africa is by far the largest and most diverse region in relation to which such a proposal has been made and whilst in theory a pan-continental union might have many advantages, in practice there would also be immense difficulties and the ultimate rejection of the idea need occasion no surprise.

The OAU was eventually established with rather more modest aims by a Conference of African Heads of State and Government at Addis Ababa on 25 May 1963. Its primary aims are stated by article 2(1) of the organisation's Charter to be the promotion of the unity and solidarity of African states and the achievement of better standards of life for their peoples. The emphasis was, and is, clearly upon 'solidarity' rather than 'unity' in the sense of pan-African government. As the absence of specifically directed reference in its Charter makes plain, the OAU is not primarily conceived as a collective security or defence organisation, but security was recognised from the outset as inherently a subsidiary dimension of its primary purposes. Amongst the basic objectives of those who founded the OAU were concerns to minimise or eliminate external interference in African affairs both by the Cold War superpowers and by colonial and former colonial powers, to expedite the progress of decolonisation and to address the problem of the existence and destabilising effects of the South African *apartheid* regime. All of these concerns carried clear security implications. Thus article 2(1)(c) of the OAU Charter includes amongst the functions undertaken by the organisation in the name of its members, 'To defend their sovereignty, their territorial integrity and independence; ...' In order to facilitate the achievement of these objectives, member states are required by article 2(2) to,

"... co-ordinate and harmonize their general policies, especially in the following fields:
...

(f) Co-operation for defence and security."

Article 20 further requires the OAU Assembly of Heads of State and Government to establish, *inter alia*, a specialised Defence Commission [35] composed of Ministers of Plenipotentiaries designated by the member states' governments.

Legally, the OAU manifestly falls within the broad category of 'regional arrangements' contemplated as peace enforcement actors by article 53 of the UN Charter. It also has the internal authority to engage in broad ranging collective security and peace support action, the political and practical capacities of the organisation are, however, considerably more open to question.

An immediately obvious difficulty lies in the nature of the OAU security commitment as it is set out in article 2(1)(c) of the organisation's Charter. It is inevitable that the 'territorial integrity' of OAU member states should be central to the organisation's security concept, not least for the reason set out above. This commitment was strengthened by the 1967 OAU Declaration Reaffirming the Principles of Respect for Sovereignty and Territorial Integrity of Member States. [36] Since, however, a significant proposition of the actual and potential conflict in the region are intra-national in character, resulting from the artificiality of some of the member states, the insistence upon territorial integrity disables the OAU from addressing at least some of the most serious security problems in the region. As N.D. White remarks,

"The solidification of the legal principle *uti possidetis juris* by this [1967 OAU] declaration, combined with the assumption that self-determination was inapplicable, cemented the *status quo* in Africa but failed to address the problems such a principle creates, evidenced by the bloody civil war in Biafra in 1967 and the many conflicts and other disasters before and since." [37]

In fairness it must be doubted whether any politically viable alternative to affirmation of the *uti possidetis* principle existed, or exists, for the OAU, but the question of post-colonial, and non-colonial, self-determination seems certain to be one of the problematic issues for public international law and international relations in the 21st century. [38] In the light of the continuing security problems in the continent, the OAU Council of Ministers at Nairobi in June 1981 approved the creation of a pan-African Crisis Response Force. [39] This was not to be a standing force, but rather an arrangement for stand-by forces to be held in readiness for OAU 'green beret' service in the manner envisaged by article 43 of the UN Charter for 'blue helmet' forces. However, like article 43 stand-by forces, the Crisis Response Force remained more theory than reality and was impeded by the fact that it was very much a US-inspired idea over which there had been inadequate regional consultation. More recently, and with much more effective consultation, an African

Security Studies Institute has been set up together with a Committee of Experts whose aim is to create the framework for multi-national regional military co-operation and to facilitate the creation of viable civil/military liaison. In the 1990s there has been a considerable extension of contact and negotiation in the area of peace support both within the OAU and between the OAU and sub-regional organisations. At the 1993 OAU Summit in Cairo the organisation resolved to create a Mechanism for Conflict Prevention, Management and Resolution. The Declaration of the Assembly of Heads of State and Government upon the establishment of the Mechanism states that,

"The Mechanism will have as a primary objective, the anticipation and prevention of conflicts. In circumstances where conflicts have occurred, it will be its responsibility to undertake peace-making and peace-building functions in order to facilitate the resolution of these conflicts. In this respect, civilian and military missions of observation and monitoring of limited scope and duration may be mounted and deployed. ... However, in the event that conflicts degenerate to the extent of requiring collective intervention and policing, the assistance or where appropriate the services of the United Nations will be sought under the general terms of its Charter. In this instance, our respective countries will examine ways and modalities through which they can make practical contribution to such a United Nations undertaking and participate effectively in the peace-keeping operations in Africa." [40]

The Mechanism comprises a Central Organ, which is the political decision maker vested with power to authorise the OAU Secretary-General to initiate appropriate action, and a Division of Conflict Management in the OAU Secretariat which assists the Secretary-General in operational implementation. Despite these significant developments, it is still unfortunately the case that the OAU's general structural base for peace support action remains weak, in part reflecting the continuing tension between pan-Africanism and sovereign independence as between the organisation's member states. In August 1995 a joint task force was established by the OAU and the International Peace Academy in order to develop and render operational the Mechanism authorised by the Cairo Summit and to develop the conceptual base of African regional peace support action. The task force reported in March 1998 [41] and, in the context of a wide ranging and thoughtful analysis, emphasised the importance of prioritisation, capacity and speed of response mobilisation. These conclusions are undeniable, although the ability of the organisation to achieve these substantial goals in the context of a highly diverse pan-continental security environment remains to be seen. It may, however, be noted that the 1997 OAU Chiefs of Staff Meeting in Harare specifically endorsed the possibility of peace support operations in concordance with the norms of the UN Charter. It may well be, however, that as considered below the true future role of the OAU will be one of coordination and policy direction, leaving robust implementation action to developing sub-regional bodies such as ECOMOG and the SADC.

In practice the OAU peace support experience to the time of writing has been founded upon *ad hoc* expedients, in much the same way as UN action during the Cold War era, and must in general be considered to have been less than fortunate. The first significant OAU peace support action was in the protracted civil war in Chad. Chad, as it currently exists, was the product of arbitrary Franco-Italian drawing of colonial boundaries and has been troubled throughout its history with divisions between the Muslim north and the Christian and Animist south and between tribal groupings in both regions. Upon independence in 1965 President Tombalbaye instituted a regime odious to the northern population who rose in revolt. The government sought French assistance between 1968 and 1971 but the troubles continued and in 1975 Tombalbaye, who had by now tried to make Animism the national religion, was deposed and assassinated. From the following year a tripartite civil war raged between forces led by General Malloum, Goukouni Oueddei and Hissene Habre. In the course of episodic civil wars, with external interventions by France, Libya and Sudan and brief appearances by the Nigerian army and forces sponsored by the OAU with a view to restoring order, there was bloodshed on a massive scale. In November 1979 Goukouni was established as President with Habre taking the defence portfolio. This uneasy alliance broke down in 1980 over negotiations for a union with Libya, which Colonel Ghadaffi abandoned in 1981, further episodic civil wars between the various factions then resumed. After early and unsuccessful attempts to mediate in the conflict the OAU Assembly agreed in 1979 to put a peacekeeping force into Chad, subject to the withdrawal of Libyan forces and to the consent of the Chad government. The OAU force in Chad from 1980 to 1982 was beset with insurmountable difficulties from the beginning. Its mandate, contained in OAU Resolution 102(XVIII) was to 'ensure the defence and security of the country whilst awaiting the integration of Government Forces'. Quite apart from the unreality of the prospect of any such 'integration' in the prevailing situation in Chad, this mandate was classically ill-conceived in that it was at once ambitious and imprecise and established no clearly viable exit strategy. In some respects, but in far more extreme degree, the force faced the same basic constitutional difficulties as UNPROFOR in the 1990s in that is was a peacekeeping force sent with an ill-defined mandate into a situation in which there was no peace to keep. In addition to this the weak direction of the OAU itself and the false and inappropriate expectations of the Goukouni regime, which tried to use the OAU force as 'its' army, greatly exacerbated the difficulties already inherent in the operation until Goukouni was overthrown and supplanted by his rival Habre. As G.J. Naldi remarks,

> "the OAU Standing Committee on Chad clarifies the role of the peace-keeping force as being to assist the government to maintain peace and security ... and to take measures to help it to form ... a ... national force. ... Thus the OAU envisaged a neutral role for the

force, an aid to the establishing of negotiations. President Goukouni, however, appeared to view the force as nothing more than another army with which to continue the fighting." [42]

The OAU also encountered serious problems of both financial and material commitment in Chad. National contingents had been promised by Benin, Guinea, Nigeria, Senegal, Togo and Zaire, but Benin, Guinea and Togo withdrew and in the event less than half of the promised number actually materialised. The financial base was also inadequate and applications for assistance were made to the UN and to external powers. [43] Ultimately the force was withdrawn in June 1982, having, hardly surprisingly, failed in all its principle objectives. The hostilities continued with various involvements on the part of Libya, Niger, the Sudan, France and the USA. Libya gave up most, but not quite all, of its claims upon Chadian territory in an announcement made by Colonel Ghadaffi to coincide with the 25th anniversary conference of the OAU on 25 May 1988, but then renewed its attacks in 1990. The OAU intervention in Chad was manifestly an abject failure, although it is difficult to imagine what intervention might successfully have been made in the given situation. Be that as it may, the next OAU peace-keeping endeavour, in Western Sahara, was little if at all more encouraging.

The crisis in the former-Spanish colony of Western Sahara embodies the profoundly difficult questions of post-colonial self-determination which are amongst the most troubling aspects of the current and foreseeable future African security environment. In the last phases of the Franco regime Spain had determined to grant independence to the Western Sahara, whilst both Morocco and Mauritania made claims to the territory. Within the territory the Polisario Front was established in 1972 initially as an anti-colonial organisation with support from Libya. In 1974 Spain proposed a referendum upon the future of the territory but King Hassan of Morocco then referred the matter of the Moroccan claim to the International Court of Justice and persuaded Spain to defer the referendum until the case had been decided. At the same time the UN sent an investigatory mission to the territory to report upon the situation there. On 15 October 1975 the UN mission declared that majority opinion in the territory was in favour of independence and on 16 October the International Court of Justice found against the Moroccan and Mauritanian claims. [44] With Franco in his protracted death throes Spain determined to vacate the territory. King Hassan organised the 'green march' of November 1975 in which some 200,000 Moroccans entered the Western Sahara at which point Spain agreed to hand the territory over to Morocco and Mauritania. On 27 February 1976 the Polisario Front unilaterally declared the Saharan Arab Democratic Republic (SADR) and its military extension, the Saharawi People's Liberation Army (SPLA) commenced guerrilla warfare, initially concentrating attacks upon Mauritania which was taken to be more vulnerable than Morocco.

The OAU attempted to provide a mediated solution to the Western Saharan crisis through an *ad hoc* Committee set up in 1978 [45] and then an Implementation Committee created in 1981. [46] The *ad hoc* committee, chaired by President Nimeiri of the Sudan was initially welcomed by Morocco and Mauritania but questioned by the Polisario Front which felt that the central question was one of self-determination and as such lay properly with the UN rather than the OAU. This view may also have been, not unnaturally, influenced by the fact that both Morocco and Mauritania are members of the OAU, as also – but with somewhat less proportionate influence – of the UN. In any event the *ad hoc* Committee reported in July 1979 and recommended, *inter alia*, that there should be an immediate cease fire in the guerrilla war to be monitored by an OAU peacekeeping force, the withdrawal of Moroccan forces from the territory and a free referendum upon the future of the territory to be phrased in terms of a choice between continuation of the *status quo* and independence. These recommendations were accepted by the 1979 OAU Assembly in Monrovia. The Implementation Committee was then formed to advance and carry through these recommendations in agreement with the parties in conflict and to arrange the emplacement of an OAU green beret force, or possibly a joint OAU/UN force, to monitor the referendum. In practice there proved to be irreconcilable differences between Morocco and the Polisario Front upon the substance of the question to be asked in the referendum and upon the prerequisite of a withdrawal of Moroccan forces.

In February 1983 the SADR attended an OAU summit but thereby precipitated a mass walk out by states sympathetic to Morocco. Subsequently Morocco and a number of other States threatened to resign from the OAU in protest over its relations with the SADR, although this did not in fact happen. Nonetheless, the OAU attempt at mediation and proposed referendum monitoring failed and further endeavours, thus far also unsuccessful, to secure a monitored referendum to determine the further of the Western Sahara have been left to the UN.

This less than fortunate body of experience tends to reinforce the suggestion made above that the OAU is not best placed as a regional peace enforcement agency, a role perhaps better left to sub-regional organisations subject to an OAU, and UN, overview. At the same time the OAU has clearly a major role to play in peace and confidence building and in the sort of supervisory roles envisaged by the 1993 Cairo Declaration. It is significant that in that Declaration the OAU Heads of State and Government thought in terms of UN action and support in cases of more robust peace making and enforcement operations and, with the additional later-1990s emphasis upon regional and sub-regional roles, this may be seen as a proper appreciation of likely patterns of future OAU peace support roles. In this context sub-regional organisations clearly take on roles of very considerable potential and actual significance, and none more so than ECOMOG in Western Africa and SADC in southern Africa. These organisations in themselves raise a number of important questions, both as regards their legal, political and material capacities and their relations with both the OAU and the UN.

ECOMOG

The post-colonial history of Western Africa was beset not only by the complications which have been the common experience of modern sub-Saharan Africa but also by divisions between Anglophone and Francophone states which has been reflected unhelpfully in the development of sub-regional institutions. The first manifestation of West African regionalism was eco-nomic in focus in the formation in 1975 of the Economic Community of West African States (ECOWAS). As its name implies, ECOWAS is founded upon the intention of fostering economic stability and development, objectives which, as in other regions and sub-regions, may themselves be conceived as part of a broader 'security' agenda. Be that as it may, the ECOWAS member states did enter into two security-related, in the military sense, Protocols in 1978 and 1981. The second of these, the 1981 Protocol relating to Mutual Assistance on Defence, provided for a collective response to external, in the sense of extra-regional, aggression and in cases of inter-state and intra-state conflict within the region. Typically, at about the same time a rival Fran-cophone security organisation, *Accord de Non-Aggression et d'Assistance en Matiere de Defense* (ANAD), was established in the sub-region. Ultimately, however, neither of these developments fulfilled their *prima facie* potential. ECOWAS did not, in fact, develop a significant military security dimension until 1990 when it was faced by the Liberian crisis. Liberia was established in 1822 as a haven for freed American slaves of African descent. The descen-dants of these freed slaves formed the political establishment of the independ-ent state upon which was set up the historic oligarchy of the True Whig Party. The country suffered economic disaster in the wake of the 1970s oil price rises and in 1980 President Tolbert was murdered in a military coup led by Master-Sergeant Samuel Doe. The Doe regime rapidly degenerated into a classic military dictatorship which yet further destabilised the already badly shaken political and economic structures of the country. Civil war broke out in December 1989 after a manifestly fraudulent election had confirmed Doe's seemingly unshakeable grip upon power. The civil war and effective collapse of government in Liberia was a humanitarian crisis within and, through a major outflow of refugees, beyond the country and also a major threat to sub-regional security. From its historic origins Liberia had looked to the USA for support but these links had weakened under the Doe regime and in 1990 the US was already strongly committed in the Gulf Crisis and disinclined to undertake new African commitments. In these circumstances ECOWAS created an ECOWAS Monitoring Group (ECOMOG) with the task of arranging and supervising a cease-fire and thereafter to establish and sustain an interim government leading to democratic elections within a period of 12 months. ECOMOG forces entered Liberia on 24 August 1990 in a rapidly deteriorating situation. Doe himself was murdered by forces of a rival faction on 9 September after which no vestige of national government remained and the ECOMOG role became much more one of enforcement. ECOMOG was from the beginning an *ad hoc* force. All ECOWAS member states were invited to contribute contingents, the initial contributors being Ghana, Guinea, Nigeria and Sierra Leone, with lead being inevitably taken by Nigeria as by far the strongest sub-regional military power. ECOMOG ultimately remained in Liberia not for twelve months but for seven years. Over this time other member states, including Benin, Burkina Faso, Gambia, Ivory Coast, Mali, Niger and Senegal contributed contingents, but the predominance of Nigeria remained an inevitable constant. Tanzanian and Ugandan forces were also brought in between 1994 and 1995 representing non-ECOWAS powers partly to offset the deleterious impression which this may have tended to convey. The *ad hoc* nature of this initial ECOMOG force generated considerable difficulties. To a large degree these were the problems all too familiar from traditional 'blue helmet' operations, but in more extreme degree. As Jean Herskovits comments,

> "Joint training did not occur; common doctrine did not exist. Each country continued to bear the expenses of its own forces; ... command and control questions, central to any military operation, were often unresolved. Not until 1994 did the Chiefs of Staff from [ECOMOG contributors] ... begin to meet on a regular, quarterly basis." [47]

A further particular problem arose from the traditional ECOWAS division between Anglophone and Francophone states, the latter group, with the notable exception of Guinea, having made a negligible contribution to ECOMOG in Liberia. Ultimately, after the failure of a number of negotiated agreements between the Liberian factions, ECOMOG was able to commence the disarmament of the warring groups in November 1996 and elections were conducted under UN and ECOWAS supervision on 19 July 1997.

The ECOMOG operations in Liberia did ultimately achieve significant positive results, but also indicated a number of serious problems in need of urgent address. These included internal problems of mandating, command and control, finance and material contribution, as well as questions of general relations between ECOWAS and the OAU and UN. In the light of the Liberian experience the 1993 revised ECOWAS Treaty was entered into which, *inter alia*, made provision for the establishment of peace-keeping or enforcement forces where necessary. This proved of some value in the Sierra Leone crisis but can be regarded as little more than an interim step in addressing the real structural problems encountered by ECOMOG.

The crisis in Sierra Leone, one of the original contributors to ECOMOG in Liberia, arose in 1992 when the oppressive regime of President Momoh was ousted in a military coup d'etat led by Valentine Strasser who then formed the National Provisional Ruling Council (NPRC) with the stated intention of preparing the way for democratic elections. Other groups within the country which had opposed the Momoh regime viewed the NPRC's claims with scepticism and escalating conflict between it and the various armed factions led to economic and political collapse within the country. In 1995 the Commonwealth Heads of Government, the OAU, ECOWAS and the UN attempted to negotiate a peace agreement leading to democratic elections. The NPRC, by now led by Julius Maada Bio, agreed that elections should be held in February 1996. Despite attempts by both the military regime and various of the armed factions to manipulate and disrupt the process, elections were held under international supervision and Ahmad Tejan Kabbah was duly elected President in March 1996.

This seemingly positive outcome was set aside barely a year later when, on 25 May 1997, a further military coup overthrew the Kabbah government and imposed authoritarian rule by the Armed Forces Revolutionary Council (AFRC). There were already nearly 1000 Nigerian troops in Sierra Leone under earlier agreements and ECOMOG moved swiftly to condemn the coup and to send further forces to reinforce the Nigerian presence and to secure the restoration of the elected Kabbah government. A military and economic embargo was imposed and overt military action was taken, *inter alia*, to secure control of Freetown airport. In parallel with these robust measures, in June 1997, ECOWAS, with the support of the UN, established a Committee of Five, involving Foreign Ministers of member states, to seek a satisfactory resolution of the situation. An agreement was brokered with the AFRC on 22 October 1997 as a result of which the Kabbah government was restored to office in March 1998. Again, the ECOMOG intervention in Sierra Leone can generally be seen in a positive light but it also highlighted the need for structural and political development in ECOWAS/ECOMOG as a major peace support actor.

Amongst the obvious institutional lessons to be learnt from the experience of both Liberia and Sierra Leone were the need for clearer planning, crisis management and implementation structures in order effectively to meet future sub-regional needs. ECOWAS has in fact taken substantial steps in this direction. Following proposals made at the December 1997 ECOWAS Summit in Rome the Heads of Member States agreed in October 1998 upon the establishment of an ECOWAS Conflict Resolution Mechanism (CRM), which has significant features in common with the equivalent OAU Mechanism. The ECOWAS-CRM includes dispute resolution mechanisms *stricto sensu*, in particular a nine member Mediation and Security Council which is also, significantly, empowered to authorise military peace support missions. In the event of any such missions provision is made for the Council to be advised upon their conduct by a Defence and Security Commission. At the same time an ECOWAS stand-by force, an institutionalised development of the former *ad hoc* ECOMOG arrangements, is to be set up. This renewed ECOMOG is conceived in the same way as the planned, but never implemented, UN stand-by forces under article 43 of the UN Charter. [48] It is thus intended that ECOWAS Member States will earmark contingents from their national armed forces for deployment in ECOMOG peace support operations at need. Crucially, in the light of experience in Liberia and Sierra Leone, it is intended that such missions would be accompanied by a Special Representative who would provide vital political liaison between ECOWAS and an ECOMOG force commander in the field. These issues and necessities are not, of course, peculiar to ECOMOG, very similar questions were also raised by the UN management of UNPROFOR in former-Yugoslavia, and the ECOWAS response in this regard may be taken to this degree as a positive indicator.

The future of the restructured ECOMOG as a sub-regional peace support actor must, at the time of writing, remain a matter for speculation. Its positive potential is self-evident, but so too are certain basic problems which will need to be overcome if a viable long-term peace support mechanism is to be maintained. The financing of ECOMOG operations seems likely to remain the responsibility of states contributing national contingents and in an economically challenged sub-region this is likely to remain a substantial impediment to sustained operational commitments. There remains also the factor of the dominant military role of Nigeria. It must be said that Nigerian commitment to ECOMOG has been vital and without this contribution it seems highly unlikely that the Liberia and Sierra Leone operations could have been mounted. At the same time the Nigerian military regime raised highly controversial issues both regionally and more widely. It is probably also the case that ECOMOG itself would benefit from a broader military resource base, which, again, feeds back to the basic question of finance.

A final question arises in the nature of the relations between ECOMOG, the OAU and the UN. This was left almost wholly unclear in the development of the CRM, including the fundamental question of mandating. There can be no doubt that legally ECOMOG would require Security Council authorisation for any non-consensual enforcement action by reference to article 53(1) of the UN Charter. The issue is real, as indicated by the experience of NATO in the 1999 Kosovo crisis, [49] and represents one of the basic questions to be considered in the general context of the development of post-Cold War regional peace support mechanisms.

SADC

The security environment of Southern Africa has perhaps changed more dramatically since the mid-1980s than that of any other region or sub-region. The end of the *apartheid* regime in South Africa in 1994 had an area impact greater even than the global effect of the end of the Cold War as the largest regional power was transformed from the principal local security threat into the potential leading area security actor. Many within and outside South Africa had feared that the racist *apartheid* regime would end only through sanguinary civil conflict, but, whilst there was indeed much bloodshed during the *apartheid* era, there was ultimately, in what President Mandela termed South Africa's 'little miracle', a peaceful electoral transition to majority rule. Although the processes of the internal South African transformation fall largely beyond the scope of this book, brief comment is called for upon the Truth and Reconciliation Commission. This proved to be a significant and innovatory peace building mechanisms which, in a deeply traumatised community, achieved remarkable results in rebuilding inter-communal relations. Naturally the process owed much to its particular circumstances, and not least to the leadership of President Mandela himself and figures such as Archbishop Desmond Tutu, but it may still be thought that the South African experience has much to teach other traumatised societies, not least at the end of the 1990s those in former-Yugoslavia.

The restructuring of security architecture after the end of *apartheid* involved two basic dimensions, the reintegration of South Africa into global and regional structures and, as a prerequisite to this, the remoulding of the country's own security institutions. The *apartheid* era South African Defence Force (SADF) and South African Police (SAP) had been amongst the principal props of the racist regime. Now the SADF, MK, [50] APLA [51] and the former 'Bantustan' militias were to be integrated into a new South African National Defence Force (SANDF) for a democratic country. Similarly a newly

integrated South African Police Service (SAPS) was being created as an
urgent priority. The difficulties in creating the SANDF and the SAPS should
not be underestimated, but significant and rapid progress has been made. The
problem was not, as in some cases of peace building in respect of infrastructure, one of developing technical competence, but rather one of defence and
police culture. As Joseph Nanveen Garba and Jean Herskovits remark,

> "In South Africa the problem would be ... one ... of how to create institutions with genu-
> inely new and different military and police cultures and goals, ... the challenge for the
> military in particular would be not just how to integrate the forces but how to ensure eq-
> uity in assigning positions of rank and responsibility." [52]

The demands of this process were, and are, considerable but not more so than
those involved in the security reorientation of the former frontline states in the
struggle against *apartheid*.

The excision of the dominant focus of *apartheid* from Southern African
security calculations demanded a reorientation from the existing sub-regional
security structures – the Frontline States and the Southern African Development Co-ordination Council (SADCC) – no less significant than that necessitated for NATO by the collapse of European communism and the former-
USSR. The initial emphasis from 1994 was upon the Frontline States, which
regrouped as the Association of Southern African States (ASAS) and
expanded their membership to take in Lesotho, Malawi and Swaziland as well
as South Africa itself, thus embracing all the powers of the sub-region. It was
anticipated that the security wing of ASAS, the Inter-State Defence and
Security Community (ISDSC), might constitute the principal pillar of the new
overarching Southern African security architecture. [53] In fact, however,
attention shifted away from the ASAS and the ISDSC towards the SADCC,
which now re-formed itself as the Southern African Development Community
(SADC) which also took in South Africa and has a membership parallel with
that of ASAS.

The reasons for the shift of emphasis in security considerations towards
SADC, which had become clear by late 1995, relate partly to structure and
partly to regional power relations. The SADC inherited from the SADCC a
clear, if rather bureaucratic, internal structure in contrast with the more
flexible and informal arrangement which ASAS had inherited from the *ad hoc*
decision-making processes of the Front Line States. Both formal and less
structured systems clearly had their respective advantages and disadvantages,
but it must be borne in mind that the flexibility of ASAS derived from the
days when *apartheid* South Africa was the principal security threat and is
perhaps less suitable for an age in which the security situation is potentially
far more complex. The factors to be taken into account include the need for a
clear framework within which a new and more complex security architecture

can be developed, remembering also the sensitivities of the regional powers, especially, but not only, South Africa and Zimbabwe, over claims to regional leadership.

In January 1996 a Summit Meeting of SADC Foreign and Defence Ministers was convened in Gabarone to resolve the shape of future sub-regional defence and security architecture and proposed as a principal mechanism a SADC Organ for Politics, Defence and Security (OPDS). The creation of such a security-focused mechanism within SADC was obviously essential since SADC is, as its name implies, much more generally focused upon economic development. It must, however, be noted that, as is for example also the case for ASEAN in Southeast Asia, [54] an expanded concept of sub-regional security includes an economic imperative at least as strong as its military dimension. The SADC-OPDS was endorsed by the organisation's Member States at a Summit on 28 June 1996. It was endowed with a complex agenda, including development of a common sub-regional foreign policy, sub-regional defence and security cooperation, conflict mediation and resolution and, most relevantly for the present purpose, the development of peace support capacity. The ASAS-ISDSC was also to be absorbed as an element of the OPDS. It was also agreed at the June 1996 Summit that OPDS should be independent of other SADC bodies, apart obviously from the political direction of the SADC Summits and Council of Ministers, and the presidency of the Organ should circulate between the 'Troika' of Botswana, South Africa and Zimbabwe.

Notwithstanding these encouraging developments, relations between SADC and ASAS remain in some degree uncertain, and visions of SADC's own future vary significantly, especially as between South Africa and Zimbabwe. So far as the latter dimension is concerned there developed a real divergence between President Mugabe of Zimbabwe, as Chairman of OPDS, and former-President Mandela of South Africa, as Chairman of SADC, the one seeing the OPDS as, in effect, a Southern African equivalent of NATO linked with but distinct from SADC, whilst the other saw it as an integral security arm of SADC. The question of leadership and ultimate authority has been the subject of fierce internal debate and no solution had been found up to the September 1998 Mauritius Summit of the SADC, although the indications in 1999 are that relations between Pretoria and Harare upon this issue are becoming somewhat less volatile. Other possible problems arise from the lack of a separate OPDS Secretariat, or even a fully developed SADC Secretariat, and the uncertainty of its relations with the OAU and, ultimately, the UN. Its relations with the OAU will presumably parallel those of ECOMOG, [55] but it may here be added that the fact that there are a number of states involved in SADC which have significant military capacity may avert the problems posed for ECOMOG by the military dominance of one member state, Nigeria. As to the UN, its primacy is accepted by the OAU and by the individual member states of the SADC and ASAS and in essence the SADC-OPDS would be a 'regional arrangement' within the broadly interpreted remit of Chapter VIII of the UN Charter. Again, however, as for ECOMOG, there is an urgent need for clarity in the nature of the organisation's relationship with the UN, the importance of which has elsewhere been shown clearly by NATO's experience in the 1999 Kosovo Crisis.[56]

Early experience of Southern African peace support, aside from the peace building process in South Africa itself, was gained in the crises in Lesotho and Swaziland. In the *apartheid* era the Kingdom of Lesotho was placed in an awkward situation as an independent African state, quite unlike the South African 'bantustans', entirely surrounded by racist South Africa to which it was to a large degree, unavoidably, economically tied. The country is in theory a constitutional monarchy. Under British colonial administration a monarchy was structured around traditional institutions headed in the post-colonial era by King Moshoeshoe II who, unequivocally hostile to *apartheid*, interacted awkwardly with the ruling Basutoland National Party (BNP) which, on pragmatic grounds, was more inclined to collaboration with the Pretoria regime. The King's relations with the opposition Basutoland Congress Party (BCP) were also poor because of his inability to prevent their being denied the fruits of electoral victory in an effective BNP coup d'etat in 1970, even though Moshoeshoe II was temporarily exiled by the BNP regime at that time. In 1986 Pretoria installed a military despotism nominally under royal authority but in fact run on pro-South African lines by Lesotho's highly politicised army. The military regime sent King Moshoeshoe back into exile in 1989 and, in violation of both cultural and constitutional traditions, replaced him with his elder son as King Letsie III. With the unravelling of the *apartheid* regime in South Africa in 1994 the regime was driven to hold elections which returned a sweeping BCP majority. The new government set about reforming and professionalising the BNP-dominated armed forces which led to military insurrection and a call from Prime Minister Kokhehle for South African military support. This was not as such forthcoming but the Presidents of Botswana, South Africa and Zimbabwe formed a 'Troika' group to attempt to mediate a solution to the crisis. This endeavour encountered many obstacles, exacerbated by differences within the troika as to the best way forward. President Mugabe of Zimbabwe favoured a military intervention to disarm and reform the Lesotho armed forces as a prerequisite for the establishment of constitutional stability, whereas President Mandela of South Africa looked for a diplomatic solution. In the midst of the crisis, on 17 August 1994, King Letsie suddenly dismissed the Mokhehle government and announced the restoration to the throne of his father, Moshoeshoe II. This restoration undoubtedly reflected majority Basotho opinion in the country, but the dismissal of the government was equally clearly a constitutional outrage and was immediately denounced as such by the Troika. In response to the escalating crisis and the royal coup the SANDF carried out major exercises on the border with Lesotho in early September and on the 14th of that month the Troika succeeded in brokering an understanding under which Moshoeshoe II was to remain King but the Mokhehle government was to be restored to power. The policy of depoliticising and professionalising the army was to be resumed as an important aspect of peace building within the country.

Sadly this process was again destabilised after the King was killed in a traffic accident a year later and finally there was a degeneration into factional fighting and mass looting broke out in the capital, Maseru. Order was restored after South African military intervention under SADC auspices, although vocal elements of Lesotho opinion attempted to blame the South African action for the disturbances – a view which may be received with some scepticism. Be that as it may, the situation in Lesotho remains fragile at the time of writing and, whilst regional inaction would be inconceivable, it is difficult to see how an effective external solution might readily be devised for Lesotho's deep seated internal problems.

On a lesser scale, rather similar issues arose from the situation in Swaziland. There difficulties sprang from the death of King Michael Sobhuza II, after the longest recorded reign of any monarch. Sobhuza II had ruled as an autocrat for the latter part of his long tenure upon the throne after abrogating the Swazi constitution. His death, leaving an infant heir and a regency under the inexperienced and little known Ndlovukazi, the Queen Mother, inevitably generated political instability. Long suppressed demands for a restoration of constitutional democracy revived and by 1996 there was widespread unrest in the country and pro-democracy strikes were seriously destabilising the economy. The same presidential Troika which had intervened in Lesotho persuaded King Mswati III to undertake meaningful consultations with a view to the restoration of the constitutional order which had been overthrown nearly a quarter of a century before. The process of democratisation in Swaziland has continued since then, although admittedly with a deliberation which has rendered the pace of change at times almost imperceptible.

Several lessons emerge for southern African security development from the Lesotho and Swaziland experiences. It may first be noted that in this sub-region, as in a number of other areas, both democratisation, in varying degrees, and economic stabilisation are beginning to enter a broadened concept of 'security', albeit in tandem with serious concerns over more overt disorders. There may here be seen some comparison with, for example, the post-Cold War development of the OAU. [57]

The future of the SADC as a sub-regional security actor remains to be seen. Clearly the SADC Organ has the material resources available to it to play a major security and peace-support role. It also compares favourably with ECOMOG in so far as it includes more than one major military power and should therefore be able to avoid any replication of the dominance of the West African organisation by Nigeria. There may also be benefits in the combination of the relatively informal tradition inherited from the former Frontline States with the more formal tradition derived from the former SADCC. This may permit a useful combination of flexible *ad hoc* diplomatic reposes with more structured military responses in cases of necessity. This said, the basic disagreement between South Africa and Zimbabwe, specifically between Presidents Mandela and Mugabe, over relations between the SADC Organ and the SADC itself and the precise *modus operandi* of the former opens a political fault line which, whilst hardly insuperable, may significantly impede the development of the SADC into the medium term future.

It is also clear from the Lesotho and Swaziland experiences, as also from the serial crises in Angola, that despite the remarkable pacification of southern Africa at the end of the 20th century, there remain diverse and deep seated problems which, as in Africa more generally, do not admit of simple solutions. Last, but by no means least, it must be remembered that major sub-regional powers, including in particular South Africa, Zimbabwe and Angola, are engaged in demanding processes of peace building and reconstruction as they emerge from traumatic recent histories. These processes also involve major shifts in bilateral relations, especially for example between South Africa and Angola. All of these factors will necessarily be the focus of immediate national priorities in preference to sub-regional security concerns in the short to medium term. The SADC Organ has, in short, a very significant peace support potential, the extent of the fulfilment of which must remain to be seen.

CONCLUSION

Africa as a region is too large and diverse in character to admit of any simple or singular solution to its security problems or peace support requirements. This would be so even without the gross exacerbation of the continent's difficulties by disastrous external interference in the colonial and Cold War eras. In this respect Africa is in some ways a significant microcosm of the global questions of post-Cold War peace support requirements and development. Of the principal institutions it seems clear that the OAU does not have, and is unlikely to develop, any rapid military response capability. It is also unlikely that so diverse an organisation will be able to sustain much in the way of effective emergency crisis management. That said, the OAU has considerable value as a facilitator and as a diplomatic and political forum in which effective peace and confidence building processes and possibly measures of peacekeeping may effectively be based. The comparative model for the OAU's future lies, perhaps, somewhere between those of ASEAN and the OSCE. Inevitably, because of the very diversity of the region, the focus for more robust action seems likely to lie with the sub-regional organisations and in particular with ECOWAS-ECOMOG and the SADC-SADC Organ. These organisations have, as suggested above, their own difficulties but are, equally, clearly capable of resolute and effective action. Whether the models for future development here are to be, in one degree or another, such organisations as NATO or the OAS remains to be seen, as does the relationship between the 'political' and 'security' arms of these organisations. From a legal and structural viewpoint there remains also the vital question of the lines of authorisation as between the UN, the OAU and the sub-regional organisations. This has not so far proved a major problem in Africa, but the potential difficulties have been clearly illustrated by the NATO experience in Kosovo in 1999.

Contrary to a conventionally dismissive response to African security and peace support structures there is in fact some reason to hope that despite the very severe political and military problems of the continent the development of post-Cold War and post-*apartheid* Africa is moving in a sustainably positive direction. An 'African solution to African problems' does not mean a radical divorce of the region from global, and specifically UN, structures, but it may indicate a development of structures with African roots through which the emergence of the continent from its troubled recent history may be smoothed. It is highly significant that the experiences of Somalia and the Great Lakes were amongst the principal elements driving the engine of peace support regionalisation and to this degree Africa must be viewed as a flagship in this process of development – with ultimate consequences which remain to be seen.

NOTES

1. UN Security Council Resolution 418 of 4 November 1977.
2. See Y. Sandoz, C. Swinarski and B. Zimmermann, eds., *Commentary on the Additional Protocols of 8 June 1977 to the Geneva Conventions of 12 August 1949* (Martinus Nijhoff, 1987), p.1351, para. 4461.
3. J. Herskovits, *Africans solving African Problems: Militaries, Democracies and Security in West and Southern Africa* (International Peace Academy, 1998), pp.5-6.
4. For discussion see Chapter 2.

5. For an early discussion of problems and perceptions see T. Hovet, *Africa in the United Nations* (Faber and Faber, 1963).
6. Ibid.
7. For a detailed analysis see G. Abi-Saab, *The United Nations Operations in the Congo 1960-1964* (Oxford, 1978); see also R. Higgins, *United Nations Peacekeeping 1946-1967, Documents and Commentary: 3, Africa* (Oxford, 1980).
8. By reason of article 27(2) of the UN Charter.
9. UN Security Resolution 157 of 1960.
10. UN Security Council 678 of 29 November 1990.
11. [1962] ICJ Reps., 151.
12. UN Security Council Resolution, 161 of 27 February 1961.
13. UN Security Council Resolution 169 of 29 November 1961.
14. See G. Abi-Saab, op.cit., Chapter IV.
15. D.W. Bowett, *United Nations Forces* (Stevens, 1964), p.180.
16. See Chapter 2.
17. H. McCoubrey and N.D. White, *The Blue Helmets: Legal Regulation of UN Military Operations* (Dartmouth, 1996), p. 53.
18. Government, even if disputed, is one of the criteria of statehood set out by article 1 of the 1933 Montevideo Convention.
19. Then known as Abyssinia.
20. Other parts having been hived off to Ethiopia and Kenya.
21. UN Security Council Resolution 732 of 1992.
22. UN Security Council Resolution 794 of December 1992.
23. UN Security Council Resolution 814 of 1993.
24. See *Re Brown and Fisher et al* 113 Dominion Law Reports (1994), 102.
25. See The Secretary-General's Report, UN doc. S/1995/231.
26. UN Security Council Resolution 846 of 1993.
27. UN Security Council Resolution 872 of 1993.
28. UN Security Council Resolution 909 of 1994.
29. UN Security Council Resolution 918 of 1994.
30. For discussion see N.J. Wheeler and J. Morris, 'Humanitarian Intervention and State Practice' in R. Fawn and J. Larkins, eds., *International Society after the Cold War: Anarchy and Order Reconsidered* (Macmillan, 1996), pp.135-171 at p.157.
31. UN Security Council Resolution 929 of 1994.
32. Op.cit., at p.159, citing Richard Dowden, *The Independent* (London) 21 June, 1994.
33. For a pointed discussion of this episode see M. Bailey, *Oilgate: The Sanctions Scandal* (Coronet, 1979).
34. See K. Nkrumah, *Africa must Unite* (Panaf. 1963).
35. Article 20(4).
36. OAU Document AHG/St.2(4) (1967).
37. N.D. White, *The Law of International Institutions* (Manchester, 1996), p.99.
38. D. Kritsiotis 'Uti Possidetis' in D. Kritsiotis, ed, *Self-Determination: Cases of Crisis* (University Hull, 1994).
39. *Keesings Contemporary Archives.*
40. 1993 Cairo Declaration of the Assembly of OAU Heads of State and Government on the Establishment within the OAU of a Mechanism for Conflict Prevention, Management and Resolution, paragraph 15.
41. See *Report of the Joint OAU/IPA Task Force on Peacemaking and Peacekeeping in Africa* (International Peace Academy, 1998).
42. G.J. Naldi, 'Peace-keeping attempts by the Organisation of African Unity' (1985) 34 *International and Comparative Law Quarterly*, pp,593-601 at p.594.
43. Voluntary assistance was authorised by the UN in Security Council Resolution 504 of 1982.
44. [1975] ICJ Reps., 12.
45. OAU Resolution 92(XV) of 1978.
46. OAU Resolution 103(XVIII) of 1981.

47. J. Herskovits, *Africans Solving African Problems: Militaries, Democracies, and Security in West and Southern Africa* (International Peace Academy, 1998), p.9.
48. For discussion see Chapter 2.
49. See Chapters 2 and 4.
50. The military wing of the African National Congress (Umkhonto we Sizwe).
51. The military wing of the Pan-African Congress (Azanian People's Liberation Army).
52. J.N. Garba and J. Herskovits, *Militaries, Democracies and Security in Southern Africa* (International Peace Academy, 1997), pp.10-11.
53. See J. Cilliers, 'The Evolving Security Architecture in Southern Africa' (1995) 4 *African Security Review*, 40.
54. See Chapter 7.
55. See above.
56. See discussions in Chapters 2 and 4.
57. See Chapter 6.

The Asia/Pacific Perspective:
ASEAN, ARF and Collective Security

Although a consideration of the ASEAN security perspective necessarily focuses upon Southeast Asia, it is also important to take into account other actual and potential major actors with interests or involvements in the region, especially those which the ARF is seeking to bring into a progressive security dialogue. For this reason this chapter is primarily concerned with, but not exclusively limited to, Southeast Asian concerns *stricto sensu*. The Cold War experience of Southeast Asia differed significantly from that of, for example, Europe or the Americas for a variety of reasons. Prominent amongst these was the fact that the region did not lie within the tacitly agreed sphere of influence of either of the Cold War superpowers, which meant that there was an increased potential for externally generated conflict – manifested in particular in the Korean and Vietnam wars and the long agony of Kampuchea/Cambodia. The situation was further complicated by the near presence of the People's Republic of China which rendered the regional Cold War confrontation, to some degree, trilateral rather than merely bilateral in nature. The Cold War security environment was thus somewhat less clearly defined in this region than was the case in some others. Nonetheless, the end of the Cold War and the demise of the former-Soviet Union was no less significant for Southeast Asia than for other regions. Notwithstanding the somewhat varied regional impact of the Cold War, the immediate consequence of its end, in Southeast Asia as elsewhere, has been the generation of a less certain security environment which proved in many respects not so much less dangerous as differently and less predictably perilous even than the preceding unstable balance of power. This has meant that some regional disputes, including not least that over the Spratly Islands, have assumed a heightened intensity once freed from the constraint of the Cold War dynamic, whilst the roles of actual or potential superpowers on the fringe of Southeast Asia, notably China and Japan, generate other grave uncertainties for the future security architecture of the region.

Any worthwhile consideration of collective security and regional peace support capabilities in Southeast Asia must be conditioned by a consciousness of the particular qualities of the security experience of the region and, in particular, by an awareness of the danger of any apparent or actual imposition of 'western' presumptions about the nature of international relations in general and collective security in particular alien to the cultural and political traditions of the region. The distorting effects of such a 'parachuting' of ideas and presumptions into analyses of Southeast Asian security concepts and structures have been clearly set out by Nicola Baker and Leonard C. Sebastian in their comment that,

> "We ... run the risk of proposing or creating security structures, agreements and processes which are irrelevant to the concerns of states in the Asia/Pacific region or, worse still, threaten to undermine their security." [1]

Such an acknowledgement by no means represents an uncritical endorsement of the unreflective arguments of cultural relativism which, in the fashionably extreme forms in which they are sometimes encountered especially in debates upon the nature and scope of human rights, are implicitly racist in their denial of the imperatives of common humanity. It rather affirms one of the central arguments advanced in this book, that, within certain core parameters, a viable post-Cold War peace support paradigm cannot be either simple or singular, but must take account of wide regional and institutional diversities. In the Southeast Asian context the ill-conceived SEATO initiative, an attempt to 'parachute' the NATO concept into a region with quite different needs, serves as an important warning illustration from the Cold War era. The Southeast Asian experience in the area of collective security has in fact been highly distinctive, not least in developing an idea of 'security' notably different from the western model which has an important contribution to make to post-Cold War debate. The distinctiveness of the experience derives, inevitably, from the complex regional historical experience and this demands preliminary examination before the present and potential future security environment can be analysed.

FROM THE SECOND WORLD WAR TO THE ASEAN WAY

The end of the Second World War was for Southeast Asia, as for most other regions, a benchmark in modern political development which shaped much of what was to follow. The 19th and the first half of the 20th centuries had been an era of colonial domination, although it is worth emphasising that this was by no means uniform in pattern or origin across the region. The principal colonial Powers were Britain, France, Japan, the Netherlands and the USA. Britain held Burma, Malaya, Singapore – established as a trading post by Sir Stamford Raffles, and Hong Kong. France held Annam (now Vietnam), Cambodia and Laos. Japan, as a comparative newcomer to colonialism, annexed Taiwan and other parts of China in the 1894-5 Sino-Japanese War and from the 1904-5 Russo-Japanese War to 1910 extended its control over the whole of Korea. The USA, for its part, seized the Philippines. There were also anomalous territories such as Sarawak, ruled by the Brooke Rajahs following cession to Rajah Sir James Brooke by the Sultan of Brunei, although this became a British colony in 1945 prior to incorporation, with Sabah, into independent Malaysia. Thailand, known for most of this period as Siam, remained free from colonial rule, although subjected to a significant degree of interference in both its domestic and external affairs by neighbouring colonial powers.

The initial defeat of the colonial powers by Japan in the Second World War is sometimes represented as having had a 'liberating' effect in demolishing the colonial ethos in the region. This is a hypothesis which must be treated with some caution. It must be borne in mind that Japan was itself a colonial power and, despite the cynical rhetoric of the 'Greater East Asian Co-Prosperity Sphere', Japanese occupation of the region was in fact a late example of colonial expansion and one which in its implementation was very far from 'liberating'. This said, the successive defeats of the colonial Powers, first by Japan and then of Japan, did deflate colonial presumptions and such episodes as the profoundly incompetent defence of Malaya and Singapore against Japanese attack virtually destroyed the imperial myth. The post-War settlement and the commitment of the United Nations to rapid de-colonisation as an expression of a newly *legal*, if still very limited, concept of self-determination, spelt the end of the colonial era.

The political and strategic environment in Southeast Asia after the Second World War was thus profoundly different from that which had existed in the 1930s. Japan had been destroyed as a military, and in the short term as an economic, power. The Kuomintong regime of Chiang Kai Shek had been driven from mainland China into the former Japanese colony of Taiwan by the communist forces led by Mao Zedong and the long and very troubled period of Chinese reconstruction was commencing. To the processes of post-War reconstruction there were added the stresses of decolonisation – the 'always messy end' as the economist J.K. Galbraith has put it, [2] and the ideological confrontation of the Cold War, here involving, as suggested above, not only the US-Soviet encounter but also the complex development of relations between the People's Republic of China (PRC) and both post-War Superpowers. These factors combined to generate a turbulent and very dangerous regional security environment. The Korean War, the Malayan 'Emergency' and the Vietnam War were amongst its several poisoned fruits.

The 1950-53 Korean War is sometimes suggested to have been the classic instance of the intended working of collective security under the UN system, this, however, is a considerable over-simplification. With the defeat of Japan in 1945 Soviet forces moved into northern Korea and established a communist regime under Kim Il Sung, whilst US forces moved into the south and established a capitalist regime under Syngman Rhee. The USSR then withdrew in 1948 and the USA in 1949, each leaving their respective client regimes on either side of the 38th parallel. In June 1950 North Korea invaded the South and took Seoul and much of the rest of the country. The UN responded swiftly to the invasion and called for assistance to be given to the Republic of [South] Korea in Security Council Resolutions 82 of 25 June 1950 and 83 of 27 June 1950. By Resolution 84 of 7 July 1950 the Security Council then stated that it,

"(2) Notes that Members of the United Nations have transmitted to the United Nations offers of assistance for the Republic of Korea:

(3) Recommends that all Members providing military forces and other assistance pursuant to the aforesaid Security Council resolutions [82 and 83] make such forces and other assistance available to a unified command under the United States of America."

The passing of this resolution was, in fact, a paradoxical instance of Cold War impediments to the operation of Security Council facilitating, rather than impeding, action. The former-USSR would undoubtedly have vetoed resolutions 82-84 in relation to Korea were it not for the fact that it had temporarily withdrawn from involvement with the Security Council in protest against the continued occupation of the Chinese seat by the Republic of China (Taiwan) despite the establishment of the People's Republic of China.

The UN mandated force in Korea was multi-national in character but nonetheless overwhelmingly US dominated and under the command of the mercurial General MacArthur. It swiftly restored the territorial integrity of South Korea but then pushed northwards towards the Chinese border whilst MacArthur uttered threats to bomb China itself. This led to a confrontation with President Truman and to his dismissal in April 1951. At the same time China intervened in order to save the Northern communist regime and to maintain a buffer State upon its own borders. Eventually an armistice was signed in July 1953 which for all practical purposes restored the *status quo* with Korea divided into two States on either side of the 38th parallel.

To say that regional peace and security was restored would be an over-statement. Strictly speaking there is, even in 1999, no peace agreement, although, despite occasional confrontations, the 'war' has, since the 1950s, been largely 'cold' in character. Be that as it may, the Korean War set the scene for an expression of Cold War confrontation in Southeast Asia which was to prove arguably more intense and certainly more violent than in most other regions.

In parallel with the Korean War the long debacle of Vietnam was commencing. The Colonial Power, France, had agreed in 1946 with the communist

leader Ho Chi Minh to the effective independence of Vietnam but in fact
France tried to re-establish full colonial control in a sanguinary war which
lasted from 1946 to 1954 and ended with French defeat at Dien Bien Phu. At
the ensuing 1954 Geneva Conference Vietnam was effectively split along the
17th parallel with a communist republic in the North and a French colony in
the South, with an intention to reunify the country with elections to be held in
1956. This did not happen and Ngo Dinh Diem was installed as head of
government in a separate State of South Vietnam with US support.

Armed conflict resumed with a claimed, although disputed, attack upon US
warships by Northern forces in the Gulf of Tonkin incident in August 1964 [3]
after some years of guerrilla activity in South Vietnam supported from the
North. The USA requested the Security Council to consider the Gulf of
Tonkin Incident but North Vietnam maintained, with the support of the USSR,
that the issue lay only with the parties to the 1954 Geneva Conference. In
practice the Vietnam War was never substantively discussed by the Security
Council and when, finally, in 1966 the USA sought a general debate upon the
issue this was, again, blocked by the USSR. The USA for its part treated the
Vietnam War initially as a parallel circumstance with the Korean War, despite
the absence of a UN decision, and under the Johnson and Nixon administrations made massive military commitments to the maintenance of South
Vietnam. In fact the parallel with the Korean War, much emphasised in initial
US thinking, was rather limited. As N.D. White comments,

> "While in the case of Korea, the Communist attack ... was a clear violation of Article 2(4)
> and a 'breach of the peace' within Article 39 [of the UN Charter], the Vietnamese situa-
> tion was more complicated, evidenced by the fact that there was considerable support for
> the Vietcong in the South. There was no ... significant event which would have enabled
> a collective response ... [and] the Soviet Union was not going to absent itself and so allow
> the collective response to become a collective United Nations' response. ... The gradual
> escalation of the conflict in Vietnam severely limited the potential of United Nations'
> action. It had not really dealt with the situation at its origin, either in 1946 or ... in the
> 1954 Conference, and thereafter it was in the untenable position of having to deal with
> the conflict from the outside." [4]

Space precludes an extensive summary of the course of the war, [5] but the
large number of American casualties and the seeming and actual weakness of
the South Vietnamese regime led to unparalleled levels of domestic opposition
in the USA which effectively derailed both the Johnson and Nixon Presidencies. [6]

Richard Nixon's policy of 'Vietnamization' and gradual withdrawal of US
forces signified that the end was in sight, even though the 1970 bombing of
Vietcong supply routes in Cambodia betokened an expansion of the conflict.
Rapprochement between the USA and the PRC, fuelled by mutual antipathy
to the USSR and sealed by Nixon's historic visit to Beijing in February 1972,

further remoulded the political parameters of the war and in 1973 the USA and North Vietnam entered into the Paris Agreement [7] under which US forces were to withdraw but South Vietnam was to be preserved. In practice, without American support, the South Vietnamese regime rapidly collapsed and by April 1975 the North Vietnamese had occupied the capital city, Saigon – renamed Ho Chi Minh City, and reunified the country under communist rule.

Vietnam had a profound impact upon Southeast Asian security architecture. In practice the Vietnam War was not only evidence of a failure of US strategic analyses and of the UN collective security system in crises in which the superpowers had or considered themselves to have major strategic interests, it was evidence for what amounted to a system of regional 'collective insecurity'. In effect the security of Southeast Asian States was being radically destabilised by inappropriate external interventions, both in the sense of the historic legacy of colonialism and in that of ideologically driven interventions by the Superpowers. Both the problem and the supposed remedies were being generated outside the region with the almost inevitable consequence that the latter were at best irrelevant and in some cases positively damaging.

An example of an inappropriate externally driven response can be seen in the creation of the South East Asian Treaty Organisation (SEATO). SEATO was established in the aftermath of the Korean War and founded upon the 1954 Southeast Asia Collective Defence Treaty, the signatories to which were the USA, Australia, Britain, France, New Zealand, Pakistan, the Philippines and Thailand. It was essentially a US-led anti-communist front and its structure closely followed the NATO model. Article IV(1) of the 1954 Treaty provides that,

> "Each party recognises that aggression by means of armed attack in the treaty area against any of the parties or against any State or territory which the parties by unanimous agreement may hereafter designate, would endanger its own peace and safety, and agrees that it will in that event act to meet the common danger in accordance with its constitutional processes. Measures taken under this paragraph shall be immediately reported to the Security Council of the United Nations."

Considerable hopes were invested in SEATO [8] but there proved to be an insufficient coherence of objectives or balance between the parties and, although the treaty relationship still exists – albeit without a Secretariat or infrastructure, ultimately the organisation proved a failure. It was in fact a classic example of the inappropriate 'parachuting' of concepts and structures to which reference has been made above and, as Bilveer Singh remarks,

> "the divergent nature of security objectives between the United States and the SEATO partners as well as incompatibility between Southeast Asian regional objectives *vis-à-vis* the global orientations of the United States doomed SEATO to failure, indicating the inadequacy of this type of regional security framework in the region." [9]

The shortcomings of SEATO were, in short, largely a reflection of the imposition of the security concerns of the Cold War Superpowers into Southeast Asian politics which had few real roots in regional concepts or experience.

Concepts of security in post-colonial Southeast Asia are in fact differently oriented from those found, for example, in Western Europe and North America and are at least as much bound up with questions of internal stabilisation and economic development as with apprehensions of external aggression. This stems in part from the troubled past of the region, including the distorting effects of historic and more recent external interventions, but also from the distinctive regional political and cultural traditions. One of the consequences of these traditions is that defensive alliances such as SEATO have tended to be perceived as exclusive and threatening rather than inclusive and protective [10] and also contrary to the urge towards consensualism which is a significant imperative of regional relations. When, in the closing years of the Vietnam War, the region began to develop its own 'security' architecture it was of a very different kind from that which the presumptions of classical Cold War international relations might have seemed to suggest. The SEATO-type model was entirely abandoned in favour of what, from the principal organisation, has come to be known as the 'ASEAN way'. Of this J.N. Mak remarks that,

> "Ultimately, ASEAN should be seen as an attempt at managing inter-state tensions so that each member could concentrate on domestic consolidation and economic development. This emphasis ... is reflected in the ASEAN concept of national and regional resilience, which equates economic development directly with stability. ... The 'ASEAN way' of conflict management and security is unstructured, informal and based on consensus. At the same time it is an inward-looking ... way of ensuring the survival of the grouping's ruling elites by emphasizing non-interference and economic progress." [11]

The so-called 'ASEAN way' is indeed characterised by calculatedly informal modes of dispute avoidance and resolution which, to a large extent, contain dangerously contentious issues through contacts which avoid any formal and confrontational reference. It is in this context noteworthy that ASEAN's dispute resolution mechanisms including, the ASEAN High Council and the 1976 Treaty of Amity and Co-operation in Southeast Asia, have hardly been utilised. This distinctive regional response to, *inter alia*, security issues and the very concept of 'security' upon which it is founded may not be suited for universal export to other regions with different traditions, but it undoubtedly has a most important contribution to make to the debate upon security in the post-Cold Era.

ASEAN AND THE S.E. ASIAN SECURITY CONCEPT

The Association of South East Asian Nations (ASEAN) was established in 1967 by Indonesia, Malaysia, the Philippines, Singapore and Thailand and presently comprises these States together with Brunei, Laos, Myanmar (Burma), Vietnam and, in April 1999, Cambodia. The expansion of ASEAN membership was neither swift nor easy. Brunei, despite its close cultural links with Malaysia, took 17 years to join and, not very surprisingly, Vietnam, fearing that the organisation might in some sense be a threatening coalition, took even longer but did ultimately join followed by Laos and Myanmar in 1997. ASEAN is not strictly conceived as a regional security organisation, still less a military alliance. Indeed, for the reasons suggested above, any such conceptualisation would from the outset have been not only unhelpful but possibly profoundly damaging in so far as the interests and understanding of both the Member States and, significantly, external actors such as the PRC differed upon the issue. As D.K. Emmerson remarks,

> "From its inception in 1967, ASEAN had kept regional security off its formal agenda – for fear of resembling a military alliance, which might have provoked outsiders and because its members' divergent views made discord on the subject too likely." [12]

Historically ASEAN has been concerned primarily to promote confidence and intra-mural amity between its members, notwithstanding the many tensions which continue to exist between them, and to minimise intervention in their internal affairs. Evident ASEAN unease with the 1999 East Timorese crisis was symptomatic of sensitivity with which such issues are invested and the cautious tradition within which they are treated.

The basic documents of ASEAN [13] make clear the nature and objectives of the organisation. The Preamble to the Bangkok Declaration of 8 August 1967 declares that the Member States,

> "Considering that the countries of South-East Asia share a primary responsibility for strengthening the economic and social stability of the region and ensuring their peaceful and progressive national development, and that they are determined to ensure their stability and security from external interference in any form or manifestation in order to preserve their national identities in accordance with the ideals and aspirations of their peoples."

No specific reference is made to collective security here or elsewhere in the Bangkok Declaration and, significantly, ASEAN itself is described in the Declaration as 'an Association for Regional Co-operation among the countries of South-East Asia'. This is not only symptomatic of an aversion to possibly threatening or destabilising discussion of 'security' concepts but also of a recognition of a different and much broader concept of 'security' from that found in an organisation such as, for example, NATO. It is noteworthy that initiatives oriented in a strictly conceived security context, such as the Malaysian sponsored Zone of Peace, Freedom and Neutrality (ZOPFAN) [14] have been treated with considerable caution. ZOPFAN was adopted as a plank of ASEAN policy at the Bali Summit in 1976 and has been included in the ASEAN Declaration of Concord. Even so, the idea incurred the suspicion of Vietnam which for a while attempted to promote an alternative ZOPFIN (Zone of Peace, Freedom, Independence and Neutrality) concept. Eventually Hanoi's fears were calmed and ZOPFIN was abandoned in favour of the original ZOPFAN approach. Nonetheless, ASEAN can in a broad sense reasonably be considered to be a regional security organisation. Amitav Acharya argues persuasively that ASEAN is a 'regional security community' in the sense referred to by Karl Deutsch in the North Atlantic context. [15] Amongst the key criteria of identification for such a community, along with the absence of actual and prospective armed conflict between members and competitive arms build up, he identifies the existence of regional mechanisms and practices for the aversion, management and resolution of conflicts. [16] ASEAN clearly fits this model of a 'security community', [17] in contrast, as Acharya suggests, with a 'security regime' or a 'defence community'. Others, including Tim Huxley, have argued that ASEAN is in fact a rather less emphatic "limited regional security community". [18]

Such an analysis is of value in admitting the distinctively different nature of Southeast Asian security concerns in comparison with those of a 'defence community' such as NATO. In particular it may serve to emphasise the different nature of security concerns in a region in which territorial disputes and external threats, whilst far from absent, are of less concern to most governments than issues of internal stability. The historical experience of ASEAN states, including in particular that of PRC-encouraged subversion in past episodes such as the Malayan Emergency, to which many of them have in one way or another been subjected has deeply ingrained the issue in regional political consciousness. The question of stability remains current, in somewhat different forms, in the post-Cold War era, not least in 1999 the potential impact of the East Timor, Ambon and Kalimantan situations, including the general question of the future stability of post-Suharto Indonesia and the recurrent refugee crises, both economic and political in origin, which have affected the region. Trans-National trade linkages have also played an important part in ASEAN institutional development, at least prior to the 1990s' recession which inevitably generated tendencies towards a greater degree of economic conservatism. [19] To some degree these developments invite comparisons with the EU, which itself originated in an endeavour to minimise the potential for conflict in a recently war-torn continent through the development of economic integration and inter-dependence. The rapid progress of the 'tiger economies' of the region in the 1980s and early 1990s emphasised this aspect of ASEAN imperatives, although the regional depression which followed the collapse of the Thai Baht has called into question at least the speed and immediate direction of this progress in the later 1990s. At the same time the environment in which the ASEAN approach has developed has been to some degree conditioned by knowledge of the implicit guarantees offered in a Cold War context by continuing US commitment in the region. This was evidenced, for example, by the large naval deployment made when PRC military exercises were used in an endeavour to exert pressure upon Taiwanese elections in 1996 – specifically to avert any abandonment of the unstable equilibrium represented by the 'one China' with two governments model. [20]

It is within this context that the conceptual framework of the 'ASEAN way' has developed, seeking to avoid intramural controversy and the raising of sensitive issues, including 'security', in the interests of maintaining stability and a viable *status quo*. Within the given context the ASEAN way has, in fact, served the region well in so far as a much greater degree of stability has been achieved than might reasonably have been anticipated in the light of the Korean and Vietnamese experiences in particular. As with any system of consensus, however, the questions still arise of what is to happen when consensus cannot be achieved and what price may sometimes have to be paid for that consensus. The latter question is perhaps painfully answered by the long agonies of Kampuchea/Cambodia and Myanmar/Burma. The genocidal Khmer Rouge regime in Kampuchea was not felt to pose a security or regional problem by ASEAN, any more – it must be added – than it was by Western Powers which were happy to see it continuing to occupy the Cambodian UN seat even after the Vietnamese intervention. Similarly the internal problems of Myanmar and Indonesia are not upon the formal ASEAN agenda although they are matters of discreet concern, although ASEAN nations were discreetly critical of the East Timorese debacle in September 1999. What then, where consensus is threatened or unattainable, as, most notably, in the case of the Spratly Islands dispute?

A system of consensus may fail not only through radical disagreement amongst its members, which on the whole ASEAN has been able to avoid, but also through the exigencies of external action. It is in this context that the most serious questions arise about ASEAN as, in some sense, a regional 'security' actor. As a process of consensus building the development of ASEAN security concepts has been slow. The general understanding is that the process is in its second stage of "Preventive Diplomacy", although there is significant doubt as to whether this concept has itself yet been adequately defined. The next stage is supposed to be one of "Conflict Resolution", although in 1999 the favoured phrasing had been reduced to the more cautious "Approaches to Conflict Resolution". Despite the continuing commitment of the organisation to 'preventive diplomacy' as an integral part of the 'ASEAN way' the 1990s have brought about a shift in the nature and direction of Southeast Asian regional security thinking. One significant response to this new and more uncertain regional security environment was the establishment, in July 1993, of the ASEAN Regional Forum (ARF). The ARF involves the overwhelming majority of the regional powers, comprising the ASEAN members together with Australia, Canada, China, the EU, India, Japan, South Korea, New Zealand, Papua-New Guinea, Russia, and the USA, the notable exceptions being North Korea and Taiwan. The central element of the ARF is constituted by the ASEAN Powers, but its credibility as an actor in the region is under-pinned by its acceptance by both the PRC and the USA, neither of which would have been happy to see a Southeast Asian security forum dominated by the other. It holds annual meetings for the discussion of regional security questions at ministerial level and meetings are held at senior official level as and when may be necessary. The practical value of the ARF may be consid-ered a somewhat open question granted that it has many of the strengths and concomitant weaknesses of ASEAN itself as a security actor. On the one hand it brings almost all of the powers likely to have an interest in Southeast Asian security questions into a consultative process which may in itself function as an efficacious mode of broadened peace and confidence building very much in line with the 'ASEAN way'. In this sense the ARF may indeed be consid-ered essentially an expansion of the ASEAN way beyond the core ASEAN territories. As Hugo J. Dobson remarks,

> "With its modest objectives of simply getting the nations of Asia Pacific talking, the ARF has demonstrated some diplomatic ability. ... Thus, it has begun modestly to achieve the undeclared goal of defusing and controlling 'regional tensions by generating and sus-taining a network of dialogues within the overarching framework of its annual meet-ings'." [21]

On the other hand, the diversity of the membership, their interests and, perhaps most importantly, their security concepts and agendas must effec-tively deny the capacity of the organisation adequately to respond to a security crisis which had gone beyond the scope of discussion and consensus seeking, if indeed it was ever actually intended to perform such extended functions. [22] As Amitav Acharya remarks,

> "to be an effective instrument of a regional security community, the ARF must overcome uncertainties and limitations. It does not have any specific 'road map' or blueprint for action. ASEAN members of the ARF want it to develop in an evolutionary and non-legalistic manner, raising concerns about its ability to provide practical solutions to re-gional security problems. Moreover, the ARF's ... 'inclusiveness' is ... a drawback, given

the sheer diversity of security concerns within the Asia/Pacific region and the obvious difficulties in achieving agreement from the relatively large membership ..." [23]

Whether this circle can effectively be squared remains to be seen. Indeed there is a lack of clear focus upon the future development of the ARF within ASEAN itself. In the Declaration of the *ASEAN Vision 2020* made in Kuala Lumpur on 15 December 1997 the references to (military) security and the ARF are at one both ambitious and carefully non-specific, although, significantly, express reference is made to the ZOPFAN concept. It is stated that,

"We envision the ASEAN region to be in 2020, in full reality, a Zone of Peace, Freedom and Neutrality, as envisaged in the Kuala Lumpur Declaration of 1971. ASEAN shall have, by the year 2020, established a peaceful and stable Southeast Asia where each nation is at peace with itself and where causes for conflict have been eliminated, through abiding respect for justice and the rule of law and through the strengthening of national and regional resilience. ... We envision the ASEAN Regional Forum as an established means for confidence building and preventive diplomacy and for promoting conflict resolution."

Beyond this level of, admittedly significant, dialogue and confidence building it is very doubtful that the ARF could function as a crisis management or enforcement agency. Quite apart from the significant political difficulties, major problems of command, control and interoperability would certainly arise. It is true that in the 1990s there have been bilateral and even some trilateral military exercises between ASEAN Member States and Malaysia was in 1999 considering the feasibility of establishing a peacekeeping centre, but there is a considerable distance to be travelled before these concepts can become a practical reality.

In the context of Vision 2020 it is again worth noting that the primary emphasis is not upon a narrowly conceived military security concept but upon issues of internal social cohesion and economic development. The flavour of the intention is given in the statement made by the Prime Minister of Malaysia, Dr. Mahathir Mohammed, that,

"By the Year 2020 Malaysia can be a unified nation, with a confident Malaysian society infused by strong moral and ethical values, living in a society that is democratic, liberal and tolerant, caring, economically just and equitable, progressive and prosperous, and in full possession of an economy that is competitive, dynamic, robust and resilient." [24]

This broad vision can fairly be seen as part of the holistic concept which is at the heart of the ASEAN "security" agenda.

At present the practical mechanism of regional peace support action would almost certainly be that of a coalition of the willing, although whether the well established tradition of the "ASEAN way" could tolerate or even survive such action must remain an open question. Whether, as D.K Emmerson suggests, [25] Indonesia, Malaysia and Singapore could represent a 'core' group in ASEAN security concerns may be debated, but these States, along with Japan and the PRC, may at least be anticipated to be key actors in the future security and defence architecture of the region. What they might do alone or together in a given situation would, however, have to be determined on a case-by-case basis. At the end of the 20th century the question of Indonesia also looms large. Quite apart from the East Timorese crisis, there remains the problem of the political stability of the country as a whole in the post-Suharto era. The worst case scenario of collapse or violent dissolution may well be an exaggerated fear but even a temporary foreign policy hiatus would be a serious problem for both ASEAN and the ARF granted the importance of Indonesia amongst the Member States. The question of the future security architecture of Southeast Asia is also inseparable from that of the future involvement and roles of other actors either beyond or upon the fringes of the region strictly conceived. These include in particular the People's Republic of China, Japan and the USA.

THE PRC AND SOUTHEAST ASIAN SECURITY

China is, by virtue of size – quite apart from anything else – the naturally dominant power in the neighbouring region of Southeast Asia. The end of the Cold War and the dissolution of the former-USSR led to the virtual disappearance of one of the post-World War II Superpowers from involvement in the region. It also brought about, for both political and economic reasons, a considerable retrenchment on the part of the USA. Both of these developments had, inevitably, considerable implications for South and Southeast Asian foreign and security policy. The post-Mao economic and structural reforms within China have also significantly increased the country's capacities as an actual or potential external actor. These various factors have made the nature of the future role of China a question of profound importance for regional security. The foreign and security policies of China are, like those of any other nation, conditioned by historical experience. In the case of China this embodies in part a determination to eradicate the memory and effects of the country's weakness in the 'century of shame' from the 1842 Opium War to the Communist victory in 1949.

Whilst, naturally, policy makers in the modern PRC do not dance as puppets upon these historical strings, it is important to understand this background as a foundational aspect of PRC international relations consciousness. In the closing years of the, Manchu, Ch'ing Dynasty (1644-1911), up to the Nationalist revolution led by Sun Yat Sen in 1911, Imperial China entered a phase of catastrophic decline. It was betrayed ultimately by an intensely conservative Confucian political tradition which led the Chinese elite to view the nation as the culturally superior 'middle kingdom' surrounded by 'barbarian' peoples from whom it had nothing to learn and who could relate to it only in terms of submission and vassalage or 'rebellious' defiance. By the 18th and 19th centuries this latter element had become more a matter of rhetoric than perceived reality – although it was still used by the Ch'ien-lung Emperor to rebuff the importunities of Sir George MacCartney's trade mission in 1793 and has lingering effects to the present time, e.g., in the official UK view of the Tibet question which rests upon an acceptance that the Dalai Lama was truly a vassal of the Chinese Emperor in the 18th century. Nonetheless, the Ch'ing were led by this tradition to fail to appreciate the dangers represented by acquisitive foreign powers, a point made manifest by a Memorandum to the Emperor from an Imperial Censor [26] entitled *The Detestable, Strong but Beatable Foreign Barbarians* [27] in which it was suggested that the tightness of European uniforms would prevent western troops from fighting effectively against Chinese forces. The lesson learnt by Japan from the arrival of Commodore Perry's 'black ships' in 1853 and implemented in the radical reorganisation attendant upon the subsequent Meiji Restoration escaped the Ch'ing Dynasty under Tzu Hsi. The result was the imposition of the notorious 'unequal treaties' and disgraceful episodes such as the Opium War. Such efforts as the Ch'ing did make to develop modern defence and security capacities were brought to nought not, ironically, by the western colonial powers but by the modern forces of Japan in the 1894-5 Sino-Japanese War in which most of the Chinese navy was either captured or destroyed. A radical process of modernisation followed the proclamation of the nationalist Republic in 1911 and after the First World War China was an active participant in the League of Nations, in which its Ambassador, Wellington Koo, was one of the more notable figures. Sadly China was dramatically failed by the League's collective security system when Japan invaded and occupied Manchuria, and subsequently substantial areas of the rest of China, in 1931 and set up the puppet state of Manchukuo under the nominal rule of the last Emperor of China, Henry Pu Yi. The Lytton Commission found that Manchukuo was indeed entirely Japanese-dominated and on February 24 1933 declined to recognise it as an independent state but resolved equivocally, *inter alia*, upon,

"(4) Recognition of Japan's interests in Manchuria ...

(7) Manchurian autonomy. The Government of Manchuria should be modified in such a way as to secure, consistently with the sovereignty and administrative integrity of China, a large measure of autonomy designed to meet the local conditions and special characteristics of the Three Provinces. ..." [28]

Typically, the League therefore indicated disapproval whilst at the same time effectively admitting the consequences of what, from any objective viewpoint, was a simple case of Japanese military aggression [29] in defiance of the League Covenant and the 1928 Pact of Paris.

At the end of the Second World War civil war broke out in China between the Kuomintong led by Chiang Kai Shek and the Communist forces led by Mao Zedong. By 1949 the Kuomintong had been confined to the island of Taiwan and in that year the establishment of the People's Republic of China was proclaimed. Under Mao Zedong Chinese foreign policy was predicated, not entirely inaccurately, upon the hostility of the rest of the world, including, after the death of Stalin and the Krushchev reforms, the 'revisionist' USSR. The aim was, on the one hand, to reverse the unequal treaties and to assert irredentist claims to territories 'stolen' in the 19th century, but also to expand communist influence in South and Southeast Asia by sponsoring subversion in non-Communist states. This was the political and ideological setting for PRC involvement in episodes such as the Korean War and the Malayan Emergency. This ambitious and, to some degree, aggressive policy was, however, set back not only by the serious internal problems inherited by the PRC from previous regimes, but also by Mao's own policies, including the disastrous Cultural Revolution which inflicted untold human, economic and political damage upon China. After Mao's death and the displacement and trial of the so-called 'Gang of Four' and their associates in the radical clique surrounding Jiang Qing, [30] the administration of Deng Xiaoping initiated major policies of economic reform and restructuring which have had a large effect upon the security stance and potential of the PRC. Denny Roy comments that,

> "Deng Xiaoping's economic and political reforms which began in 1978 brought historic changes to China, ... [W]ith an ongoing economic growth rate close to 10 per cent yearly, China now has the potential to become the world's largest economy in the medium term. With a strong economic and technological base combined with a large population, China could become the strongest power in the region, if not the world. If this occurs, the current international order in the Asia-Pacific will be completely overturned." [31]

This remains at least potentially the case in the longer term, even though China has not remained unscathed by the Southeast Asian currency crisis of the late 1990s. The future place of China in the security architecture of the Asia/Pacific region, whether as hegemon or guarantor, must remain unpredictable, but there is at least some room for hope that the PRC may ultimately play a stabilising role. Since the initiation of the Deng reforms in 1978 significant progress has been made towards the achievement of the basic Chinese foreign and security policy goal of eliminating the products of the 'century of shame'. This includes, notably, the peaceful return of Hong Kong to Chinese sovereignty in 1997, effectively ending the era of colonial intervention apart from the slightly longer survival of Macau. Within the area of metropolitan China there remains, however, the question of Taiwan.

The issue of Taiwan has a large regional significance both in terms of the island's status and its continuing importance in Sino-American relations. When in 1949 the Chinese Communist Party established its authority over mainland China the Nationalist Kuomintong government fled to Taiwan and there maintain themselves as the Republic of China (ROC). From an external viewpoint it might be thought that the PRC and the ROC could quite simply be separate states, certainly both essentially meet the basic requirements of article 1 of the 1933 Montevideo Convention on the Rights and Duties of States in so far as each has a defined territory, population, government and *prima facie* capacity to enter into relations with other states. [32] The problem lies in the fact that neither the PRC nor the ROC currently desire such separate recognition. Both the Beijing and Taipei governments claim to be the legitimate government of all China, including Taiwan, with the consequence in effect that Beijing considers Taiwan to be a rebellious province whilst Taipei considers the mainland to be in a condition of disaffection. In practice a tense *status quo* has been established founded upon the idea of 'one China with two governments'. The PRC has on occasion indicated its willingness to deploy military force against Taiwan, including periodic confrontations over scattered islands between Taiwan and the mainland. More particularly in the mid-1990s the electoral gains of the opposition Democratic Progressive Party in Taiwan, which advocates the establishment of a formally independent Republic of Taiwan led to menacing PRC military manoeuvres across the straits from Taiwan and eventually to the deployment of US naval forces to guarantee the island's security. In July 1999 the proclamation by President Lee of the ROC that a "two States" policy would now be adopted was declared unacceptable by Beijing and warning was given of a possible military response. Thus, China has indicated that it will prevent any move towards Taiwanese independence, by force if necessary. At the same time the USA somewhat awkwardly accepts a 'one China' policy whilst simultaneously acting as a guarantor of ROC security. As Robert Scalapino remarks,

"At present, US policy rests somewhat uneasily on two different principles ... . On the one hand ... American and Chinese leaders accept a one-China policy. On the other hand, the Taiwan Relations Act, passed by the Congress and signed by President Carter, stipulates that unification should be by peaceful means, and that prior to that time, the security of Taiwan is a matter of concern to the United States." [33]

An easy solution to this problem is difficult to envisage and the situation has at least the potential seriously to destabilise not only East Asian security but that of the whole Asia-Pacific region.

Other potential and actual problems arise from combinations of irredentist and economic aspirations. The Paracel Islands were seized from [South] Vietnam in 1973 and the multilateral dispute over the Spratly Islands remains a major regional security issue in the late 1990s. The Spratly islands dispute is the centre of a wider contention over the potential oil and gas reserves as well as the fishing resources of the South China Sea. [34] China makes large territorial claims in the sea primarily by virtue of its 1992 Law on the Territorial Sea and the Contiguous Zone, [35] although it has signed but not ratified the 1982 UN Law of the Sea Convention which would to some degree be incompatible at least with their maximum apparent extent. Significantly China sets this dispute also in the context of the expurgation of the 'century of shame', arguing that the Spratlys form part of China's ancient patrimony into which acquisitive foreigners have intruded. This interpretation is highly debatable, a number of ASEAN states also make territorial/economic claims over the islands, and Chinese claims have generated a range of conflicts over the issue. Most alarmingly in 1995 the Philippines found that the PRC had established a small base on Mischief Reef, well within Manila's area of jurisdiction, and had arrested fishermen in the area. The Philippines responded with parallel arrests of Chinese fishermen. Further confrontations, including the sinking of a Chinese fishing boat, occurred in 1999. Although in military terms the confrontations were both indirect and small in scale, they indicated a willingness to use force in circumstances which suggest ominous precedents from elsewhere. The Falkland Islands are also remote and fairly barren territories of considerable economic significance and, whilst the strength of Argentine feeling on the territorial claim can no more be doubted than that of the UK's commitment to the right of self-determination of the islanders, there is some reason to think that the 1982 Anglo-Argentine Falklands Conflict centred to a significant degree upon the rich offshore resources associated with the islands. Commonly linked with, but actually distinct from, the Spratlys dispute, the confrontation over the Paracels has an even more alarming potential in that it involves a direct disagreement between the PRC and Vietnam of unpredictable potential. Nonetheless, the received wisdom in the region is that the Spratlys and the Paracels will generate tension and discord but are not in themselves likely to cause major regional armed conflict. Significantly, the concerned ASEAN Members favour claimant-to-claimant bilateral settlements of these issues in preference to placing them upon any overt ASEAN agenda.

In this context constructive engagement with the PRC has many advantages from the viewpoint of the Southeast Asian states. As remarked above China has joined the ARF, as also the Council for Security and Cooperation in the Asia-Pacific Region, and this in itself, with the co-presence of the USA, indicates a potentially positive degree of balancing and engagement in regional security. At the same time it is clear that the PRC is limited in its enthusiasm for organisations such as the ARF, partly because like any regional superpower, like indeed the USA in South America, it has a preference for bilateral relations with its smaller neighbours in contrast with collective multilateral arrangements in which its relative power and influence might be less.

China proclaims its peaceful intentions and there is no reason to consider these any less, or more, sincere than similar protestations made by most modern states. As a major and ultimately probably dominant regional power there can be little doubt that the PRC will play a peaceful and even pacificatory role unless and until it feels that its substantial interests are threatened. The fundamental question then is what those substantial interests are conceived to be. The episodes of Tibet, Taiwan and the Spratlys suggest the probable answer. In foreign affairs China will seek to exert its power wherever it feels that it has been driven from its historic role of regional pre-eminence by acquisitive foreign powers during its era of eclipse. To this degree it probably does harbour hegemonistic aspirations, whether or not they are conceived as such. At the same time the emphasis of post-Mao Chinese administrations has been primarily upon economic development and whilst this has had a significant expansionary effect upon the technological capacities of the People's Liberation Army, [36] it is as an economic power that Chinese influence is most notably likely to expand in the immediate future. It seems rather unlikely that the PRC would play a major role in Southeast Asian peace support action at least in the medium term and, even if it were willing, the acceptability of action by the People's Liberation Army in many countries of Southeast Asia must be considered very doubtful. Much will turn upon the progress of economic, and possibly political, reforms within an authoritarian Communist system and the ultimate outcome of the present dichotomy between the historic and modern elements of PRC policy formation. Both engagement with and balancing of an increasingly powerful China within ASEAN-generated mechanisms such as the ARF must seem the most immediately positive way forward for Southeast Asian collective security development in this context. It might be hoped ultimately that China will play the role of a benign regional superpower that can be seen, for example, in the post-Cold War development of relations between and through the European nations, the USA, NATO and the WEU. This, however, will require that ASEAN nations in particular refuse to bow to implicit or explicit Chinese threats over incidents such as that at Mischief Reef and whether this will in fact occur remains to be seen. Even if such an ASEAN engagement does work in this way [37] it will come about not only through China-ASEAN relations but also through the developing future roles of the two other principal 'external' actors in the region, Japan and the USA.

JAPAN AS A SECURITY ACTOR

Japan is potentially a highly significant security actor both within and potentially beyond the Asia/Pacific region, its defence forces are indeed amongst the largest, excepting those of the USA and PRC, and best equipped in the region. Whilst the military qualities of the Japanese defence forces can hardly be doubted, Japan, like China but from an opposite perspective, carries a large historical burden which would for the foreseeable future render any external operations by these forces highly problematic both within Japan and beyond. As in the case of the PRC, an adequate review of the possible future security role of Japan is necessarily prefaced by a brief consideration of the historical background.

Japan as a modern state dates from the Meiji Restoration when, in 1868, the Emperor Mutsohito resumed political power displacing the Tokugawa Shogunate whose policy of feudal isolationism had been discredited by the forced opening of the country by the US Navy in the shape of Commodore Perry and his 'black ships'. Rapid economic, industrial and military development followed and by the 1890s Japan had acquired large, well equipped and trained modern armed forces. It adopted western models not only in the economic and technical sectors but also in foreign policy, assuming extensive ambitions as a regional colonial power. Territorial gains were made from China in the 1894-5 Sino-Japanese War, some of which were then lost under pressure from the European powers, particularly Russia which, rightly, saw the rising East Asian power as a threat to its interests in the region. This perceived set back led directly to the 1904-5 Russo-Japanese War and overwhelming victory on land in the siege of Port Arthur and at sea in the battle of Tsushima in which the Russian Baltic Fleet which had sailed half way round the world to relieve Port Arthur was largely destroyed. [38] The principal fruit of the Russo-Japanese War was the establishment of Japanese rule over Korea. Further gains were made in the First World War, in which Japan played a largely passive role, [39] primarily through the seizure of some of the German colonies in the region. In the 1930s Japan underwent a significant political change in relation to which certain popular misconceptions require to be corrected. The aggression and military brutality which these developments later engendered have commonly in the West been attributed to a surviving pre-modern Samurai spirit in the Japanese government and armed forces. This is an absurd analysis. There undoubtedly was, and still is, a fascination with the historical resonance of the pre-Meiji restoration Samurai warrior class in Japan, but to suggest that the Samurai *bushido* military code was a real formative influence upon Japanese military practices in the Second World War is as much an exaggeration as to suggest that the medieval fantasies of the Nazis genuinely moulded the practices of the Third Reich. It was rather the case that Japan fell victim to the same urges toward fascistic militarism which engulfed much of Europe at the time and also affected, albeit in lesser effect and degree, the Kuomintong in China. It is worth noting that whilst the senior commanders of Japanese forces in World War II were too young to have experienced the Samurai era other than through romanticised histories, the commanders in the Russo-Japanese War, General Nogi and Admiral Togo, who on the whole conducted their operations in scrupulous compliance with the then prevailing norms of the international *jus in bello*, actually were former Samurai. The cruelty displayed to prisoners was founded upon a sense that surrender was 'dishonourable', but this was a convenient reinvention, as was the brutal conduct of occupation policy which was at least in part founded upon racist disdain for the conquered peoples.

For Japan the Second World War was largely a campaign of colonial expansion coupled with a desire to seize the opportunity to eclipse the USA as a Pacific Power during a time of American military engagement in Europe. Japanese endeavours in this direction commenced well before 1939, with the invasion of Manchuria in 1931 after which Japan left the League of Nations in the light even of its very temporising response to the 1931 invasion, despite the fact that Japan was one of the five Permanent Members of the League Council.

After its catastrophic defeat in the Second World War, culminating in the nuclear bombardment of Hiroshima and Nagasaki, Japan was purged and reconstructed under American occupation, albeit with significant elements of constitutional continuity – including not least the preservation of the monarchy, the Emperor having been deemed to have played no culpable role in the criminal wartime regime. [40] In the security sector the initial American intention was one of absolute demilitarisation but within a short time, especially after the 1949 Communist victory in China, the possible advantages of a docile Japan as a subordinate Asian security actor became apparent. A small but symbolic evidence of this change of emphasis may be seen in the restoration and preservation of the pre-dreadnought battleship *Mikasa*, Admiral Togo's flagship at Tsushima, with American encouragement and financial assistance. A change of this nature was, however, resisted by the post-war Premier, Yoshida Shigeru. He retained the American-drafted article 9 of the Constitution which states that,

"In order to accomplish this aim of [international peace and renunciation of war] ... land, sea and air forces, as well as other war potential, will never be maintained. The right of belligerency of the State will not be recognized."

This provision has been much debated and opposition parties have traditionally taken the view that it must actually outlaw all Japanese military forces. The government view has however been essentially that whilst aggressive forces or the use of forces in an aggressive manner is clearly proscribed, self-defence capacity is not as such either 'war potential' or a right of belligerency in the sense implied by article 9. Prime Minister Yoshida thus agreed to the creation of a lightly armed national force, pointedly entitled the Japanese Self Defence Force (JSDF), but through the 1951 US-Japan Mutual Security Treaty secured a US guarantee of Japanese security in exchange for the continuing presence of US bases and forces in Japan after the ending of occupation.

This was the basis of the Yoshida doctrine which became the foundation of Japanese security policy in the Cold War era. The essence of this was that Japan would strive to regain its pre-War status as a power by economic rather than military means and, with the very limited exception of the JSDF, would entrust its external security to the US guarantee. From the late 1950s this policy became entrenched as article 9 was interpreted to preclude not only military aggression but any overseas military deployment whatsoever, including collective security action or UN peace support operations. This almost absolute demilitarisation was symbolised by the practice of restricting defence expenditure to not more than 1% of gross national product [41] although it must be added both that 1% of Japanese GNP is a very significant resource and greater sums than this implies were anyway later devoted to the JSDF which is, in the 1990s, one of the major military forces of the region. Within the Cold War context Yoshida had astutely shed both the financial burden and the divisive politics of defence by delegating national defence to a foreign power. Japan thus gained most of the benefits whilst avoiding almost all of the dangers of a *prima facie* pacifist stance.

For all its apparent, and indeed actual, advantages, the Yoshida doctrine was not entirely without cost. As Kenneth Pyle remarks,

"the [Yoshida] strategy did have an Achilles heel. In its ... acceptance of becoming a military protectorate of the United States, and its required deference to US foreign policy: Japan ... [had] warped and unbalanced ... institutions for the making of foreign policy. ... Thus, while the Yoshida strategy gave rise to powerful economic institutions in the post-war state, it left an undeveloped political dimension of foreign policy making and a nation unprepared to deal with the political consequences of the economic power it had acquired by the 1990s." [42]

The end of the Cold War, and the somewhat changed foreign relations stance of the PRC under the Deng administration, radically changed Japan's security environment and increasingly brought the Yoshida doctrine into question.

Uncertainty concerning the PRC and the possible dangers posed by a potential future militantly nationalist Russia all suggested a change of position in Tokyo. Further, American retrenchment and increasing discontent of US-Japanese trade imbalances led to increasing pressure for a more active Japanese participation in collective security and peace support mechanisms. The 1990-91 Gulf Conflict was a key stage in this development. Japan was much criticised for its refusal, pursuant to the established interpretation of article 9 of the Constitution, to send forces to the Gulf. In response to this unprecedented international criticism the 1992 UN Peacekeeping Operations Co-operation Act was passed [43] permitting the JSDF to engage in overseas operations but only in non-combat roles, including humanitarian assistance, election monitoring and logistical support. The 1992 Act signalled a shift in domestic Japanese politics of very considerable significance in which even the opposition Social Democratic Party finally recognised the lawfulness of the JSDF and accepted at least limited overseas deployment. More confrontational roles, including cease fire monitoring, are also admitted by the Act, but the relevant section has not been brought into force at the time of writing and seems unlikely to be so in the foreseeable future. Despite these limitations there is now support for the development of a more visible Japanese peacekeeping presence, emphasising provision of high technology logistical support rather than infantry combat units. [44] The 1992 Act thus admits only very limited JSDF involvement in overseas operations, but it has, nonetheless, borne far from insignificant fruit. Since the passage of the Act JSDF units have been involved in election monitoring in Cambodia, mine clearance in the Gulf and refugee assistance in Zaire. [45]

Such operations, and any further actions permitted by the 1992 Act, fall well short of combat operations in support of collective security and peace enforcement and the Act could be extended further to relax the interpretation of article 9 of the Constitution. The article could anyway be argued not inherently to preclude at least the latter type of operation since the legality of the JSDF is accepted and UN authorised peace support action can properly be seen as international 'policing' which does not strictly involve war capability in sense intended by article 9. However, any such involvement by Japan in Southeast Asia would raise extremely sensitive questions. The legacy of the Second World War remains a real burden to Japan in its relations with its East Asian neighbours. Although Japan has largely sanitised its own consciousness of its involvement in the global conflict [46] and satisfied itself, and much western liberal opinion, that it was a victim state upon the basis of the Hiroshima and Nagasaki bombings, that perception is not shared by the states which formed part of the 'Greater East Asian Co-Prosperity Sphere' as Japan termed its wartime conquests. Despite Japan's constructive post-war history and its large economic penetration of the region, the residual bitterness of the war years remains a serious problem. Imperial visits are still bedevilled by the question of 'apology' and issues of material compensation, for example for the so-called 'comfort women', [47] even though the present Emperor and Government had no part in the Second World War. Even after more than half a century the presence of Japanese soldiers, certainly in any combat role, would almost certainly have a profoundly negative impact upon any regional collective security or peace support operations. Granted also Chinese sensitivities, any involvement of the JSDF in, for example, a hypothetical flare up of the dispute over the Spratly Islands would be almost inconceivable. An even more difficult question might arise if China were to decide to use force in any territorial dispute with Japan, for example over the Diauyutai/Senkaku Islands, in the light of the potential for direct confrontation between the JSDF and the PLA and, beyond that even for Sino-American confrontation in consequence of the US-Japan security guarantee. Fortunately in present circumstances it seems improbable that any such hypothetical confrontation would escalate beyond the stand-offs which have from time to time occurred over the Taiwan strait.

In fact, and very wisely, Japan has proceeded cautiously in developing its security contacts with Southeast Asia. It was involved from the outset in the ARF and whilst, as pointed out above, this forum has only a rather doubtful potential as an active regional peace support agency, its value as a confidence building mechanism in a security extension of the 'ASEAN way' may prove to be very considerable.

The future role of Japan as a security and peace support actor, both generally and in Southeast Asia, is uncertain. Its history and internal politics will for the foreseeable future continue to impose severe limitations upon its development in this direction, but the 1992 UN Peacekeeping Operations Co-operation Act indicates a significant initial movement. Nonetheless it is highly unlikely that Japanese combat troops in an enforcement role would be welcomed in the region and such a further development would receive a very ambivalent response in the USA. Parallel US concerns with potential regional Chinese hegemony and with the uncomfortable resonances and possible consequences of a full Japanese remilitarisation combine with Japanese politics to suggest that, despite US retrenchment and Japanese discomfort with the US military presence in Okinawa, the US security umbrella is likely to remain the linchpin of Japan's security planning. This will be subject both to Japanese political development and the consequences of US ambivalence as between security and economic imperatives in its Japan policy. [48] After half a century these various post-Second World War sensitivities are, however, now much reduced amongst ASEAN Members, as elsewhere, although they linger in Singapore as also in China. Evidence of greater Japanese engagement with security matters may be seen in the enunciation of the Hashimoto doctrine by Prime Minister Ryutaro Hashimoto during a visit to Singapore in 1997. In a lecture given to the Institute of South East Asian Studies (ISEAS) on 14 January 1997 he indicated a greater willingness on Japan's part to become involved in Southeast Asian security matters, whilst also emphasising the fundamental importance of the continuing US role in the region and the Japanese determination to facilitate and encourage it. [49] In a key passage he stated that,

> "The Japan-US security arrangements are a very important framework for engaging the US presence. ... Japan will continue to do its best to maintain confidence in the arrangements ... as [an] ... infrastructure for stability and economic prosperity in the Asia-Pacific, and ... in no sense targeted against any specific country." [50]

These ideas were on the whole well received by ASEAN Member States, although the elements of constructive engagement and US involvement would seem to have played a not insignificant part in this. The delicate policy balances involved in the US-Japan security relationship have been shown in successive discussions in the 1990s, the conclusion of which has in essence been that the security status quo will be retained with an increased emphasis upon Japanese defence responsibility and some concessions over the Okinawa bases. This gradual 'normalisation' of Japan as a security actor is no doubt in some respects long overdue and, certainly, the 1950s Yoshida doctrine has lost both its viability and utility in the post-Cold War era. If, however, it is asked whether Japan is likely in the short to medium term to become a major collective security or peace support actor the answer must seem to be in the negative. Japanese aspirations to a permanent seat on the UN Security Council, finally undoing the consequences of the 1931 invasion of Manchuria, are also intimately linked to questions of deployment potential. While Japan has very influential support within the UN, including majority support within the current permanent membership of the Council, it cannot expect to be able to secure such a position unless and until it demonstrates itself willing and able fully to participate in peace support operations. However, the pace of UN reform is such that the immediacy of this question is to say the least limited. Nevertheless Japan and its East Asian neighbours must come to terms with and resolve the traumas of their historic past if Japan is to assume a security role commensurate with its economic and military capacity.

THE US ENGAGEMENT WITH EAST ASIA

The USA is, by virtue of its geographical situation, a Pacific as well as an Atlantic power and as such is inescapably concerned with the security environment on the far side of that ocean. It is also deeply, and not necessarily always comfortably, engaged with East and Southeast Asian economies in the Asia-Pacific rim context. American engagement with East Asia goes at least back to the first half of the 19th century. The original penetration of the region was through trans-Pacific trade, with more forceful intervention developing from the mid-century when Commodore Perry forcibly opened Japan to the world, ironically in anticipation that this would open a valuable new market opportunity. At the end of the century, and with very considerable internal political controversy, the USA became a colonial power in the Asia-Pacific region [51] with the annexation between 1898 and 1902, primarily under the McKinley administrations, of Hawaii, Samoa, Puerto Rico, the Philippines and Guam and also the authorisation of the development of the extra-territorial Panama Canal zone. These annexations were by no means all either invited or unresisted. There was fierce opposition in the Philippines led by a nationalist movement under General Aguinaldo which fought for independence not only from Spain but also from the USA. The modern engagement of the USA with East and Southeast Asia has, however, been primarily shaped by the Second World War and Cold War experiences.

As remarked above, the Second World War signalled the end of the colonial era in Southeast Asia, whether that colonialism was European, Japanese or American. It also unequivocally established the USA as the dominant Pacific power. Despite PRC perceptions, it was, however, very far from establishing hegemonic US power in the region. On the contrary, the post-1949 tripartite Cold War confrontation between the USA, USSR and PRC in East Asia involved these states in a balance of power structure which was, for the reasons set out above, less predictable and in some respects more dangerous than that which was maintained over the bilateral spheres of influence structure in Europe.

During the Cold War era US policy in Southeast Asia, as elsewhere, was founded upon the containment of communism and the limitation of both Soviet and PRC spheres of influence. US-sponsored endeavours to deal with this situation, including the ill-fated SEATO, were not always well conceived in terms of the political and strategic context of the region. The post-war situation was further complicated by the ill-managed processes of decolonisation, especially as regards the inter-Allied treatment of the former Japanese colony of Korea and the very reluctant, and war torn, French disengagement from Vietnam. In both cases the countries were split between a Soviet-sponsored northern sector and a US-sponsored southern sector and the Korean and Vietnam wars resulted when the northern communist regimes attempted to re-unify the countries under their rule to the exclusion of the southern capitalist regimes. This endeavour failed in Korea, where an uneasy status quo prevails, but succeeded in Vietnam after a long war which had profound affects upon US domestic and foreign relations policy. Space precludes a detailed analysis of the political fall out from Vietnam, suffice it to say that but for the assassination in Dallas the Kennedy administration, which took America into the war, would probably have been dislocated by it, the Johnson presidency was stifled by it and the Nixon administration, which took the USA out of Vietnam, was destroyed by the Watergate scandal to which the embittered internal politics generated by the war contributed not a little.

Strategically the impact of the Vietnam war has been the subject of considerable over-simplification. The domino theory, which had considerable currency in contemporary US analyses and which suggested that if one Southeast Asian state was allowed to fall to communism the rest would surely follow was to some degree naive. A number of Southeast Asian states had in fact faced down PRC-inspired subversion, as for example in the Malayan emergency, and the final collapse and absorption of South Vietnam did not bring about a sweeping communist take over of the region. South Vietnam, especially after the deposition and assassination of President Diem, was a weak entity almost entirely dependent upon ultimately unsustainable US support. It would also be a mistake to view the Cold War strategic history of the region simply as a battle between communism and capitalism. As in any multilateral balance of power system there were shifts of interest and relationship between the participants. The most dramatic of these was the realignment of relations between the USA and the PRC in the 1970s. As China's relationship with [North] Vietnam cooled to the point of actual military confrontation later on in the 1970s and dangerous disputes erupted with the USSR over the Amur river frontier, the USA and PRC found a limited common cause in concern with the objectives of the USSR and its client states in the region. These same complex considerations led also to the curious position adopted by the western powers over Kampuchea/Cambodia in the era of the Pol Pot regime. Whether the Khmer Rouge government was technically genocidal may be open to question. Article 2 of the rather inadequately drafted 1948 Genocide Convention defines genocide as,

"acts committed with intent to destroy, in whole or in part, a national, ethnical, racial or religious group as such:"

Whether the destruction of a group which is economically defined as in the case of the victims of the Khmer Rouge would fall within this definition is somewhat uncertain. Be that as it may, however, the, admittedly variously motivated, Vietnamese invasion of Kampuchea which put an end to the slaughter of the killing fields was disapproved largely because it involved Vietnam. The USA, many of the EU powers and the PRC all sustained support for the Khmer Rouge's retention of the Cambodian seat in the UN long after its removal from actual power in the country.

Post-Cold War retrenchment and the weakening of formerly clear ideological fault lines in the region have, together with a relative lack of foreign policy emphasis under the Clinton administration, rendered US attitudes towards Southeast Asian security rather unpredictable in the late 1990s. A number of issues do, however, present themselves as evidently significant for the determination of future direction. Firstly continued US economic and political engagement must be considered certain, if only because disengagement from the Asia-Pacific rim would in the long term economic view, even in the context of the late 1990s recession, be inconceivable. At the same time, the end of the Cold War has reshaped the parameters of that engagement, even whilst certain continuities remain. Amongst these are the continuing questions of the Koreas, the foreign and military relations of Vietnam and the status of Taiwan.

In the 1990s Korea presents particular difficulties. The economic collapse, and indeed outright famine, suffered by North Korea has called the continued viability of the communist northern state into question, in dangerous combination with what appears to be significant military nuclear development by the country. Whether in time Korea may be reunified under the more stable American-backed southern government must remain a matter for speculation but for the time being the US commitment to South Korea retains a self-evident importance which may indeed be no less significant than at any time since the 1950s. The question of Vietnam is rather different. The painful memory of the Vietnam War has long impeded the normalisation of relations between Washington and Hanoi and at the time of writing [52] continues to do so. In a post-Cold War strategic setting this is probably ill-advised from the viewpoint of both Vietnam and the USA. Vietnam is a considerable regional power and one which has by no means even relations with a potentially hegemonic PRC. It may therefore play a significant role in achieving that stabilising balance of power and interests upon which the future stability of the region may depend. Richard K. Betts suggests pointedly that,

> "In the bipolar Cold War world, it may have made sense to want Vietnam [as a Soviet client state] to be weak and vulnerable. In the new postwar world, there is no reason to want that unless Chinese dominance is preferred to some measure of balance." [53]

In this sense a rapprochement with Vietnam, in which significant progress has been made, including developing military contacts in the 1990s and, in 1994, the lifting of the economic embargo, could be a positive contribution to both confidence and peace building in the region. The Taiwan issue has been considered in the context of the Chinese strategic position but it is worth re-emphasising that there is to be here found the best evidence of US willingness to engage militarily when real commitments are threatened, as in occasional PRC menaces to the ROC.

The overall picture from the US viewpoint appears, unsurprisingly, to be one of continuing commitment coupled with a scaling down of actual presence in a way congenial to both the USA and the host states. The 1990s commenced with the Bush administration's East Asian Security Initiative (EASI) which was predicated upon a phased reduction of the fixed US military presence in the region and its replacement with bilateral flexible access arrangements with ASEAN states. ASEAN has made it clear that the majority of the membership do not desire a US withdrawal from the region but whilst EASI remained a major plank of US-East Asian security dialogue under the Clinton administration, the foreign policy disarray which characterised it for a variety of reasons caused its potential for the maximisation of the US role as a balancing power in the region not really to be achieved. [54] The closure of US bases in the Philippines and reductions in the scale of presence in Okinawa are both symptomatic of the EASI led policy and in fact the emergence of a more flexible response mode must seem appropriate in a much less predictable and more dynamic structure of regional relations. The historically favoured bilateral approach – typical of great powers with its implicit element of *divide et imperare* – may, however, be less appropriate in the post-Cold War world in which multilateral engagement with or through regional organisations may be seen as an emerging dominant theme not only in the collective security and peace support sectors but in international relations generally. This sensitive realignment is also clouded by disagreement between the USA and many of the authoritarian South and Southeast Asian governments upon issues of human rights. What is seen from Washington as an essential element of both international law and democratisation is seen in many capitals in the region as unwarranted 'western' interference and even quasi-imperialism. The question enters large issues of legal and political theory pertaining to universalism and cultural relativism [55] but there are nonetheless implications for security responses, not least in relation to the situation of SLORC rule in Myanmar and to that in East Timor, both of which issues are effectively excluded from consideration by ASEAN through its tradition of avoidance of conflict by sidelining. At the same time the security guarantees offered to Japan, even with increased Japanese willingness to engage in both its own defence and UN peace support operations continue, as, in effect does the protection of Taiwan. In at least the medium term knowledge of the US presence in and commitment to the region seems set to remain a vital dimension of the security architecture of the region and indeed the development of the ASEAN way of conflict aversion and management may be argued to depend, at least in part, upon that background reassurance. Whether politically or militarily the USA would be willing to intervene directly in, e.g., a flare up of open conflict over the Spratly Islands must remain open to very considerable doubt, but the sense that it *might* do so is paradoxically in itself possibly a peace building, or at least conflict aversion, factor in the dispute.

THE FUTURE OF PEACE SUPPORT IN SOUTHEAST ASIA

The future of regional peace support in Southeast Asia must remain rather uncertain in the short to medium term. The regional organisations, including the security offspring of ASEAN – the ARF, have considerable potential and indeed successful practice in conflict aversion, and peace and confidence building. Their strengths in those sectors, essentially those of inclusiveness and consensuality, may however become weaknesses where consensus and peace building fail and an actual military crisis erupts. It is highly unlikely that the ARF could in its present form operate as an effective peace enforcement agency, granted both the institutional traditions from which it sprang and the diversity of its membership. In some respects it is reminiscent of the League of Nations Assembly as a peace support agency – too large, too divided and potentially too slow to react in the case of an emergency, even whilst having great promise for the aversion of at least some emergencies. Unfortunately the region is by no means lacking in sources of potential security breakdown. The Spratly Islands, the Diauyutai/Senkaku Islands, Taiwan, North Korea and East Timor and the possible destabilisation of Indonesia are all potential flash points. In both the Spratlys and across the Taiwan strait there have been minor armed confrontations, in the latter case leading to an indicative placement of US naval forces. The September 1999 "independence" referendum in East Timor, supervised by the UN, led to a massive vote in favour of independence accompanied and followed by campaigns of violence and intimidation by pro-Jakarta "militias" which the Indonesian police and armed forces were either unable or unwilling to restrain. In this situation most of the foreign UN staff were withdrawn in early September 1999 leaving a sanguinary chaos behind whilst Indonesia, on 10 September 1999, initially refused any immediate permission for the entry of an international peacekeeping force. This position was changed shortly thereafter with acceptance of the deployment of an international force, partly as a result of pressure exerted at the Asia-Pacific

Forum meeting in New Zealand. By Resolution 1264 of 15 September 1999 the UN Security Council authorised,

> "... the establishment of a multinational force under a unified command structure, pursuant to the request of the Government of Indonesia conveyed to the Secretary-General on 12 September 1999, with the following tasks: to restore peace and security in East Timor, to protect and support UNAMET [the Election monitoring group] in carrying out its tasks and, within force capabilities, to facilitate humanitarian assistance operations, and authorizes the States participating in the multinational force to *take all necessary measures* to fulfill this mandate."

The emphasis is added, and the phrases "all necessary measures" means use of armed force in combat if that should be necessary. The force was, in short conceived as at least in part a robust enforcement force. The Foreign Minister of Indonesia, Ali Alatas had urged that the multinational force should contain a large ASEAN element,[56] although, as remarked above, this is not actually a role for which ASEAN is really conceived or structured. In fact the force was Australian-led and very largely Australian composed, but it did also include contingents from other States, including a UK Gurkha contingent and logistic and communications support from the USA and an ASEAN presence. It may again be noted that where "peace building" had become a manifest impossibility and, in some sense, "enforcement" was required, the situation was not one calculated for ASEAN, or even ARF, intervention but rather for that of an *ad hoc* "coalition of the willing".

In the end it is probable that for general purposes, at least in the immediate term, the maintenance of international peace and security in the region will depend upon a multilateral balance of power system in which crises are likely to be resolved by the balancing of interests as between the ASEAN powers, the PRC and the USA, with a normalising Japan possibly playing an expanded but still limited role. It is highly unlikely that other external powers, such as in particular India, would become involved, not least because for the foreseeable future Indian security concerns are likely to remain focused upon the continuing tensions over the Himalayan frontier region with China and the developing nuclear arms race with Pakistan and the dangerous dispute over Kashmir. [57] Peace enforcement action in Southeast Asia would, therefore, seem necessarily to rest upon *ad hoc* foundations with an essential foundation in bilateral or multilateral "coalitions of the willing" including in some cases possibly other major neighbouring powers such as Australia. Regional organisations are unlikely to play a large part in any such action, subject to any, rather unlikely, development of the ARF in this direction, but ASEAN and the ARF will no doubt continue to play a vital role in peace and confidence building, in short in conflict avoidance, which should by no means be discounted.

NOTES

1. N. Baker and L.C. Sebastian, 'The Problem with Parachuting: Strategic Studies and Security in the Asia/Pacific Region' in D. Ball, ed., *The Transformation of Security in the Asia/Pacific Region* London: Frank Cass. 1996, p.15 at p.29.
2. J.K. Galbrath, *The Age of Uncertainty* (BBC/Andre Deutsch, 1977), Chapter 4, especially at p.128.
3. It seems that this followed an engagement between Southern Forces and Northern held islands in the Gulf, which has led some to denounce the response as a mere pretext for war. This is a harsh judgment, it is possibly more accurate to say that the Gulf of Tonkin incident was Vietnam's 'Archduke', an incident minor in itself which served to spark a conflict waiting to happen.
4. N.D. White, *Keeping the Peace*, 2 ed., (Manchester University Press, 1997), p.19.
5. For discussion see, amongst many others, S. Karnow, *Vietnam: A History* (Penguin, 1984).
6. How far the Watergate scandal would have gone in the absence of the Vietnam involvement must remain an open question.
7. See (1973) 67 *American Journal of International Law*, 389.
8. For a highly optimistic assessment of SEATO and the hopes invested in it see G. Modelski, ed., *SEATO: Six Studies* (F.W. Cheshire for the Australian National University, 1962)
9. Bilveer Singh, *ZOPFAN and the New Security Order in the Asia-Pacific Region* (Pelanduk Publications, 1992), p.5.
10. This is of course to some degree a matter of the inevitable difference between internal and external perceptions.
11. J.N. Mak, 'The Asia-Pacific security order' in A. McGrew and C. Brook, *Asia-Pacific in the New World Order*, Routledge, 1998, p.88 at pp.113-4.
12. D.K. Emmerson, 'Indonesia, Malaysia, Singapore: A Regional Security Core?' in R.J. Ellings and S.W. Simon, eds., *South East Asian Security in the New Millennium* (M.E. Sharpe, 1996) p.35 at p.75.
13. A useful collection will be found in *ASEAN Documents* (ASEAN National Secretariat, Indonesian Department of Foreign Affairs,).
14. For discussion see below; also Bilveer Singh, op.cit.
15. See K.W. Deutsch et al, *Political Community and the North Atlantic Area: International Organization in the Light of Historical Experience* (Princeton University Press, 1957, 1968)
16. A. Acharya, 'A Regional Security Community in Southeast Asia' in D. Bell, ed., op.cit., p, 175 at pp.176-9.
17. See Chapter 1 for discussionn of these concepts.
18. See T. Huxley, *Insecurity in the ASEAN Region* (Royal United Services Institute for Defence Studies, 1993)
19. Amongst the most important examples of ASEAN trading measures have been the 1977 ASEAN Preferential Trading Arrangements, the 1992 ASEAN Free Trade Area (AFTA) plan and the develop-ment of Subregional Economic Zones, such as the Singapore-Johor-Riau (SIJORI) triangle, linking the economies of contiguous regions across national boundaries.
20. For discussion, see IWAC Adre, 'China and the "Springtime of Nations": Next Steps?' (1993) XL *International Relations*, p.435-450.
21. H.J. Dobson, "Regional Approaches to Peacekeepiong Activities: The Case of the ASEAN Regional Forum" (1999) 6 *International Peacekeeping*, p.152 at p.16 citing Michael Leifer, *The ASEAN Regional Forum*, Adelphi Papers No.302 (Brassey's Defence Publishers, 1996), p.55.
22. Some thoughts upon this have been outlined by T. Huxley in "Regional Security – Enhanced or Eroded: W(h)ither ASEAN and the ARF? (Unpublished RUSI Paper, June 1999).
23. Op.cit., at p.187.
24. Dr. Mahathir Mohammed, *Vision 2020* (ISIS Malaysia, 1991), p.2.
25. Op. cit.
26. The Imperial Censorate (Tu Ch'a Yuan) was one of ther Nine Chief Ministries of the Imperial administration, the Censors were not concerned with suppression of political or literary dissemination in the western sense but were in effect Government auditors who had a general brief to inspect the

functioning of the government and bureaucracy and reported directly to the Emperor upon matters which they considered to be of concern.

27. The text will be found in translation in H.E. Schurnam and D. Schell, eds., *China Readings,* (Penguin, 1968), Vol. I.
28. LNOJ, Special Supplement, No.101, 43. The text is reproduced in F. Knipping, H. von Mangoldt and V. Rittberger, *The United Nations System and its Predecessors* (Oxford, 1997), Vol. II, p.627 at p.634.
29. The Imperial Japanese Government claimed that the army in Manchuria had acted without its authority. Granted the turbulent politics of Japan in the 1930s the authority may at the very least have been strained, but it is nonetheless extraordinary for a modern state, and one which at the time was for all practical purposes a totalitarian system, to deny that it had control over its own armed forces.
30. For an official Chinese view of the trial see *A Great Trial in Chinese History* (New World Press, 1981).
31. D. Roy, 'Restructuring foreign and defence policy: the People's Republic of China' in A. McGrew and C. Brook, eds., *Asia-Pacific in the New World Order* (Routledge, 1998), pp.137-157 at p.137.
32. Recognition of the ROC is now relatively limited, but by no means negligible, in scale and many states which do not accord *de jure* recognition to it nonetheless engage in 'informal' relations with the Taipei government.
33. R.A. Scalapino, 'The US Commitment to Asia' in D. Ball, ed., op.cit., p.68 at p.79.
34. For discussion see M.G. Gallagher, 'China's Illusory Threat to the South China Sea' in M.E. Brown, S.M. Lynn-Jones and S.E. Miller, eds., *East Asian Security* (The MIT Press, 1996), at pp.133-158.
35. For discussion of this see Hyun-Soo Kim, 'The 1992 Chinese Territorial Sea Law in the Light of the UN Convention' (1994) 43 *International and Comparative Law Quarterly*, pp.894-904.
36. The PLA embraces the navy and air force as well as the army *stricto sensu*.
37. For a highly sceptical view of this see G. Segal, 'East Asia and the "Costrainment" of China' in M.E. Brown et al., eds., at pp.159-187.
38. The only significant vessel to remain operational in Russian hands was the cruiser *Avrora* which was later to play an important symbolic role in the 1917 October Bolshevik Revolution.
39. A request by Britain that the four powerful *Kongo* class battlecruisers should sail to assist the Royal Navy in the North Sea was turned down, not unreasonably, on the grounds that the Japanese public would not understand such a deployment of such expensive units.
40. This view remains somewhat open to question, for a general discussion see T. Crump, *The Death of an Emperor* (Oxford, 1991); see also A.C. Brackman, *The Other Nuremberg* Collins, 1989), especially at pp.392-5
41. K. Pyle, 'Restructuring Foreign and Defence Policy: Japan' in A. McGrew and C. Brook, eds., *Asia-Pacific in the New World Order* (Routledge, 1998), p.121 at p.125.
42. Ibid.
43. For discussion of this see P.J. Katzenstein and N. Okawara, 'Japan's National Security' in M.E. Brown, S.M. Lynn-Jones and S.E. Miller, eds., *East Asian Security* (The MIT Press, 1996), p.265 at pp.290-292.
44. See Masashi Nishihara, 'Japan-US Cooperation in UN Peace Efforts' in S.S . Harrison and M.Nishihara, eds., *UN Peacekeeping: Japanese and American Perspectives* (The Carnegie Endowment, 1995), pp.163-175.
45. Now the Democratic Republic of Congo.
46. For discussion see S. Ienaya, 'The Glorification of War in Japanese Education' in M.E. Brown et al., eds., op.cit., pp.332-351.
47. These were women in occupied territory forced into prostitution for the service of Japanese military personnel.
48. See below.
49. See R. Hashimoto, *Reforms for the New Era of Japan and ASEAN for a Broader and Deeper Partnership* (ISEAS, 1997), especially at p.14-16.
50. Ibid., at p.14.
51. At the same time the USA was making colonial inroads in South America, notably through the acquisition of Puerto Rico and Guam and also the authorisation of the development of the extra-territorial Panama Canal zone.
52. March 1999.

53. R.K. Betts, 'Wealth Power and Instability: East Asia and the United States after the Cold War' in M.E. Brown et al. eds., op.cit., p.32 at p.61.
54. For discussion see D.K. Emmerson, 'US Policy Themes in Southeast Asia in the 1990s' in D. Wurfel and B. Burton, eds., *South East Asia in the New World Order* (Macmillan, 1996), p.103 at pp.108-12
55. It is of interest that the 1993 Bangkok NGO Declaration on Human Rights affirmed the importance of universal standards in contradiction of many esatblished government views in the region.
56. Reported in Security Council Press Release SC/6727 of 15 September 1999.
57. For discussion see Chapter 8.

In the Absence of Regional Organisations

One of the evident difficulties to be found in the development of a regional peace support paradigm, or paradigms, for the 21st century is the possibility that in any given case there may be no, or no suitable, regional organisation or arrangement to which requisite action might be delegated. It is important to stress from the outset that the issue is not one of an absolute absence of regional organisations. There are, indeed, very few parts of the world which are wholly devoid of international or trans-national arrangements of one sort or another. The question is rather one that focuses upon an extreme point in the spectrum of appropriateness, or practical possibility, of utilising whatever organisations might be available in a given situation. Such circumstances represent, in short, the outer edge of the possibilities covered by the caveat of "appropriateness" which is set to the requirement of article 53 of the UN Charter that regional arrangements should be employed in peace-support action. A situation in which there either are no organisations or those which do exist are incapable, for whatever reason, of taking useful action in the given case is in the sense of article 53 merely the ultimate expression of "inappropriateness".

The preceding chapters have outlined the diversity of character and capacity to be found amongst regional organisations. These are, naturally, the product of differing historical and political experiences in the various regions and their consequent security concerns. The quite different processes of development, foci of interest and *modi operandi* of, for example, ASEAN, NATO, the OAS and the OAU make the point very clearly. In this general context it need occasion no surprise that amongst the regions and sub-regions which have developed no, or no significantly effective, security organisations are to be found a number which have been prey to long-running and dangerous political and military instability which acts in itself as a major impediment to any such institutional development. It may be added that it is no less unlikely that in any such situation an appropriate regional "coalition of the willing" could be generated to perform a viable peace-support or enforcement role in the event of a crisis. In this event the UN Security Council would in effect have no regional options amongst which to choose for the purposes of article 53. The UN itself would then be left as the only available peace support agency, which returns the debate to the issues of resourcing, capacity and Security Council politics which originally generated consideration of a revival of regionalism in the post Cold War UN context.

The two principal foci of this chapter are the security situations in the Middle East, including the extended Arab-Israeli confrontation, and in South Asia, including the long-running Indo-Pakistani dispute over, *inter alia*, Kashmir. These situations are not, in either case, unique in character and in both cases there are well established regional organisations, respectively the Arab League and the SAARC. For a variety reasons, but in each case primarily the structure of regional relations, these organisations are precluded from effective action in relation to the fundamental security problems faced in their respective areas of interest. They therefore represent, for the present purpose – although not for others, the type of functional absence referred to above and, in differing ways, they represent significant failures of both the global and regional dimensions of post-war security architecture. With their continuing instability and their potential for nuclear exchange these are problems of vast significance for the 21st century and, to that degree, are amongst the sternest tests to be faced by the emerging post-Cold War global and regional security structures.

THE MIDDLE EAST

The Middle East is, in a number of respects, the most pointed example of the failure of post-Second World War international security mechanisms, combining in one bloc a range of negative features to be found variously in other regions. In the immediate post-war years there was an attempt to "parachute" the NATO concept into the Middle East in the form of the Central Treaty Organisation (CENTO). This developed from the Baghdad Pact, itself a cause of dissension within the Arab League over Iraqi participation in the 1950s, and proved not only as unsuitable as was SEATO in Southeast Asia [1] but was doomed from the outset by the realities of the Arab-Israeli dispute. Some of the region's problems derive, nearly a century later, from the aftermath of the imperfectly conceived and executed dismemberment of the Ottoman Empire at the end of the First World War, together with the variety of inter-State disputes which are found in many other regions and sub-regions. There are, thus, a number of territorial disputes, as for example between Saudi Arabia and Qatar, some of which have even led to sporadic small scale armed conflict. On a much larger scale the Ba'ath dictatorship in Iraq has had a serious destabilising effect upon the region, including the great disaster of the 1980-88, Iran-Iraq, Gulf War and the 1990-91 Gulf Conflict. The latter, following the Iraqi invasion and occupation of Kuwait, generated the only major 20th century peace enforcement operation in the region in the shape of the UN authorised Coalition action. This, indeed, was the beginning of the post-Cold War restructuring of global security architecture, although it proved to be a very misleading precedent and one which was far from representing the outset of the "new world order" so confidently asserted by President Bush. Serious as these issues were, and are, the overarching feature of the Middle Eastern security equation has from the very outset of the UN era been the long-running Arab-Israeli confrontation. The principal regional organisation, the Arab League, was indeed created very much in the context of this problem, although never with that sole focus. The League is *prima facie* both a regional organisation in the proper sense of that term and also, in practice, a regional military alliance, but, again, its development and practice has been so much shaped and distorted by the Arab-Israeli confrontation that its efficacy in both respects has been severely, if not fatally, compromised. The UN Security Council has also effectively been excluded from effective action, not least by the certainty of a US veto upon any action seen as contrary to Israel's interests and, formerly, the likelihood of a Soviet veto upon any decisions of the opposite tendency. For these reasons the Middle East has, since 1945, largely lacked both regional and global peace support resources of any practical effect and there is little evidence that the post-Cold War order holds out any immediately greater promise.

THE FORMATION OF THE ARAB LEAGUE

The Arab States had emphasised the importance of regionalism in the emerging post-war security architecture from an early stage and at the San Francisco Conference which shaped the structure of the UN joined with the South American States in advocating a strong regional element in the security structures to be developed under the global organisation's aegis. They shared to a large degree South American concerns over fears of the implications for national autonomy – and Superpower domination – which a Great Power dominated Security Council indicated and this sensitivity can be seen in the structures of the League which were emerging at the same time. [2] After a preliminary exchange of notes the Arab League originated in July 1944 when Nahhas Pasha, Prime Minister of Egypt, announced the calling of an Arab Conference to be held in Cairo to facilitate post-war Arab unity and to resolve the Palestine question. The Conference, actually held in Alexandria, with delegates from Egypt, Transjordan, Lebanon, Iraq and Syria and observers from Libya, Palestine, Morocco, Saudi Arabia and Yemen met in September 1944 and produced the preliminary Alexandria Protocol setting out the aims and objectives of the proposed organisation. The Protocol stated, *inter alia*, that,

> "A League will be formed of the independent Arab States which consent to join the League. ... The object of the League will be to control the execution of the agreements which the above States will conclude; ... [and] to protect their independence and sovereignty against every aggression by suitable means; ... In no case will resort to force to settle a dispute between any two member states be allowed. ... The Council [of the League] will intervene in every dispute which may lead to war between a member state of the League and any other member state or power, so as to reconcile them." [3]

The League was finally created a year later on 22 March 1945 when the Pact of the League of Arab States was concluded, originally between Syria, Transjordan, Iraq, Saudi-Arabia, Lebanon, Egypt and Yemen, establishing the organisation with its seat in Cairo, a League Council and a permanent Secretariat. The Pact makes somewhat equivocal provision for matters of defence and security, specifically in articles 5 and 6. [4] Article 5 provides that,

> "Recourse to force to resolve disputes between two or more League States is inadmissible. If a difference should arise between them, not pertaining to the independence, sovereignty or territorial integrity of (any of the) states (concerned), and the contending states have recourse to the Council to settle it, then its decision is executory and obligatory. ...'"

Article 6 then adds that,

> "Should aggression by a state against a member of the League take place or be apprehended, it is for the state which has suffered, or is threatened with aggression to demand that the Council be summoned to meet immediately. The Council shall decide upon the appropriate measures to check the aggression, and shall issue a decision by unanimous assent. If the aggression emanates from one of the League states, the view of the aggressor shall not affect unanimity of assent ...'"

The problematic nature of these provisions will be immediately obvious. They are in the first place of limited potential effect. The ban upon resort to armed force as a means of international dispute resolution contained in article 5 merely restates the principle of the 1928 Pact of Paris which was at the time of the creation of the League in the process of reaffirmation by the International Military Tribunals at Nuremberg and Tokyo and restatement by article 2(4) of the UN Charter. The extensive exclusions built into the substantive provision of the article effectively ensure that any threat actually likely to lead to armed conflict is removed from its scope, thereby rendering its value in addition to general international law rather slight. The more specifically directed provision of article 6 is no less problematic, although in a somewhat different way. In the actual event of aggression the article provides only for a right to demand the convening of the Council of the League. The apparently mandatory requirement that the Council then "shall" unanimously determine the measures to be taken suggests a process with all the defects of UN

Security Council procedures with more in addition. The requirement of unanimity amounts in effect to a power of veto on the part of any member, apart from the aggressor should it be one. No provision is made for the not unlikely eventuality of unanimity being unattainable. It is also not very clear how any such decision, particularly if it involves use of armed force, is to be implemented, although this would presumably be through action by a "coalition of the Arab willing" initially pursuant to article 51 of the UN Charter. This view is conformed by the limited peace support action which the League has undertaken, notably in the Lebanon. [5]

The general, and less than robust provision, of article 5 of the Pact is significantly supplemented by the 1950 Treaty of Joint Defence and Economic Cooperation Among the States of the Arab League, the key provision of which is article 2. It provides that,

> "The Contracting States shall consider that an armed aggression committed against any one or more of them, or against their forces, to be an aggression against them all. For this reason, and in accordance with the right of legitimate self-defence, both individual and collective, they undertake to ... aid ... the State ... against whom an aggression is committed, and to take immediately ... all measures ..., including the use of armed force, to repulse the aggression and to restore security and peace. ... In application of Article 6 of the Arab League Pact and Article 51 of the United Nations Charter, the Council of the Arab League and the (UN) Security Council shall immediately be notified of the act of aggression and of the measures ... adopted ...."[6]

This is of course the classic language of collective defence and is closely similar to that of, e.g., article 5 of the 1949 North Atlantic Treaty or article 4 of the Warsaw Pact. Again, however, it is the misfortune of the Arab League and the Middle Eastern region that this commonplace international concept has been overtaken by the Arab-Israeli conflicts.

The idea of collective defence is in some respects peculiarly appropriate to the Arab League in so far as it has deeper roots in Islam than in most other faiths and cultures. The doctrine of *Jihad*, commonly misunderstood in the West as an advocation of aggressive "Holy War" and abused as such by some in the Islamic world – including by Iraq in the 1990-91 Gulf Conflict, [7] is, properly understood, precisely a doctrine of collective self-defence. It originated in the *Hejirah*, the flight of the Prophet and the early Muslim community from the attacks of the Meccans to refuge in Medina and is expressed as a dimension of struggle with the opponents of faith. Collective military defence is seen, upon the basis of a comment made by the Prophet when returning to Medina from battle, as the lesser *jihad*, in contrast with the greater *jihad* of struggle against spiritual weakness, and is limited to defence of the Muslim community against external assault. [8] The key Qu'ranic text is found in Chapter 9:123 which in translation reads,

O you who believe, fight the unbelievers who gird you about, and let them find firmness in you: and know that Allah is with those who fear Him.

Jihad is ultimately linked with the Islamic division of the world into the *Dar ul-Islam*, the House of Faith, and the *Dar al-Harb*, the House of War. This does not, other than in an eschatological end-time sense, imply a duty to wage war against all non-Muslims, but in a present time frame refers to those outside the Islamic *Ummah* as a source from which aggression might come. In this context significant elements of Middle Eastern, and other, Islamic opinion considers Israel to be a classic manifestation of the *Dar al-Harb*. Whilst the League is far from being a "fundamentalist" [9] organisation, the idea of *jihad* has undoubtedly contributed to the organisation's policy sense of the Arab-Israeli situation, especially since 1967 in relation to the West Bank. This is in a sense the counterpoint to some of the expressions of religious Zionism and a contributor to the difficult of resolving the crisis.

Be that as it may, forces of circumstance, religious and political, have left the Arab League and its Member States in the position not of actual or potential peace support actors but as belligerents in conflict with a major regional power which would neither wish nor be welcome to become one of their number. This is the fundamental flaw in present Middle Eastern security architecture and one to which no easy solution suggests itself.

THE ARAB LEAGUE AND THE ARAB-ISRAELI CONFLICT(S)

This is not the place for a detailed analysis of the Arab-Israeli conflicts but certain fundamental issues require to be outlined. The long and troubled history of the Jewish people from the Roman suppression of the Jewish Revolt [10] in 70 CE [11] and their dispersal from the territory of Israel was marked by successive, more or less violent, phases of anti-Semitic persecution. These persecutions reached a climax in the late 19th and early 20th centuries with the Russian pogroms and, ultimately, the Nazi holocaust in German and German-occupied territories under the Third Reich. These appalling events are well enough known but, in an age in which it has become fashionable for "revisionist" academic historians to play down and even to deny the reality and the significance of the holocaust, it is worth re-emphasising the unequivocal nature of the evidence both for the hideous mass slaughter and the personal responsibility of the leaders of the regime for it. [12]

This tragic history goes some considerable way towards explaining both the urgent desire for a secure Jewish homeland and the seeming intransigence of a significant element of the modern Israeli political spectrum. The situation, both within and beyond Israel, is however by no means so simply structured as this might appear to suggest and there are other fundamentally important factors which cannot safely be ignored.

Modern Zionism has complex roots, including groundings in basic teachings of Judaism – in particular the idea that God anciently granted the land of Israel to the Jewish people as their homeland and affirmed it to them in their flight from Egypt in the Mosaic era. [13] Many world faiths hold certain sites to be in some sense sacred by virtue of historical or claimed events associated with them, it is in the present context both the glory and the tragedy of Jerusalem that it contains sites variously sacred to all three of the world monotheistic religions – in temporal order, Judaism, Christianity and Islam. Judaism is, however, unique in its profound, indeed foundational, sense of a theology of place, a sense reinforced by the persecution which the Jewish people have suffered in their long diaspora since 70 CE. The importance of the land of Israel is thus a religions as well as a political imperative in Israeli understanding and this has had a significant impact upon the understanding and application of international law in this context.

The Zionist movement was originally founded upon ideas of Jewish resettlement in Palestine rather than necessarily upon aspirations for a Jewish State as such. Interestingly the Basle Programme of the World Zionist Organisation issued on 29 August 1897 referred to "a home in Palestine secured by public law" [14] but not directly to a "State". Increasing resettlement in fact took place, with varying and sometimes intense levels of local Arab resistance, from the 1860s onwards and by 1900 the first modern wholly Jewish city, now Tel Aviv, had been established near to Jaffa. [15] The more "political" dimension of Zionism developed in parallel with the resettlement movement and is especially associated in its earlier period with the writings of Theodore Herzl. [16] Herzl advocated the creation of a Jewish State in Israel/Palestine and sought the support of both the Ottoman Sultan and the Kaiser for this project. Not very surprisingly he was unable to generate much enthusiasm for the idea in either Istanbul or Berlin. The Sultan could not be expected to welcome the carving of yet another sovereign State out of his decaying Empire and the Kaiser was little more likely to wish to offend an Empire which, however distressed its condition, was the key to the Dardanelles and a major potential obstacle to the Anglo-Franco-Russian Coalition which was in fact to oppose Germany in 1914. The work of Herzl nonetheless sowed seeds which were to come to fruition over the following half century and to lead to the eventual creation of the State of Israel.

The first substantial building block was the Balfour Declaration on 2 November 1917 by the British Foreign Secretary, Lord Balfour, to Lord Rothschild as President of the British Zionist Federation. The substantive part of the declaration read as follows,

"His Majesty's Government views with favour the establishment in Palestine of a national home for the Jewish people, and will use their best endeavours to facilitate the achievement of this object, it being clearly understood that nothing shall be done which may prejudice the civil and religious rights of existing non-Jewish communities in Palestine, or the rights and political status enjoyed by Jews in any other country." [17]

This carefully worded statement offered no guidance as to just how existing civil and religious rights were to be conserved as the new "national home" was created and it is the inability to square this circle which has plagued Israel/Palestine and the region ever since. The Balfour Declaration was also, at least implicitly, as Istvan Pogany points out [18] already inconsistent with assurances given to Arab leaders, including the Sheriff of Mecca who had given important sanction to Allied operations against Ottoman forces in the Middle East.

The waters were further muddied in the aftermath of the First World War when the dismemberment of the Ottoman Empire was undertaken in part through the imposition of League of Nations Mandates under article 22 of the Covenant of the League, that in respect of Palestine being granted to the United Kingdom on 24 July 1922. The Preamble to the Mandate referred expressly to the Balfour Declaration and effectively repeated its terms whilst article 2 required the creation of conditions for a "Jewish national home" whilst safeguarding the rights of all the inhabitants of Palestine. [19] Again, no indication was given of the means by which these increasingly incompatible objectives were to be achieved.

From the mid-1930s onwards conflicts between the rapidly expanding Jewish settlements and their Arab neighbours frequently erupted into violent confrontations which were repressed with considerable difficulty. In 1937 a British Royal Commission chaired by Lord Peel actually recommended a partition of the territory into autonomous Jewish and Arab States, but this was acceptable to neither party and was rejected as impractical.

In the later years of the war and shortly afterwards British resistance to massive Jewish immigration into Palestine generated terrorist activity by extreme Zionist organisations, such as the Stern Gang, including the assassination of Lord Moyne and the King David Hotel massacre. At about the same time the Truman Administration in the USA, partly through genuine and creditable sympathy with the sufferings of the Jewish people under the Nazis but also with an eye to domestic political advantage, adopted the policy of uncritical support which has been the basis of US-Israeli relations ever since. Finally, in May 1947, the United Nations General Assembly resolved to establish the UN Special Committee on Palestine (UNSCOP). Following further debate and reference to an *Ad Hoc* Committee the General Assembly resolved on 29 November 1947 to recommend partition more or less along the lines that the majority on UNSCOP had advised. [20] The United Kingdom then agreed to surrender its Mandate over Palestine by 15 May 1948 but declined to supervise the implementation of the partition. The establishment of the State of Israel was proclaimed in Tel Aviv on 14 May 1948 and was almost immediately recognised by both the USA and the USSR.

The hostility of the Arab League to Israel has been unequivocal from the outset. Annex I to the 1945 Pact of the League states that,

"Its [Palestine's] existence and *de jure* independence is a matter on which there is no doubt as there is no doubt about the independence of the other Arab countries. Therefore, although external manifestations of that independence have continued to be obscured by overriding circumstances, it is not admissible that this should by an impediment to its participation in the proceedings of the [Arab] League Council." [21]

A rather more explicit statement was included in the Alexandria Protocol which remarked also that,

"The Committee also declares that it is second to none in regretting the woes which have been inflicted upon the Jews of Europe by European dictatorial states. But the question of these Jews should not be confused with Zionism, for there can be no greater injustice and aggression than solving the problem of the Jews of Europe by another injustice, i.e. by inflicting injustice on the Arabs of Palestine of various religions and denominations." [22]

This sense that in 1945 Europe and the West expiated its sins at Arab expense remains a source of Arab outrage and has been one of the major impediments to the positive development of the League's general external relations.

The day following the establishment of the new Israeli State the forces of Egypt, Iraq, (then) Transjordan, Lebanon and Syria, invaded the territory, initiating the first Arab-Israeli War. Despite numerous UN Security Council calls for cessation, hostilities dragged on until 20 July 1949 when, very belatedly pursuant to a final Security Council Resolution [23] and as a result of military exhaustion, an armistice, but not a peace settlement, was agreed. This set the pattern for the Arab-Israeli confrontation to the end of the 20th century, characterised by mutual intransigence, sporadic outbreaks of actual hostilities, stalling peace processes, UN impotence and a fundamental inability to settle the core issues – failing, that is, to square the circle originally propounded by the 1917 Balfour Declaration.

The subsequent history is well known. The 1967 Six Day War commenced with pre-emptive Israeli air strikes against Egypt, following a build-up of tension in which attempts had been made to close the Straits of Tiran to Israeli shipping and the United Nations Emergence Force (UNEF) which had been monitoring the cease-fire was withdrawn from Sinai after Egypt had retracted its consent to its presence. Hostilities with Jordan and Syria immediately followed. At the end of six days, when a new cease fire was agreed, Israel was in occupation of Sinai, the West Bank and the Golan heights, having more than doubled the extent of its territories up to the *de facto* boundaries which it has, except Sinai, maintained to date. The balance of legalities in the Six Day War is confused, other than to say that some if not indeed all the parties involved violated article 2(4) of the UN Charter. Whether the Israeli attack was a valid exercise of "anticipatory" self-defence which might be brought within the meaning of article 51 of the UN Charter may be debated with reference to the notoriously ambiguous criterion of the "occurrence" of an armed attack for that purpose granted the manifestly menacing prior actions of the Arab states. On further complication arises in relation to the status of the territories seized in 1967, and especially the West Bank. Israel claims the West Bank as legitimately its territory, partly upon implicit grounds of security necessity but also upon historic and religious grounds which have much less, if indeed any, basis in international law.

The question of the "occupied" or other status of the West Bank is highly significant and merits brief exploration in the present context. From the viewpoint of the international *jus in bello*, military occupation has historically been considered a short term phenomenon with the permanent status of the affected territory being presumed to be determined by the post-conflict settlement. The problem in the present case is that there has been no post-conflict settlement and the interim condition has therefore continued for a much longer time than would normally be expected. This generates an apparent difficulty of legal interpretation. The Land Warfare Regulations annexed to 1907 Hague Convention IV provide by article 42 that,

> Territory is considered occupied when it is actually placed under the authority of the hostile army. The occupation extends only to the territory where such authority has been established and can be exercised.

The requirement is thus simply one of adverse military occupation of territory formerly lawfully held by another sovereign State or States. A significant caveat however arises with article 6 of 1949 Geneva Convention IV which provides that,

> ... In the case of occupied territory, the application of the present Convention shall cease one year after the general close of military operations: however, the Occupying Power shall be bound, for the duration of the occupation, to the extent that such Power exercises the functions of government in such territory by the following Articles of the present Convention: 1 to 12, 27, 29 to 34, 47, 49, 51, 52, 53, 59, 61-77, 143. ...

The one year limitation refers to perception of occupation as effectively limited to the period of armed conflict and its immediate aftermath. In cases such as that of the Palestinian territories, which is not in fact unique in post-1945 experience, it is, however, clear that the minimum code represented by the articles listed in article 6 will remain applicable "for the duration of the occupation", however long that may prove to be. Despite trenchant Israeli and US denials it is difficult to see why this should not be the case for the West

Bank, even making all allowances for the evident security necessities of Israel pending a satisfactory resolution of Arab-Israeli relations. [24]

In fact Arab-Israeli disagreement upon the point remained absolute. In the 1973 *Yom Kippur* War, the Arab States neighbouring Israel launched a sudden attack with a view to "driving Israel into the sea". Some small Arab gains were initially made, after which Israel regained all the lost grounds and at the end of the war the *de facto* Israeli frontiers remained what they had been before. In both the Six Day and *Yom Kippur* Wars the Arab League proved unable to act as an effective regional agency and, in so far as the Arab-Israeli crisis was one of the spurs to its creation, it definitively failed as a forum for resolution or even as a military alliance. Since 1973, and the endeavours of the USA in the person of Henry Kissinger as Secretary of State in the Nixon Administration, stability of a sort has returned to the region. The peace concluded between Egypt, under President Sadat, and Israel was highly controversial within the Arab League and dangerously soured relations between Cairo and Damascus in particular. Steps forward were taken in the 1990s with the establishment of a partially autonomous Palestine under President Arafat, but the Wye River agreements stalled and nearly failed under the Netanyahu government, a coalition which included some of the more intransigent religious parties, in Israel. At the time of writing under the Barak administration, the peace process may again be moving forward, although by no means swiftly or smoothly. If, as it is devoutly to be hoped, a stable and sustainable peace settlement guaranteeing security and justice to both Israel and its Arab neighbours can be achieved, the credit will in present circumstances belong to neither the UN nor regional organisations such as the Arab League. It will be attributable rather to the war-weariness of the parties and, in this as in some other matters, ultimately to major power brokerage – here specifically by the USA.

THE ARAB LEAGUE AND OTHER SECURITY ISSUES

If, by the circumstances of its origin and political environment, the Arab League has not been able to have a significant positive impact upon the Arab Israeli situation, it does have a somewhat more positive record in some other regards. It has had some success as a forum for inter-Arab dialogue and peace and confidence building. Prior to the crises associated with the policies of the Ba'ath dictatorship in Baghdad, R.W. Macdonald could write with justification that,

> "The Arab League states have effectively policed their own region during most of the League's history [to 1965]. Despite bitter propaganda exchanges between rival Arab states, there have been surprisingly few breaches of the peace by Arab League members.

And despite somewhat inadequate machinery, most of the breaches of the peace that have occurred have been settled satisfactorily. The Lebanese crisis of 1958 was eventually settled within the Arab League family ... [and] [i]n 1961 the League's handling of the Kuwait incident was efficient and expeditious. Most other internal threats ... have been settled amicably ... usually by means of arbitration and mediation, and often by the direct intervention of the League's Secretary-General." [25]

The League has in fact since that time undertaken some limited peace-support action, notably in 1975-6 in the Lebanon. Lebanon has been one of the major victims of the Arab-Israeli strife, its territory having been partly taken over by PLO units in conflict with Israel and then dragged into hostilities with Israel. The resulting tensions brought about an effective collapse of government in 1975 and in 1976, following Syrian military intervention, an extraordinary session of the Arab League Council was held in Cairo on 8-9 June 1976 and called for an immediate cease-fire and Lebanese national reconciliation. It was also resolved to form a "Symbolic Arab Severity Force" to replace the Syrian forces in Lebanon and to maintain security and stability. A few days later, with some considerable reluctance, the Lebanese interim government agreed to this. In October 1976, in a further Conference in Riyadh, the "Symbolic Arab Security Force" was redesignated the Arab Deterrent Force. The legal authority of this force is debatable. [26] No authorisation from the Security Council was either sought or received, but it is questionable whether this was actually "enforcement action" within the meaning of article 53, even whilst it was also manifestly not self-defence within the meaning of article 51. *Prima facie* it may be regarded as a consensual "peacekeeping" action assisting an allied state in the restoration of internal security and order. The 1950 Treaty of Joint Defence and Economic Cooperation provides by article 3 that,

"The Contracting States shall consult together at the request of any one of them, whenever the territorial integrity, independence or security of any one of them is threatened."

In the light of this, and the unwelcome Syrian intervention, the *prima facie* consensual action of the League may, even without considering the sovereign capacities of the participating Member States, be considered *intra vires* the organisation. In the event both the scale and complexity of the situation in Lebanon ultimately defeated the Arab Deterrent Force which, with gradual withdrawal of other contingents, reverted to being in effect a Syrian force. Eventually in the context of the violent disruption of the State of Lebanon the Arab Deterrent Force was wound up in 1983 and a Multinational Peacekeeping Force comprising British, French, Italian and US contingents was deployed in Lebanon. The Arab League's endeavours in Lebanon cannot be considered successful, partly by reason of the endemic political background and partly because the small and under-resourced force was sent with a "peacekeeping" mandate into a situation in which there was no peace to keep. This was hardly the fault of the Arab League, nor an experience unique to it, but the case again illustrates the impediments faced by the League in any endeavours to function as a regional peace support agency.

Finally, the 1990-91 Gulf Conflict, between two Arab League Members, Iraq and Kuwait, did not ultimately involve the Arab League in any significant way. Indeed such has been the dissension created within the League by the successive crises generated by Iraq in the 1980s and 90s that it is doubtful whether such a role could have been played. In the event the occupation of Kuwait was ultimately terminated by UN-authorised action by a coalition of external Powers. [27] The role of a powerful "coalition of the willing", and the role of the USA therein, will be noticed and is especially significant in the context of a region in which the local security actor is, largely by circumstances beyond its control, disabled from effective action.

It must be concluded that whilst the Arab League can and does play a useful role as an Arab forum, its potential as a regional security actor is and will remain slight so long as the region is burdened by the Arab-Israeli dispute. Even when, or if, a stable and secure peace is established between Israel and its neighbours and the Palestinian issue is satisfactorily resolved, it is unlikely that Israel would want or be invited to join the League and a regional security organisation which excludes the region's strongest military power is at some disadvantage, even leaving aside current internal dissensions. Whether an Arab-Israeli settlement would permit enhancement of the so far dismal performance of the UN in the region, with the possible exception of the 1990-91 Gulf Conflict, remains to be seen. Certainly as the region in relation to which President Bush first asserted the existence of a "new world order" the present security architecture of the Middle East is at best disappointing and classically reliant upon major power brokerages and *ad hoc* "coalitions of the willing" – which may in itself be indicative of an important continuing element of post-Cold War regional and global security development.

REGIONAL COOPERATION IN SOUTH ASIA

South Asia is not unique in having experienced colonial rule, but the nature of that experience, and in particular the manner in which the region emerged from its colonial past, have been particularly influential in shaping the current security environment and architecture. [28] The nature of this political emergence has taken different form throughout the region. India is the world's largest democracy and while it has been forced to develop against a background of considerable internal division which has often manifested itself in political and religious violence, the institution of democracy in India would appear to be secure. Sri Lanka also boasts a democratic political system, though inter-communal violence has often been so intense as to threaten its continuance. Pakistan, Bangladesh and the Maldives have been less successful in democratic forms of government, and each has experienced prolonged periods of military rule. The Himalayan kingdoms of Bhutan and Nepal which make up the remainder of the South Asian region have, in the relatively recent past, made significant moves toward democratisation. In the 1990s democracy remains fragile, as fledgling political institutions seek to gain a foothold within the dominant traditional value system and a society in which internal cohesion is threatened by divisive political practices. Nepal has, in this regard, fared rather better, its slow progress toward democratic rule reaching its peak in 1990 with the adoption of a new constitution providing for a parliamentary system of government, multi-party democracy based on universal suffrage and civil rights.

South Asia's population accounts for over one-fifth of the world's population. It is also home to three major world religions, Hinduism, Buddhism and Sikhism, though it is Islam which has had the most marked effect upon inter-state relations. The latter is the state religion of Pakistan, Bangladesh and the Maldives. Hinduism is practised extensively throughout India and Nepal, and by the Tamil population of Sri Lanka, though the majority Singhalese population there are Buddhist, as is the majority of the population in Bhutan. Throughout the region's post-colonial history religion has proved divisive both domestically and internationally and it is a significant factor in many of the tensions and cleavages which continue to hamper regional cooperation, particularly with regard to security issues. Religious division, however, is far from being the only obstacle with which the states of South Asia have had to contend since gaining independence. The region lies toward the bottom of almost all of the statistics tables relating to issues such as poverty, child mortality, malnutrition and illiteracy; the total number of people within the region who live on or below the World Bank's "poverty line" is estimated to be greater than the total population of Africa. [29] The impact of such socio-economic factors cannot be disregarded in any discussion of regional development, cooperation and security.

The region has also had to contend with a geographic location which is not wholly conducive to stable security relations. In this regard China presents perhaps the most obvious complication, but instability in Afghanistan and Central Asia, the somewhat precarious nature of intra and inter-state relations in much of Southeast Asia and the prospect of Russian and, more likely, US involvement must all be factored into a discussion of Indian sub-continental politics.

With particular regard to security one final factor must be highlighted, namely the preponderance, territorially, economically, demographically and militarily of India. India accounts for over 75% of the regions population, for an almost equal amount of its landmass and for an even greater percentage of its GDP. It is unassailably the region's great power and has the potential, at least in the long term, to assume such a status at the global level. Intra-regional security relations and cooperation are, accordingly, dominated by bilateral relations between India and its neighbours and by the nature of those between India and extra-regional actors such as China and the United States. India's relationship with its neighbours is not, in this regard, dissimilar to that of the United States and other American states under the Monroe Doctrine and, indeed, beyond. According to Devin Hagerty, "[a]lthough it was never enunciated explicitly or officially, successive Indian governments have systematically pursued an active policy of denial in South Asia similar to that applied to the Western Hemisphere by the United States in the nineteenth century." [30] While Hagerty can, perhaps, be criticised for suggesting too early a terminal point in regard to US pursual of the Monroe Doctrine [31] his basic contention would appear to be accurate. India's regional security policy would thus appear to have two central, inter-connected, objectives, firstly to ensure stability within the region and, so far as possible, the assumption or continuance in power of friendly regimes, and secondly to prevent extra-regional interference by other powers. This has led to a situation in which, in the words of Shelton Kodikara, "[w]hile India perceives neighbours as being integral to its own security, the neighbours perceive India itself as a threat against which security is necessary." [32]

The relationship between India and Pakistan is perhaps the most significant factor in intra-regional security and presents the greatest obstacle to improved cooperation in this area. The greatest issue of contention between the two states is that concerning the State of Jammu and Kashmir (hereafter Kashmir) the status of which, at the time of partition and independence, remained unresolved. [33] The British refused to consider partition of Kashmir itself, though with the benefit of hindsight and notwithstanding the question of its Buddhist population and the opposition of the maharaja, this may, given the relatively clearly defined areas occupied by both the minority Hindu and majority Muslim populations, have had much to commend it. Despite the conclusion by the maharaja of "standstill" agreements with both India and Pakistan the two countries went to war over the territory in 1947 and again in 1965. The first of these conflicts brought about the accession by the maharaja to Indian rule, subject to consultation with the people of Kashmir regarding the territory's future status. In 1948 India raised the issue of what it termed "Pakistani aggression" at the United Nations where the Security Council formulated plans for a withdrawal of forces of both sides and for the holding of a plebiscite. A ceasefire became effective at the beginning of 1949 but despite this, and the interposition of a UN peacekeeping force, to date no solution to the conflict seems forthcoming. Neither party to the conflict appears willing to make meaningful compromises, the population of the territory is still to be consulted regarding its future status and, in the meantime, a UN presence has failed to prevent military exchanges of varying degrees of severity, the most recent of which occurred in the summer of 1999.

India and Pakistan also came into conflict over East Pakistan, the result of which was the creation, in 1971, of the state of Bangladesh. [34] The conflict arose after elections throughout Pakistan raised the spectre of secession on the part of the eastern half of the non-contiguous state. The Pakistani military government refused to countenance the demands for greater eastern autonomy proposed by the victorious Awami League and ordered a military response which resulted in the deaths of hundreds of thousands – some estimates claim millions – of Bangladeshis and an outpouring into India of approximately ten million refugees. India, in addition to providing equipment and training to the Bangladeshi *Mukti Bahini* (national army) became ever more embroiled in the conflict until finally open conflict between India and Pakistan erupted. Pakistan also initiated conflicts in Punjab and Kashmir, but the outcome on all fronts was a crushing defeat. One positive result of this most desperate situation was the installation of a civilian government in Islamabad, though this in no way signalled the end of the country's domestic political problems and the overall impact of the crisis was a further deterioration in Indo-Pakistani relations.

The nature of Indo-Pakistani relations has, since the two states gained independence, stood as the single greatest impediment to the construction of a meaningful collective security mechanism in South Asia. Both states have, as part of this confrontation, sought to develop their military capabilities, and in so doing throughout the years of the Cold War found both the USA and the USSR to be, in accordance with political allegiances, willing assistants. The possibility that this relationship could develop a character of even greater potential destructive power became a reality in the early summer of 1998 when first India, and then Pakistan, detonated nuclear devices. The full implications of these actions are, and hopefully will remain, unrealised, but as William Walker comments:

> "By conducting nuclear tests, and by the tenor of its announcements, India is the first state to overtly have proclaimed itself a nuclear power since China made its move in 1964. It has therefore crossed a political threshold, followed by Pakistan, that most people hoped would never be crossed again.
>
> In fact, the high emotions aroused by India's actions have quickly led India and Pakistan to cross not one but two thresholds: from an ambiguous to an unambiguous commitment to nuclear arms; and from non-weaponized to weaponized deterrence."[35]

The tests were lamentable in that they ran contrary to the international regime – essentially comprising the Comprehensive Test Ban Treaty (CTBT) and the Nuclear Non-Proliferation Treaty to which neither state is, in fact, a party – the primary intention of which is to prevent the spread of a nuclear weapons capability. However, the general context of Indo-Pakistani relations, and the specific rhetoric which surrounded the tests, raises even greater trepidation. As Walker notes:

> "[T]he Indian government provocatively asserted that 'India has a proven capacity for a weaponized nuclear programme' ... the Pakistani government even more provocatively asserted that 'the long-range Ghauri missile is already being capped with the nuclear warhead [*sic*] to give a befitting reply to any misadventure by the enemy.'"[36]

The current state of relations between the two states bears comparison with those between the USA and the Soviet Union during the darkest days of the Cold War. The fact that the arsenals are so much smaller is counter-balanced, if not even out-weighed, by the greater intensity and degree of animosity, by the presence of shared borders and disputed territories over and in which the militaries face and not irregularly engage one another, and by the lack of a secure second strike capability which increases the likelihood of a pre-emptive strike. The negative international response to the nuclear tests was welcome in its unanimity, but is likely to prove limited in its impact. Moreover, the nations of South Asia will be no more able than was the international community *en masse* to provide a mechanism to mitigate the now nuclear tensions which exist between India and Pakistan. In this regard the prospect for regional collective security is, perhaps, more bleak in South Asia than in any other region of the world.

The acrimonious nature of Indo-Pakistani relations have since independence been the most significant issue in intra-regional politics and it remains so to this day. There have, however, been other developments in intra-regional relations which have also undermined regional cooperation. Two major factors have conditioned relations between India and Bangladesh, firstly a sense of indebtedness and gratitude on the part of the former stemming from the means by which it gained independence and secondly water. The first of these factors clearly established a predisposition toward cordial relations, as did the existence of a common "enemy" in the form of Pakistan, but this was to prove a temporary phenomenon, the cessation of which was signalled by the putsch which resulted in the establishment of a military regime in Dhaka. Indeed the most tangible remnants of the 1971 conflict which gave rise to independence, namely the Indian forces stationed in Bangladesh, came to be resented as an occupying force and thus contributed to the deterioration in bilateral relations as did dispute as to the exact location of the border between the two states. It is however the construction of the Farakka Dam and its impact upon Bangladeshi water supplies and agriculture which has proved most divisive. The waters of the Ganges are sufficient to satisfy the needs of both countries in all but the dry season, but during this period India takes advantage of its upstream location to the detriment of its eastern neighbour. Solutions to the dispute so far suggested have proved fruitless, and while tensions between the two states cannot, in either intensity or potential consequences, be compared with Indo-Pakistani relations, they do provide a further hurdle to closer cooperation within South Asia.

Sri Lanka's relationship with India has benefited from the island status of the former, which has, with a limited number of minor exceptions, precluded the possibility of territorial disputes. Physical separation has not, however, prevented a process which, over time, has resulted in a significant number of Sri Lankans being able to trace their ancestry back to the Indian mainland and, in so far as these people represent a minority dissatisfied with central government control, the two states have been drawn into conflict. Sri Lanka's predominantly Hindu Tamils, who constitute approximately one-fifth of the county's population, have, since Sri Lankan independence in 1948, sought a greater degree of political autonomy than that afforded them by the government in Colombo. Lack of progress in this regard resulted in a radicalisation of political agendas in the late 1970s and the outbreak of civil war in 1983.

Following the outbreak of conflict India became progressively more involved. [37] Initially India acted as a mediator between the Tamil separatists and the Sinhalese government, although it did so while simultaneously allowing the separatists, in the form of the Liberation Tigers of Tamil Eelam (LTTE), to train in bases in the Tamil Nadu province of India. This latter aspect of Indian involvement was motivated by a desire to placate domestic sympathy for the LTTE and Sri Lanka's Tamil population, but the policy became unsustainable with the advent of direct Indian military involvement in the conflict. Domestic sympathy was also responsible in part for the decision by India to parachute relief supplies into Tamil areas of Sri Lanka against the wishes of the Colombo government which, at the time, was looking to press home a decisive military advance. The Indian government, for its part, feared that a conclusive military defeat, accompanied as it was likely to be by widescale loss of life, would trigger civil unrest in Tamil Nadu and the airdrop was thus part of a wider policy to ensure the return of the Sri Lankan government to the negotiating table. The Indians were successful in securing this return to negotiations the result of which was the Indo-Sri Lankan peace accords singed in July 1987. Under the terms of the accords an Indian "peacekeeping" force was deployed, tasked with guaranteeing and enforcing a cessation to hostilities. The force failed in this aim and instead found itself both engaged in heavy fighting with the LTTE which it had previously helped to train, and facing a violent backlash from Sinhalese nationalists. Having been in place for little over two years New Delhi agreed, under considerable pressure from the government in Colombo, to withdraw its forces. The process of withdrawal was completed by the Spring of 1990, official Indian estimates putting casualties amongst the peacekeepers at 1,100 dead and 2,800 wounded.

According to Devin Hagerty India pursued three inter-connected, though not always compatible, objectives during the civil conflict in Sri Lanka. The first of these was to assist in the stabilisation of Sri Lanka, the second to protect the Tamil minority from government security forces and the final objective was to forestall the intervention of external forces. [38] In pursuing these policies India's actions are, as Hagerty himself notes, reminiscent of those of the United States in its relations with the states of the Western Hemisphere. These parallels can be seen once more in Indian intervention in the Maldives in 1988 when New Delhi acted in support of the Maldivian President whose tiny country had been threatened by a coup. Strung out across the Indian Ocean some 500 miles south west of the mainland, the atoll's significance lies in its strategic location attested to by the attention paid to it by the Superpower adversaries of the Cold War. In this also lay the motivation for Indian intervention in 1988, for the coup, irrespective of its outcome, could only serve to enhance the attraction of great power backing. The significant likelihood that a state other than India may be prepared to lend such patronage and so gain a foothold in South Asia was reason enough for India to act. As Hagerty comments:

"The Maldives mission ... illustrated New Delhi's willingness to intervene in a neighbouring state to ensure regional stability. The quickness with which it responded, moreover, indicates that in light of reports that [the Maldivian President] had also approached the United States and Great Britain, the Indians were anxious to arrive first. As diplomats in the region noted at the time, the action 'underscores India's supremacy and its readiness to move quickly to head off intervention from outside the region."[39]

India's relations with Bhutan and Nepal have, in one significant regard, to be differentiated from those of the other states within South Asia, for these Himalayan kingdoms border not one but two regional powers, sandwiched, as they are, between India and China. Shortly after gaining independence India sought to assume the responsibilities of the former colonial power with regard to Bhutan, Nepal and Sikkim and in so doing incorporate them within an Indian controlled Southern Himalayan external policy network. This objective was secured, between 1949 and 1950, with the conclusion of bilateral treaties between India and the three Himalayan states under the terms of which India would abstain from intervening in the domestic affairs of its smaller neighbours but would assume effectively responsibility for their external relations. The Indo-Himalayan security system has failed, however, to provide India with the security blanket *vis-à-vis* China which provided the ultimate rationale for the treaty framework and has, in relation to the respective Himalayan parties, had a somewhat mixed history. As Shelton Kodikara comments

> "Th[e] policy eventuated the absorption of Sikkim in the Indian Union in 1975, and the stabilisation of Bhutan to the virtual status of a protectorate, with a foreign policy profile which was formally independent, but which towed the Indian line on major subcontinental security-related issues."[40]

Whilst in the cases of Sikkim and Bhutan India has, through different means, secured compliance with its security objectives, from an Indian perspective, Nepal has proved far less compliant. The strategic importance of Nepal to India had long been recognised by both parties. As Nehru famously commented:

> "From time immemorial, the Himalayas have provided us with a magnificent frontier. ... We cannot allow the barrier to be penetrated because it is also the principal barrier to India. Therefore, as much as we appreciate the independence of Nepal, we cannot allow anything to go wrong in Nepal, or permit that barrier to be crossed or weakened because that would also be a risk to our security."[41]

The intensification of Sino-Indian rivalry has, however, to a degree been exploited by Nepal so as to provide the government in Kathmandu with greater diplomatic manoeuvrability. This policy of playing the two regional powers off against one another culminated in the 1988-89 purchase by Nepal of Chinese arms, including anti-aircraft weaponry and a consequent deterioration in Indo-Nepalese relations. India claimed that the purchase violated bilateral arrangements between the two countries and perceived the affair as a case of Chinese interference within an established Indian sphere of influence. In response, India effectively imposed a trade blockade upon Nepal, but the shortages which ensued, rather than serving as intended to demonstrate to whom Nepal owed its "true" allegiance, showed signs of having the opposite effect. Realising the dangers inherent in the blockade policy, New Delhi resumed negotiations, the outcome of which was an agreement reached in 1990 which effective restored bilateral relations to their pre-dispute standing.

The Indo-Nepalese dispute illustrates well the difficulties faced by India in pursuing a security policy a principal objective of which is the exclusion of external actors from South Asia affairs. By virtue of its geographic location the region is one within which India, whatever its perceived interests and intentions, is unlikely to enjoy an unfettered role. It is rather the case that India will have to act, as it currently does, as the principal regional power, but in so doing it must formulate and pursue policies with a view to extra-regional responses, most immediately those of China. As the 20th century draws to a close China is often cited as a prime candidate to assume the role of a global superpower and while, both in terms of capabilities and aspirations, such claims may be exaggerated, it is self evidently the case that China does constitute a major security actor in South Asia. [42] Despite initially good Sino-Indian relations, this has manifested itself most clearly in the form of direct conflict between China and India, most notably in the 1962 border war which ended in a humiliating defeat for the latter. China has made extensive claims to Indian territory in both the northeast and northwest of the country, as well as to parts of Bhutan and Nepal which, as discussed above, have treaty relations with India regarding their external affairs. Some progress has been made over the issue of border demarcation, including agreements over parity of border forces, transparency in troop movements and mutual force reductions, [43] but despite this tensions remain in relations between the two Asian giants.

Several other, not wholly unconnected, factors have also served to impair Sino-Indian relations. The closeness of Sino-Pakistani relations is one such factor, not least because the warmth of the relationship is fuelled by the party's common animosity toward India. That all three states are known to possess a nuclear military capability only serves to accentuate the tensions in the region. Both China and Pakistan contest Indian title to parts of Kashmir, disputes which can have only been exacerbated by Pakistan's agreement in 1964 to hand part of the territory which it occupies over to China which, for its part, has assisted Pakistan, both through the provision of arms and at the diplomatic level, in its numerous conflicts with India. Sino-Indian relations have also suffered as a result of China's close involvement with the SLORC regime in Myanmar (Burma). [44] India has looked on with considerable anxiety as China has provided Myanmar with military and economic assistance, though most concern is no doubt generated by reports that Myanmar has accepted a Chinese offer to build a deep-water port on its western coast providing access to the Bay of Bengal and that this facility may be used as a Chinese military base. [45]

Whilst China, by virtue of its proximity, constitutes the most significant extra-regional actor, other states also play a significant role in regional affairs, notable amongst them the United States. The relationship between the two states has been characterised by a marked divergence in strategic objectives, though since the end of the Cold War these have receded somewhat. During the years of the US-Soviet confrontation India, despite its proclamations of non-alignment, enjoyed close relations with the Soviet Union, the two states signing the Indo-Soviet Treaty of Peace, Friendship and Cooperation in 1971. The treaty did not constitute a full military alliance but rather bound the two countries "to refrain from giving assistance to any party taking part in an armed conflict with the other party", [46] but this distinction carried little weight in Washington (or Beijing). The parties to the Indo-Pakistan conflict, which in 1971 was at the level of open hostility, thus assumed the roles of proxies in the superpower confrontation, Soviet support for India being countered by US (and Chinese) assistance to Pakistan. The early 1970s represented a low-point in Indo-US relations, but throughout the years of the Cold War the two states often found themselves in opposing camps. The Cold War provides much by way of the account for this, but it was also a result of India's (self proclaimed) role as leader of the Third World and non-aligned movement – a role for which it found itself, not by coincidence, in competition with China.

Soviet and subsequently Russian influence in the region lessened significantly with the end of the Cold War, though the United States has, in South Asia as in almost every other region of the world, maintained its status as a major security actor. In the absence of the Cold War confrontation US-Indian relations improved, though the issue of nuclear proliferation mitigated against the assumption by Washington of closer ties with New Delhi, as well as creating new tensions in its relationship with Islamabad. For the region of South Asia the end of the Cold War heralded a significant change in security dynamics, but the continuation, and indeed in so far as it became a nuclear confrontation the intensification, of the Indo-Pakistan conflict prevented the region from realising the benefits of cooperation which elsewhere proved less elusive. The absence of a regional security mechanism is both indicative of, and contributory to, this problem.

South Asia is, in fact, not wholly devoid of a regional cooperative mechanism, but in practice this has proved to be less than efficacious and in the field of South Asian inter-state and regional security there exists no organisation possessed with competence to act. [47] The Charter of the South Asian Association for Regional Cooperation, whilst citing in its Preamble the desire of member states to promote "peace, stability, amity and progress in the region through strict adherence to the principles of the United Nations Charter ..." makes no reference to issues of security. This silence is made all the more deafening by the General Provisions of the SAARC Charter which provide that decisions must, in all cases, be made on the basis of unanimity and that "bilateral and contentious issues shall be excluded from the deliberations." [48] There was at the time of the SAARC's formation in 1985 little, if any, desire to establish a regional security mechanism, a clear reflection of the precarious state of intra-regional relations. The presence of a nuclear dimension to the Indo-Pakistan conflict singles it out as the greatest threat to security at the regional level – and potentially far beyond – but, as has been highlighted above, this is far from being the only source of regional instability. In the absence of a regional mechanism for dealing with such conflagrations it may be that India itself will come to act as the guardian of regional security.

Following its intervention in the Maldives Indian Prime Minister Rajiv Gandhi, when asked in Parliament if India would "extend help whenever any government is in trouble and if it was laying down a 'Gandhi Doctrine' ... along the lines of the US Monroe Doctrine." replied that India had acted because the SAARC was incapable of doing so. [49] That India then, and it may be suggested now, sees itself constituting the regional security mechanism for South Asia may provide a solution to the specific variety of crisis experienced by the Maldives in 1988, but, as noted at the outset of this discussion, it is likely to do little other than exacerbate the security concerns of the majority of states within the region.

CONCLUSION

The modern experience of both the Middle East and South Asia tends to confirm one of the fundamental weaknesses of any general regional analysis of security concerns. That is to say that the more fragile or unstable a regional security structure, the less likely it is that an actually or potentially effective regional defence or security system will develop. Whether this is the direct product of instability in itself, as in the case of the Arab League, or of an inherently hegemonistic regional structure, as in the case of South Asia, the end result is that, in effect, no regional peace support or enforcement option exists. If nothing else were to dictate the continuing centrality of the UN role in peace support mechanisms, this alone would suffice to do so. Even in such an attenuated role regional organisations may still perform some valuable work, even if as no more than potential "talking shops", but these cases serve starkly to warn against an simplistic resort to regionalism as a universal panacea.

NOTES

1. See Chapter 7.
2. For discussion see R.W. Macdonald, *The League of Arab States* (Princeton University Press, 1965), p.9-12.
3. The full text in English will be found in Khalil II at pp.53-56.
4. Full text in Khalil II at p.58.
5. See below.
6. Text in English in Khalil II, pp.101-2.
7. See below
8. For detailed discussion of *Jihad* see Abdur Rahman I. Doi, *Shahr'ia: The Islamic Law* (Ta Ha Publishers, 1984), Chapter 25.
9. This term has come to be used in the West to describe certain forms of extreme Islamic political movement, although this usage is in fact a misunderstanding. Fundamentalism refers strictly to a

Christian literalist approach to Biblical interpretation and is otiose so far as Islamic approaches to the *Qu'ran* are concerned. In particular, many of the extremist movements characterised as "fundamental-ist" can be argued anyway not to adhere to orthodox Muslim teaching in any event.

10. For a near contemporary account see Josephus, *The Jewish Revolt*.
11. "Common Era", this term is used in reference to Jewish history in preference to the Christian "Ante Dominum" (AD) formula. The year count is the same.
12. A complete answer to the "revisionists" will be found, amongst many others, in G. Hirschfeld, ed., *The Policies of Genocide* (Allen and Unwin, 1986).
13. See, e.g., Genesis 12:1-7; Exodus 3:16-17 and Deuteronomy 1:6-8.
14. The text will be found in English in Muhammad Khalil, *The Arab States and the Arab League: A Documentary Record*, Vol. II (Khayats, Beirut, 1962), hereinafter Khalil II, in English at p.483.
15. For general background P. Brogan, *World Conflicts* (Bloomsbury, 1992), p.294 ff.
16. Herzl is now regarded as one of the founding Fathers of the State of Israel, although this, like many such reputations, is a little overstated.
17. Khalil II, p.484.
18. See I. Pogany, *The Security Council and the Arab-Israeli Conflict* (Gower, 1984), p.17.
19. The test will be found in Khalil II, at pp. 493-4.
20. UN General Assembly Resolution 181(II) of 29 November 1947. A minority on UNSCOP had favoured a Federal Israeli-Arab unified State in Palestine.
21. Khalil II, p.61.
22. Ibid., p.55.
23. UN Security Council Resolution 62 of 16 November 1948.
24. A Conference held in Geneva in July 1999 under the auspices of the ICRC concluded that the West Bank is an occupied territory and that the relevant provisions of 1949 Geneva Convention IV are applicable therein for the protection of the civilian population, *inter alia*, against reprisals and collective punishments.
25. R.W. Macdonald, op.cit., pp.285-6.
26. For detailed discussion see I. Pogany, *The Arab League and Peacekeeping in the Lebanon*(Avebury, 1987), Chapter 6.
27. See UN Security Council Resolution 678 of 29 November 1990; for discussion see H. McCoubrey and N.D. White, "International Law and the Use of Force in the Gulf, (1991) X *International Relations*, pp.347-373.
28. For a general discussion of South Asian politics see C. Baxter *et al*, *Government and Politics in South Asia*, (Westview Press, 1998). For more specific discussion of security related issues see S. U. Kodikara (ed.), *South Asian Strategic Issues: Sri Lankan Perspectives*, (Sage, 1990) and M. S. Agwani *et al* (eds.), *South Asia: Stability and Regional Co-operation*, (CRRID, 1983).
29. See C. Wagner, "Regional Cooperation in South Asia: Review of the SAARC", *Aussenpolitik*, 1993, Vol 44(2), pp.182-3.
30. D. T. Hagerty, "India's Regional Security Doctrine", *Asian Survey*, 1991, Vol 31, p.363.
31. See Chapter 5
32. S. U. Kodikara, quoted in See C. Wagner, "Regional Cooperation in South Asia: Review of the SAARC", p. 184.
33. See S. Johal, *Conflict and Integration in Indo-Pakistan Relations*, (University of California Press, 1989) and S. Ganguly, *The Origins of War in South Asia; Indo-Pakistani Conflicts Since 1947*, (Westview, 1986)
34. See D. K. Patil, *The Lightning Campaign: The Indo-Pakistan War, 1971*, (Compton Press, 1972); R. Jackson, *South Asian Crisis: India-Pakistan-Bangla Desh* (Chatto and Windus, 1975); and O. Marwah, "India's Military Intervention in East Pakistan, 1971-72", *Modern African Studies*, 1979, Vol 13(4), pp. 549-80.
35. W. Walker, pp. 517-18.
36. Ibid, p.518.
37. See A. Sivarajah, "Indo-Sri Lanka Relations and Sri Lanka's Ethnic Crisis: The Tamil Nadu Factor", in see S. U. Kodikara (ed.), *South Asian Strategic Issues: Sri Lankan Perspectives*, pp.135-59; and D. T. Hagerty, "India's Regional Security Doctrine", pp. 353-8.

38. D. T. Hagerty, pp. 353-4.
39. Ibid, p. 359.
40. S. U. Kodikara (ed.), *South Asian Strategic Issues: Sri Lankan Perspectives*, pp. 24-5.
41. Ibid, p. 25
42. H. C. Hinton, "China as an Asian Power", in T. W. Robinson and D. Shambaugh (eds.), *Chinese Foreign Policy: Theory and Practice* (Clarendon Press, 1997), pp. 348-72 and G. Klintworth, "Greater China and Regional Security", *Australian Journal of International Affairs*, 1994, Vol. 48(2), pp. 211-28.
43. G. Klintworth, p. 222.
44. See A. Selth, "Burma and the Strategic Competition between China and India", *Journal of Strategic Studies*, 1996, Vol. 19(2), pp. 213-30.
45. Ibid., p. 215.
46. M. S. Agwani *et al*, p. 95.
47. See A. Ahsan, *SAARC: A Perspective* (University of Dhaka Press, 1992); and A. M. Reed, "Regionalization in South Asia: Theory and Praxis", *Pacific Affairs*, 1998, Vol. 70, pp. 235-51.
48. Article X(2).
49. D. T. Hagerty, p. 360.

CHAPTER 9

The Potential and Dangers of
Regional Peace Support Action

The foregoing regional analyses have shown the diversity of character, objectives and capacities to be found amongst regional organisations which are, or might potentially become, involved with security or peace support action. These differences are the natural product of the differing historical and political experiences of the various regions and sub-regions and their consequent security concerns. The dangers, and even the practical impossibility, of "parachuting" inappropriate models from one region into another were pointedly demonstrated by the less than fortunate histories of, e.g., the SEATO [1] and CENTO [2] organisations which were, respectively, endeavours to import the NATO concept into Southeast Asia and the Middle East. Indeed in some cases, such as the Middle East and South Asia, [3] both the origins of the existing organisations and the nature of regional relations effectively preclude the adoption of any practical or useful regional peace support option. This diversity of institutional provision and availability is the foundation of one of the principal themes of this book, that no simple or singular solution to global, or regional, security problems is offered through the utilisation of regional organisations and arrangements. It is rather the case that the regional option affords a range of choices which have been contemplated, at least in principle, from the outset of the UN era, and indeed are *required* to be taken up by the Security Council "where appropriate" under the terms of article 53 of the Charter. To this degree the effect of the resource-driven post-Cold War UN peace support crisis has not been in some fashion to generate a regional peace-support option, or necessity, but rather to refocus attention upon an aspect of UN security architecture which had not so much been neglected as distorted, along with much else, by the Cold War ideological dynamic.

In principle the greater utilisation of regional organisations and arrangements in peace support action does not require a reshaping of legal understanding, since article 53 of the UN Charter already makes *prima facie* adequate provision for the possibility. Some greater degree of political and strategic reorientation may be conceded to be necessary, but in fact, in this as in other matters, the international relations, international organisational and international legal perspectives are inextricably linked. The possible legal complications, especially as between regional arrangements and the UN, in the new peace support context were pointedly illustrated in the 1999 Kosovo crisis is which the NATO air strikes prior to the establishment of KFOR were effectively left in an unsatisfactory legal limbo – not explicitly authorised but also not, when the opportunity arose, denounced as unlawful. [4] The exploration of the regional option in the developing post-Cold War global security architecture in fact returns the debate to the fundamental issues of the dichotomy between globalism and regionalism which were first explored at the outset of the UN era in the 1940s.

It will be recalled that although the collective security concept of the UN Charter rested upon the idea of the capacity of the collective power of the States gathered together in the UN to outface the individual power of any actual or potential aggressor, it was clear from the beginning that the practical functioning of the Security Council would rest upon the backing, or at least the acquiescence, of the major Powers. This was enshrined in the veto power, which Cordell Hull considered to be a *sine qua non* for the involvement of the major Powers with the Council. [5] It was indeed in the concern of the smaller Powers that their security interests might be overlooked or even imperilled in this context that the preserved "self-defence" provision of article 51 of the Charter and the initial impetus for regional security development had their genesis. Significantly, regions which feared the continuing impacts of regional hegemonism or neo-colonial interference, such as South America and the Middle East, were leaders in relation to both self-defence provision and the regionalist debate. This is not to suggest any simple dichotomy between big power globalism and small/medium power regionalism, the interaction involved in reality a far more complex balance of interests. The end result was, as outlined in earlier discussion, essentially a compromise which embodied the ultimate primacy of the globalist UN concept, of which Inis Claude remarks that,

> "The finished UN Charter conferred general approval upon existing and anticipated regional organizations, but contained provisions indicating the purpose of making them serve as adjuncts to the United Nations and subjecting them in considerable measure to the direction and control of the central organization. The Charter reflected the premise that the United Nations should be supreme, and accepted regionalism conditionally, with evidence of anxious concern that lesser agencies should be subordinated to and harmonized with the United Nations. ... [It] involved permissive concessions to regionalism; it did not, as Churchill had urged, involve fundamental reliance upon regional agencies as the 'massive pillars' of the world system." [6]

The primacy of the UN over regional security arrangements was thus accepted from the outset, and indeed was necessarily so. Such organisations or arrangements which include the possibility of the non-consensual deployment of armed force within their remit expressly rely upon article 51 of the UN Charter and acknowledge the need in all other cases to secure Security

Council authorisation. It has been contended above that the arguments seeking to qualify this proposition in the context of the NATO air strikes in the 1999 Kosovo crisis were neither adequate nor necessary. [7] The development of regional structures, like that of the UN itself, were then moulded, or distorted, by the Cold War confrontation. Organisations such as NATO and the Warsaw Pact emerged as mirror image collective defence structures on either side of the "iron curtain" ideological divide, the end of the Cold War then caused a reorientation of the one and the dissolution, following that of the former-Soviet Union, of the other. Others, such as the OAS and the OAU, were less directly shaped but still strongly influenced by the Cold War context, whilst ASEAN in particular emerged from the aftermath of regional disasters generated by the combination of the last phases of colonialism and the new external interference of the Cold War. The processes of reorientation and invitation to an expanded peace-support role, or roles, following upon the end of the Cold War did not, and could not, simply return the debate upon collective defence and security to the 1940s. In contrast with the situation described by Inis Claude at the outset of the UN era, the resource-driven crisis of peace support in the post-Cold War era means that in fact, if not in theory, a greater reliance upon regional agencies is inevitable. They may not have assumed the Churchillian role of "massive pillars" of the international security system, but the basic issues of globalism and regionalism which underpinned the original debates at Dumbarton Oaks and San Francisco have returned for renewed debate in a different context and with rather different foci of interest.

GLOBALISM AND REGIONALISM: THE CONTINUING CONTEXT OF DEBATE

Although the context of consideration in the post-Cold War era differs very significantly from that which moulded discussion in the years immediately following the Second World War, there is a clear continuity in the underlying imperatives. A powerful and effective regional organisation may, on the one hand, serve as an effective guarantor of peace and security, but it may also threaten to become a vehicle for a hegemonistic distortion of regional relations. The UN faces a rather different problem. The UN is hardly a credible global hegemon, even if it wished to become such, but its essential and continuing role in peace support and enforcement is one of sustaining a system founded upon universal international norms applied, to the greatest possible extent – albeit with all too many defaults, in a uniform fashion. The UN will almost certainly retain the option of peace-support and even peace enforcement action, indeed it will in practice have to do so, but the maintenance of universally applicable governing norms may properly be seen as its irreducible core function in this area. Ultimate control by and answerability to the United Nations is essential if a meaningful global security structure is to be maintained. Without such control and accountability a policy of peace support regionalisation would essentially be a first step along a road which leads back to the fragmented balance of power structures of the pre-1914 era, with incalculable but almost certainly disastrous consequences.

These basic issues were explicitly recognised by Boutros Boutros-Ghali in *Supplement to Agenda for Peace* in remarking that,

> "The experience of the last few years has demonstrated both the value that can be gained and the difficulties that can arise when the Security Council entrusts enforcement tasks to groups of Member States. On the positive side, this arrangement provides the Organization with an enforcement capacity it would not otherwise have and is greatly preferable to the unilateral use of force by Member States without reference to the United Nations. On the other hand, the arrangement can have a negative impact on the Organization's stature and credibility. There is also the danger that the States concerned may claim international legitimacy and approval for forceful actions that were not in fact envisaged by the Security Council when it gave its authorization to them. ..." [8]

Strictly speaking, these remarks were addressed to *ad hoc* "groups of States" but may properly also be applied to the more formal "groups of States" gathered together in regional organisations and arrangements. Boutros Boutros-Ghali went on to add pertinently that,

> "The capacity of regional organizations for peacemaking and peace-keeping varies considerably. ...Given their varied capacity, the differences in their structures, mandates and decision-making processes and the variety of forms that cooperation with the United Nations is already taking, it would not be appropriate to try to establish a universal model for their relationship with the United Nations. Nevertheless it is possible to identify certain principles on which it should be based.

> Such principles include: (a) Agreed mechanisms for consultation should be established, but need not be formal; (b) *The primacy of the United Nations, as set out in the Charter, must be respected.* ..." [9]

The emphasis is added. It would indeed, for the reasons suggested above, be neither possible nor desirable to implement any universal pattern of regional peace support. The requirement is rather to establish a mechanism of choice amongst such options for means and methods of action as may be available in a given case which is capable of achieving the optimum balance between efficacy on the one hand and control and accountability on the other. Once again the 1999 Kosovo crisis affords a type example of both the possible benefits and the certain dangers of regional peace support devolution.

The 1999 Kosovo crisis has been considered above [10] and its detail requires no further rehearsal here. The development of the international response to the crisis, from the NATO air strikes to the deployment of KFOR, however, clearly demonstrated both the benefits and the dangers arising from a regionalisation of peace enforcement action. The analysis which follows must be prefaced by two vitally important caveats. Firstly the Kosovo crisis arose in the context of a UN system in transition from the Cold-War mixed collective security and balance of (Super)power paradigm to one the precise shape of which is as yet far from clarified. The dangerous uncertainties and ambiguities, both legal and political, which beset the situation and the respective Security Council and NATO responses should thus be seen against this background and treated with due caution in consideration as a precedent for future peace support/enforcement development. Secondly, to reiterate a point already well established, the NATO military alliance is in a number of respects markedly atypical amongst regional arrangements and for the present purpose its actions in Kosovo offer an important example for analysis but not a universal model of possible modes of action.

As it has been remarked above, the Kosovo crisis represented in its essentials a situation in which the Security Council should have acted but faced major political impediments in doing so, whereas NATO was able act but was unable to show any unequivocal authority for its immediate response. From the Security Council viewpoint, the crisis was not only an internal Yugoslav (Serbo-Montenegrin) humanitarian disaster involving at least quasi-genocide, it was also manifestly a threat to regional peace and security potentially involving conflict between Albania, FYROM, Greece and Serbia and, in a worst case scenario, a broader European war. In this regard it manifestly fell within the meaning of article 39 of the UN Charter. The historic Russo-Serbian connection, going well back into the Tsarist era and in 1914 one of the mainsprings of the First World War, together with ingrained Russian and Chinese sensitivities over minority populations within national borders, rendered the issue supremely delicate as between the Permanent Members of the Council and rendered a veto upon any initial decision upon robust enforcement act highly likely. NATO, in contrast, had the material capacity to act and, subject to general international law, there is no reason to doubt its internal constitutional capacity. Again, as remarked above, the NATO action in former-Yugoslavia, in all its respects [11] fell outside the core NATO remit of self defence action under article 51 of the Charter, as set out within strict geographical limits by articles 5 and 6 of the 1949 North Atlantic Treaty. This core remit may, however, be considered as defining the *obligations* of the Member States, but cannot limit the inherent powers of the Member Sovereign States. There is thus no reason why NATO Members should not undertake other, lawful, action by consent using the infrastructure which they themselves have set up. It may be emphasised that this is indeed the only internal legal basis upon which NATO could engage in any peace support or peace enforcement action *stricto sensu*. The immediate key question is therefore not one of internal authorisation but that of external control and accountability, to and by the UN.

It is here that the real dangers of the Kosovo experience emerge. The claims of NATO to have acted upon an extension of earlier Security Council Resolutions were at best thin and the arguments of "humanitarian intervention", whilst far from without ethical grounding, enter an area of grave legal doubt. The special arguments of "legal dissociation" between a government and the people, or some part of them, who are governed [12] may sit well in specific relation to Kosovo. However, as a general invitation to intervention in any State which some other (powerful) State deems to be "unrepresentative", it is fundamentally subversive of the whole idea of collective security, especially when the UN is effectively excluded. Such arguments should not be linked with the adoption by, e.g., the OAS of ideas of democratisation as a part of a regional security concept – the focus there being upon the impact of the overthrow of a democratic regime rather than a claimed right of intervention to create such a government. It is also much to be regretted that, presumably for reasons of media "spin", some NATO political leaders adopted a rhetoric of "just war" which has no place in modern international law or international relations analysis and is of most sinister potential significance. It does not follow from this that the NATO air strikes were therefore unequivocally a violation of article 2(4) and hence unlawful. Although they were clearly aimed to some degree, at the "territorial integrity" of Serbia, in so far as they were undertaken to halt the genocidal practices of the Serbian regime they cannot be said to have been actions "inconsistent with the purposes of the United Nations". When the Security Council considered a Russian motion that the NATO action was unlawful, the proposition was defeated on a 12:3 vote. Even so, the impetuosity of NATO decision-making is open to considerable political question. The ground commitment ultimately accepted in June 1999 as part of the agreement brokered by President Ahtisaari of Finland and Prime Minister Chernomyrdin of Russia, and finally implemented in the deployment of the NATO-led KFOR, must seem to have been *ab initio* a necessary part of any final resolution of the crisis. That, in the case of Kosovo, this should take the form of a NATO-led endeavour with Russian involvement may also be seen in retrospect as both appropriate and inevitable. Whether Serbia could have been brought to abandon its genocidal policies in Kosovo, with their inherent horrors and their regional security threat, without robust military action must be doubted. It must also, however, be asked why the action, merging perhaps into what became the KFOR operation, could not have been attempted under an OSCE umbrella, whilst remaining NATO-led, thus including Russia – with its ability to put pressure upon Belgrade – from the beginning? The matter must now remain speculative but it is possible that had this approach been adopted the impediments to straightforward Security Council authorisation might have been avoided with manifest legal, political and practical advantage.

What lessons are then to be learnt from this episode? The potential dangers of Kosovo as a precedent are self-evident. The apparent sidelining of the Security Council in the initial NATO action inevitably raises the perils of fragmentation and hegemonism to which Inis Claude implicitly refers in his analysis of the regional UN debates upon the globalist/regionalist dichotomy. This is not to suggest that NATO in Kosovo actually entertained hegemonistic ambitions, the problem arises rather in respect of what the initial NATO position might later be used to support. The ideas of "just war" and "fundamental dissociation" which are already, in late 1999, emerging from the crisis are symptomatic of this. By the same token the Security Council found itself impeded by power bloc politics similar to those of the Cold War from effective action in the face of a manifest threat of South East European security, granted the possible entanglement of, e.g., Albania, FYROM [13] and Greece, as well as a gross humanitarian crisis. In this respect it was initially prevented from fulfilling its most basic purpose, as defined in the Preamble to the UN Charter, of " [uniting] strength to maintain international peace and security." The seeming choice between a technically lawful inaction which would have permitted a dangerous exacerbation of regional destabilisation and, at least, quasi-genocide to run its course and robust regional "enforcement" action upon the thinnest and most questionable of initial authorities illustrates pointedly the opposing perils which regionalisation must avoid if it is to generate a viable new peace-support paradigm or paradigms. If the signals from Kosovo actually indicated a movement towards uncontrolled and unaccountable regional military action, dragging the Security Council helplessly in its train with little role beyond that of retrospective validation, the outlook would be bleak indeed. Such a development would in fact mark the end of any meaningful global collective security system and would threaten a relapse into the abyss of competing hegemonic power blocs upon a scale far more dangerous even than that of the Cold War and bringing to belated fruition the worst fears entertained at Dumbarton Oaks and San Francisco at the beginning of the UN era. Fortunately, to advance so dismal a conclusion upon the basis of the Kosovo experience would be an excessively pessimistic over-reaction.

The Serbian allegations that NATO flagrantly ignored international law and the Security Council in its response to Kosovo may be suggested to have been, at best, over-stated. The argument that the air strikes were a violation of article 2(4) of the UN Charter in particular had very little objective foundation. The air strikes were not an attempt to settle an international dispute through unlawful aggression, as, for example, was the Argentine invasion of the Falkland Islands in 1982 or the Iraqi invasion of Kuwait in 1990. They were, rather, an ambiguously founded attempt to resolve a serious threat to regional security and to stop grave violations of international law, including the commission of actual or quasi-Genocide, following the failure of diplomatic attempts to end the crisis. At the same time the political, and arguably the military, strategy pursued may be thought to have been flawed, not least in reference to the failure to use an OSCE mechanism as suggested above. Be that as it may, the ultimate result was one entered into under Security Council authority and, in effect – although not expressly, within the letter and spirit of article 53 of the Charter. The processes which led to the June 1999 agreement and the deployment of KFOR were far from ideal but they may be suggested to have represented a faltering exploration of a new form of security crisis management at a particular and difficult point in international political and legal development. The long term procedural answers undoubtedly lie in the processes of development of both the relationship between regional arrangements and the Security Council and the structure and *modus operandi* of the Security Council itself. In this respect the Kosovo crisis may ultimately point to a positive way forward.

THE BROADER REGIONAL PERSPECTIVES

The lessons to be learnt from the Kosovo experience include both matters closely particular to the specific situation and, as suggested above, conclusions of a much more general application. The most general suggested resultant norm, that of procedural flexibility in selection amongst such peace support options as may be available in a given situation is, by its nature, conditioned by the diverse range both of the agencies and the situations which may be involved. The prospects and dangers may readily be illustrated by reference to other post-Cold War security crises.

The 1990-91 Gulf Conflict and its aftermath may be seen as highly significant in this context. The initial dispute over oil rights as between Iraq and Kuwait, in which respect Iraq may have had a case, led to the Iraqi invasion and occupation of the Emirate in flagrant violation of article 2(4) of the UN Charter. In this context the UN had, perhaps, four *prima facie* possible options. These were, in an admittedly crude categorisation, (i) diplomatic pressure perhaps backed by non-military sanctions under article 41 of the UN Charter, (ii) the creation and deployment of a UN "Blue Helmet" enforcement force, (iii) enforcement action under the aegis of the Arab League, the regional organisation of which both Iraq and Kuwait are members, or (iv) action through some "coalition of the willing". Of these apparent options the first and second may be dismissed in the circumstances as both impractical and almost certainly inefficacious. The third, that of the genuine regional option, might at first sight seem to have offered rather more hope had it been pursued. In practice, however, the Arab League is far more a peace and confidence building than an "enforcement" organisation [14] and, in part but not entirely because of the distortions occasioned by the Arab-Israeli conflicts, has a very uncertain capacity for co-ordinated military action upon the scale and degree of immediacy called for in the circumstances. The 1950 inter-Arab Treaty of Joint Defence and Economic Co-operation was not invoked by the parties in conflict and the Emir in fact sought the aid of friendly States, including the USA and other Western Powers as an act of collective defence under article 51 of the UN Charter. The resulting action, in effect by a powerful "coalition of the willing" was then "adopted" by the UN Security Council under Resolution 678 of 19 November 1990 authorising "all necessary means" – a euphemism for armed force – for the expulsion of the Iraqi occupying forces from Kuwait. [15] The initial coalition action was successful in that the national sovereignty of the Emirate was indeed restored and the Iraqi occupiers were expelled. This appeared to be, and indeed was, a significant confirmation of the actual and potential value of "coalitions of the willing" in terms of immediate response to aggression. The more difficult questions arise in relation to the aftermath of the conflict.

Notwithstanding the self-evidently demanding nature of the task of enforcement, it is commonly the case that the tasks of post-conflict restoration and peace-building are yet more difficult. In the case of the 1990-91 Gulf Conflict there remained a dynamically unstable and aggressive State which had generated two major regional conflicts against its neighbours in the 1980-88 Gulf War and the 1990-91 Gulf Conflict and had, at least in the former, demonstrated its willingness to employ chemical weapons of mass destruction against both the victims of its international aggression and against its own people in Iraqi Kurdistan. The long and unsatisfactory record of UN weapons inspections in Iraq after 1991 requires no further recitation here, although it stands as an example of the generic difficulties of arms control verification. In the present context more troubling questions arise from the continuation of sanctions over a period, at the time of writing, of nearly a decade from the end of the hostilities and occupation of Kuwait. Comment upon this subject must be prefaced by acknowledgement of the fact that, like the Milosevic regime in Serbia during the 1999 Kosovo crisis, the Baghdad Ba'ath regime proved adept at manipulating elements of the Western media and laying the blame for the effects of the sanctions entirely upon the Western Powers and the UN. In fact the intransigent uncooperativeness of the Iraqi government and their unwillingness to distribute, e.g., the medical supplies which had been made available had a very large role to play in the very real consequent sufferings of the Iraqi people. Nonetheless, the value and effect of the sanctions regime raises serious questions about this mode of enforcement and the more so where one of the linchpins of the willingness of the "coalition of the willing" in the first instance lay in the actual and perceived threat posed by the attack upon Kuwait to powerful Western economic interests. The idea that the non-military sanctions provided for by article 41 of the UN Charter, and especially economic sanctions, can properly be seen as an initial and milder response in comparison with more coercive measures has increasingly come to be questioned in the post-Cold War era. The experience of post-1991 Iraq, as also Haiti, has strongly reinforced these doubts. [16] Indeed, in all too many cases economic sanctions may prove to be ineffective in their impact upon delinquent governments whilst devastating local economies and inflicting suffering upon some of the very peoples whom the UN seeks to protect [17] and even raising the levels of domestic political support for the regimes concerned. In the case of the post-1991 response to Iraq it may be suggested that the routes of diplomatic and political pressure had more to be said for them than damaging and ineffective sanctions accompanied by sporadic military action which in many cases did little more than offer the Saddam Hussein regime propaganda opportunities whilst putting other Middle Eastern governments, with little sympathy for Baghdad, into an increasingly embarrassing situation. The impression was given of a weak UN permitting the continuance of a *modus operandi* which had had its proper and successful role in the early stages of the crisis but which had lost much of its point in the later stages. It may here be noted that whilst the use of the provision of article 6 of the UN Charter that

> "A Member of the United Nations which has persistently violated the Principles contained in the present Charter may be expelled from the Organisation by the General Assembly upon the recommendation of the Security Council"

might presently be politically impractical, a reformed and reinvigorated Security Council and General Assembly may one day wish to consider its use as a diplomatic and political weapons of far greater potential efficacy than the, to date, universally unavailing article 41 mechanism. More immediately, the

Western Powers could, and should, ponder the folly of their earlier policy of arming and supporting the Iraqi military machine. [18]

For the present purpose the ultimate lesson of the 1990-91 Gulf Conflict, with its immediate success and much less satisfactory aftermath, is ultimately not one of the exercise of choice – which may here be argued to have been initially exercised both effectively and appropriately – but rather that of the need for continuing and effective engagement with the issues by the Security Council. In short, it may be said that the evolving exigencies of long-term crisis management render the processes of choice and option selection a continuing necessity and not a matter of single decision.

The debacles of the Somali experience and the African Great Lakes crisis reinforce this message but do so with significant additional elements. The detail of these events has been outlined above [19] but certain points require to be re-emphasised for the present purpose. The failure in Somalia of UNOSOM, by reason in large part of inadequate direction and the familiar affliction of under-resourcing, led to the creation of the largely US UNITAF force ("Operation Restore Hope") which itself became mired in the Somali factional conflict as did its final successor, UNOSOM II. Although there was an achievement of significant humanitarian relief, the record of UN, and in effect US, peace support action in Somalia must be reckoned to have been one of abject failure. Indeed the Somali experience was one of the building blocks for the developing concept of regional peace support, although the extent to which the particular policy of an "African solution to African problems" must in the case of Somalia be thought to be no more encouraging than the experience of attempted external "solutions" proved to be.

The genocidal conflicts in Rwanda and Burundi seem at first sight to offer an even more doleful message. The failure of the UNAMIR force in the face of the renewed political crisis following the double assassination of the Presidents of Burundi and Rwanda in 1994 cannot fairly be attributed to the peace support mechanisms in themselves, but the response of the international community thereafter was disastrously ineffective. The replacement UN force, UNAMIR II, was accorded a manifestly inadequate mandate in the circumstances and offered such slight resources and support by the UN Member States that its viability in any shape or form was rendered deeply questionable. The end result, the French-led, and almost entirely French-constituted, "Operation Turquoise" was approved by the Security Council with the greatest reluctance and by the narrowest of margins. Whilst France undoubtedly had genuine humanitarian motives it also had an extensive post-colonial agenda which more than justified some of the doubts entertained by the Security Council. "Operation Turquoise" did again achieve some slight measure of humanitarian success, but was in other respects short-lived and a manifest failure. The final deployment of UNAMIR II, after further scenes of genocidal slaughter and even then still grossly under-resourced was the final scene of a scandal of incompetence and unconcern which raises serious questions not only about peace-support mechanisms but also about the value and future of the Security Council itself. In effect, faced with an inability to create an effective "Blue Helmet" force and the lack of any practically available regional resource, the UN Security Council attempted, *faut de mieux*, to avail itself of a neo-colonial interventionist force, with predictably disastrous results. The lesson, apart from rather dispiriting conclusions about the international community as a whole and the Permanent Members of the UN Security Council in particular, would seem to be the rather obvious one of the necessity for effective contingency planning. It clearly is not possible to predict where the next security crisis might emerge, Yugoslavia would have been a low priority in any such list complied in the early 1980s, it is however possible to develop a sense of the available resources in the various regions and how they might properly be deployed, and more importantly not deployed, in any hypothetical case of need. This perhaps is the most important of all the lessons to emerge from the post-Cold War peace-support experiences and is one which will be explored further in the concluding chapter.

THE POTENTIAL BENEFITS OF REGIONALISM

In the light of the above considerations it is possible to suggest the outline of both the benefits and the dangers of a regionalisation of peace-support action. In the first place it is clear from the experience, *inter alia*, of Yugoslavia, Somalia and the African Great Lakes that *some* use of regional organisations in peace support is not so much an option as a necessity in the context of the resource-driven crisis of post-Cold War peace support.

The principal virtue of this necessity lies precisely in the availability of resources. The capacities of the various regional agencies are, as earlier chapters have made clear, highly various in their character and quality and in this lies the key to any ultimate analysis of the balance of benefits and dangers represented by a regionalisation of peace support. In terms of purely military capability the most immediately obvious example may be found in the contrasts between the capabilities of the ill-mandated and under-resourced UNPROFOR "Blue Helmet" force and the various NATO-led forces, IFOR, SFOR and KFOR, in former-Yugoslavia. An established military alliance such as NATO has the obvious advantages over any *ad hoc* arrangement, be it "Blue Helmet" or otherwise, of effective joint command structures, developed, if not perfect, interoperability and practical experience of combined exercises and operations. These several advantages are especially marked in the case of NATO, although the rapid post-Cold War expansion of the alliance may generate future questions over interoperability and, possibly, command structure. Nonetheless, it seems likely in at the very least the medium term that NATO will remain much the most operationally capable of the various regional arrangements. At the same time, in much more difficult circumstances and with much less joint operational experience, the multinational, albeit predominantly Nigerian, ECOMOG forces [20] – essentially the "enforcement" branch of ECOWAS, and more distantly of the OAU in West Africa – is developing a considerable potential.

It would of course be a mistake to presume that the resource advantages of regional organisations are limited to military capabilities. To take an obvious example, ASEAN and, in practice, even the ARF, have an extremely limited joint military enforcement potential, but they have played a considerable and beneficial role in regional peace and confidence building. In this regard the East Asian experience of external intervention, from the colonial era through Korea, Vietnam and Cambodia, has strongly influenced and enhanced the development of this dimension of the "ASEAN way". [21] In the comparison between Europe and Southeast Asia there are obviously very different balances of actual and potential advantage. The strength of NATO on the military side contrasts with the weakness of the ARF, if indeed the ARF had ever actually been intended to play such a role, whilst the diplomatic strength of ASEAN contrasts with the weakness of the OSCE in the practical dimension of peace and confidence building. Again the OAU affords a varied example of significant peace and confidence building potential, but little in the way of realistic military or "enforcement" potential, except tangentially through sub-regional organisations such as ECOMOG or the SADC Organ.

In addition to the specific advantages which the various regional and sub-regional organisations and arrangements may have to offer in given situations, there is also to be considered the general advantage, with a mirroring disadvantage, of the "local" nature of such bodies in peace support processes and operations. This is the factor of close familiarity with and commitment to the region in question. Amongst other practical potential benefits deriving from this are the avoidance of inappropriate methodological "parachuting" [22] and an, almost, necessary commitment to the often neglected "tail" of post-enforcement peace and confidence building.

These several advantages of a regionalisation of peace support action might be elaborated region-by-region but the instances offered above may suffice to indicate the nature of the benefits which might be expected to be gained. Again, however, the diversity in the balance of benefits to be sought must be emphasised as an essential point of the analysis. The optimal exploitation of these various possible advantages involves, by definition, an effective and appropriately founded selection amongst the available options in each given case. Wise choices may prove to be highly beneficial, whilst unwise or inadequately informed choices may carry the seeds of potential or, as in the African Great Lakes crisis, actual disaster. This potential, or actuality, represents the negative term in the equation of the benefits and dangers of a regionalisation of peace support strategies and requires to be accorded no less attention than the potential advantages.

THE POSSIBLE DANGERS OF REGIONALISATION

The dangers which may be discerned in a move towards a regionally based paradigm, or paradigms, of peace support action are various in their detail but all turn ultimately upon the simple fact of the diverse character of the severally available regional options. The most obvious dangers are at first sight contradictory in nature, being predicated on the one hand upon excessively robust regionalism and, on the other the weakness or even vacuity of regional organisations and arrangements.

The danger of regional strength is in essence that of actual or potential hegemonism. The point was central to the debates over the relative merits of regionalism and globalism at Dumbarton Oaks and San Francisco at the outset of the UN era. It will be recalled also that the point was recognised by Boutros Boutros-Ghali in *Supplement to Agenda for Peace* in remarking that,

"The experience of the last few years has demonstrated ... the difficulties that can arise when the Security Council entrusts enforcement tasks to groups of Member States. ... There is ... the danger that the States concerned may claim international legitimacy and approval for forceful actions that were not in fact envisaged by the Security Council when it gave its authorization to them. ..." [23]

The danger here canvassed is, in short, that of a hijacking of actual or supposed peace support action by other domestic or regional political agendas. This danger has been expressly or implicitly ranged in reference to much of the robust regional action undertaken in the closing years of the 20th century, for example in connection with ECOMOG action in West Africa and the pre-KFOR NATO action in the 1999 Kosovo crisis. There is no sound foundation for accusations of actual or intended hegemonism to be levelled against either ECOMOG or NATO, but there is more generally a genuine danger in future hypothetical cases of the UN becoming a helpless passenger in a train driven by an organisation which has ceased to follow a globally framed agenda and is following one, of positively sinister potential, of its own devising. The real danger of UN weakness upon which this peril is predicated was very clearly indicated in Kosovo, as has been suggested above, and is one of the most basic considerations to be entertained in any analysis of future development of peace support methodologies.

The opposite danger arises from the possibility of a United Nations which may be tempted to treat the regional option as in some sense a global solution to its resource-driven peace support difficulties. As the preceding chapters show, the capacities and potential of the various regional organisations are highly diverse and in some cases very slight. The impediments to significant peace support action under which the Arab League and the SAARC labour [24] are important but not unique instances of this phenomenon. It is, of course, also the case that even where an available regional organisation may have some important potential it may not necessarily be appropriately equipped or conceived to deal with the crisis in question.

In both cases the emphasis returns to the importance of the primacy of the United Nations in peace support operations, even if the primary operational role is in many cases taken by regional arrangements and/or "coalitions of the willing". This is, of course, precisely the imperative embodied in article 53 of the UN Charter and the future design of peace support paradigms will drift from this basic provision only at grave peril to the United Nations organisations and, much more importantly, to the very concepts of collective security and defence.

THE BALANCE OF BENEFITS AND DANGERS

The benefits and the dangers of a regional peace support paradigm or paradigms are in themselves fairly obvious and in many ways equally balanced, being, indeed, in a number of respects mirror images of each other. The important question is not one of whether the benefits outweigh the dangers, or vice versa, but one of how structures can be guaranteed which will optimise the benefits to be gained and minimise the dangers to be feared. The key element here is the future role of the United Nations Security Council and how in a changed post-Cold War international relations context an increasingly important regional option is to be developed, controlled and managed. This issue will be the principal concern of the concluding chapter.

NOTES

1. See Chapter 7.
2. See Chapter 8.
3. See ibid.

4. See Chapter 4.
5. See I. Claude, *Swords into Plowshares*, 4 ed., (McGraw Hill, 1984), p.143.
6. Ibid., p.114.
7. See Chapter 4.
8. *Supplement to Agenda for Peace*, S/1995/1, 3 January 1995, paragraph 80.
9. Ibid., paragraphs 87-88.
10. See Chapter 4.
11. I.e. including the NATO-led IFOR, SFOR and KFOR Forces as well as the pre-KFOR 1999 air strikes against Serbia.
12. See M. Weller, "Armed Samaritans", *Counsel*, August 1999, pp.20-22. For a discussion of the general proposition of "democratic legitimacy" see T.M. Franck, "The Emerging Right to Democratic Governance" (1992) 86 *American Journal of International Law*, p.46; for critical analysis see S. Murphy, "Democratic Legitimacy and the Recognition of States and Governments" (1999) 48 *International and Ciomparative Law Quarterly*, pp.545-581.
13. The Former Yugoslav Republic of Macedonia.
14. See Chapter 8.
15. For discussion see N.D. White and H. McCoubrey, "International Law and the Use of Force in the Gulf" (1991) X *International Relations*, pp. 347-373.
16. For a detailed discussion of the sanctions issue in the 1990-91 Gulf Conflict see L. Freedman and E. Karsh, *The Gulf Conflict 1990-1991* (Faber and Faber, 1993) pp. 129-228; For an analysis of the Security Council debates over the imposition of sanctions in Haiti see J. Morris, 'Force and Democracy: UN/US Intervention in Haiti', *International Peacekeeping*, Vol 2 (1995), p.391 at pp.403-406.
17. For discussion of the potential impact of economic sanctions see N.D. White, "Collective Sanctions: An Alternative to Military Coercion?" (1994) XII *International Relations*, 75.
18. See K.R. Timmerman, *The Death Lobby: How the West Armed Iraq* (Bantam Books, 1992) and J. Sweeney, *Trading with the Enemy: Britain's Arming of Iraq* (Pan Books, 1993).
19. See Chapter 6.
20. See ibid.
21. See Chapter 7.
22. This term is here used in the sense employed by Nicola Baker and Leonard C. Sebastian in "The Problem of Parachuting: Strategic Studies and Security in the Asia/Pacific Region" in D. Ball, ed., *The Transformation of Security in the Asia Pacific Region"* (Frank Cass, 1996) p.15 ff.
23. S/1995/1, 3 January 1995, paragraph 80.
24. See Chapter 8.

CHAPTER 10

Regionalism and Peace Support in the 21st Century

However the specific pattern of 21st century peace support and enforcement may develop, and the variable exigencies of international relations would render a detailed prediction an ill-advised venture, it may be presumed with confidence that regional agencies will play an enhanced and powerful role therein. At least two principal factors lend powerful support to this conclusion. The resource-driven crisis in post-Cold War UN peace support capacity which precluded the global organisation from meeting effectively the increased demands of the late 1980s and 90s generated by the collapse of the Cold War balance of (Super)power structure seems unlikely to receive any early or significant alleviation. By the same token, the dynamics of post-Cold War politics are no more conducive to an assumption by UN Members of their obligation to hold substantial forces on stand-by for UN service under articles 43 and 45 of the Charter than were those of the Cold War itself. Whilst this should not be taken to mean that classical "Blue Helmet" forces have no future role, especially in peacekeeping rather than peace enforcement, it is also clear that substantial other resources are needed if the increasing demands placed upon global security mechanisms are successfully to be met. As Boutros Boutros-Ghali foresaw in *Supplement to Agenda for Peace,* [1] the regional option will be an important variable in this developing peace support equation. The need for development of this form was shown early in the post-Cold War era with the debacles in former-Yugoslavia, Somalia and the African Great Lakes region, all of which, in various ways, demonstrated a fatal UN incapacity.

At the same time, as the regional analysis advanced in earlier chapters has made clear, the regional option is unable to offer any simple or singular solution to global security problems. The wide variety of the character and objectives of the organisations and arrangements manifestly precludes any such approach. Indeed, it is by no means to be assumed that any, or at least any functionally suitable, regional agency will be available in any given security crisis. [2] The variety of organisational structures and their unavailability in some highly significant cases may seem to be evidence of a major defect in the regional argument. This is not, however, necessarily the case. The fact that no absolute and unreflective devolution of peace support and enforcement action to regional agencies is possible affords the best available guarantee against an abdication of functions and the peril of local "Big Power" hegemonism which has always lurked at the heart of the regionalist argument.

Rather than offering a complete, or even a "new", solution to global security problems, the regional option is suggested instead to afford a very significant extension of the peace support/enforcement resources which *may* be available in any given case. This does not, and should not, mean that regional agencies afford the only available resource, they are instead one amongst a number of possible continuing and future peace support options. The most important issue for the concluding part of this study is thus that of the mechanisms and parameters of selection amongst the various, or in some cases very limited, peace support options. To this degree contemporary, post-Cold War, debate in this area substantially returns to the issues which were rehearsed in the globalist/regionalist debate at Dumbarton Oaks and San Francisco at the outset of the UN era, [3] albeit in a radically changed international relations context.

The key peace support and enforcement issue for the early and middle years of the 21st century will not, it is suggested, lie in a crude choice between global and regional mechanisms but, rather, in the structuring of modes of selection amongst potential actors in order to secure the optimum balance between both modes of operation. The nature of such an optimum modality is not, in itself, difficult to anticipate. It would involve an informed process of selection between arguably available options capable of securing appropriate delegation of peace support actions to available and suitable regional agencies whilst sustaining ultimate UN oversight but avoiding the urge to micro-management which did so much damage in the 1990s. The achievement of this desirable result will emerge, if at all, from a complex interaction between, by no means categorically exclusive, legal, political, strategic and military factors.

The key element in a positive interaction of this type is manifestly that of a selection of agencies and a *modus operandi* in each given case according to criteria of predictive efficacy. Above all, the *ad hoc* grasping at seeming "solutions" merely because they happen to be "available", seen to such doleful effect in "Operation Turquoise" [4] in the African Great Lakes crisis, must be avoided. In practice the most effective decision making processes in future peace support action will, *ex hypothesi*, rest upon a realistic appreciation of the real potential, in contrast with the inflated aspirations of a given agency. It may be added that this rather basic imperative applies no less to the UN itself than to the regional organisations and arrangements. Effective analysis requires individual consideration of the legal, political, strategic and military variables of the equation. However they may be perceived it must, nonethe-less, be recalled that the ultimate focus is upon an interactive modality and that these "areas" of concern by their nature overlap to a considerable degree, however unpalatable some practitioners in all of these fields may find that proposition.

PUBLIC INTERNATIONAL LAW AND REGIONAL PEACEKEEPING

The development of a significant 21st century regional peace support dynamic presents no difficulty in principle from the viewpoint of the UN Charter. The idea of a globalist system with an important but carefully subordinated regional element was established in the 1940s and is precisely reflected in the "collective defence" dimension of article 51 and in Chapter VIII, especially article 53, of the UN Charter. It will be recalled that the terms of article 53 are mandatory rather than permissive in so far as the Security Council is actually *required* to make use of regional organisations and arrangements in peace support action where these are "appropriate". In this sense the modern, resource-driven, revival of interest in regional peace support represents no more than a reactivation of an important potential which was inherent in the UN system *ab initio*. During the Cold War era this potential was largely marginalised by the emergence of the mixed collective security and balance of (Super) power system and consequent significant sidelining of the Security Council itself.

The Cold War shaped, and arguably distorted, not only the operation and development of the Security Council but also that of the regional agencies. Post-Second World War alliances, such as NATO and, to a lesser degree, the WEU, [5] as well as actually or practically defunct organisations such as SEATO [6], CENTO [7] and the Warsaw Pact, were all conceived in and shaper by the context of the ideological confrontation. Other regional organisations such as ASEAN [8] and the OAU [9] were less directly shaped by the Cold War but some, like the OAS [10] with its US-led equation of "democracy" and "security" with non-communism, were perhaps even more radically distorted than the military alliances themselves. To a greater or lesser degree many of these organisations and arrangements, no less than the UN itself, have had to reorient their objectives in the changed patters of post-Cold War international relations and security concerns.

NATO offers an obvious, but not necessarily unique, example. As considered in Chapter 4, NATO is a defensive military alliance whose core remit, set out in articles 5 and 6 of the 1949 North Atlantic Treaty, is expressly founded upon the collective self-defence provision of article 51 of the UN Charter. Its involvement in the peace support operations of IFOR, SFOR and KFOR in former-Yugoslavia in the 1990s fell manifestly outside this remit. It does not, however, follow that the organisation is legally precluded from undertaking such operations. As has been argued in this book, whereas operations falling within the remit of articles 5 and 6 of the North Atlantic Treaty are *mandatory* for NATO Member States, other operations may, subject to general norms of international law, still be undertaken with their *consent* in their sovereign capacities using the infrastructure which they themselves have created. Where such consent is not forthcoming, those Members which were agreeable to the proposed action could, of course, still act as a "coalition of the willing" with all the advantages of joint operational experience and material interoperability, but could not do so under a NATO aegis. Such action might, however, be undertaken under the formal aegis of the WEU or even the OSCE, as might be more appropriate in a given case. Several important points flow from this.

As NATO's original rationale weakened as the Soviet, although not necessarily the Russian, threat dissolved in the late 1980s and was not supplanted by any new immediately obvious single external menace, a significant reorientation became necessary if the organisation was to be maintained. The core defence remit remains in place but other activities, including "out of area" peace support, are being developed by consent. Given that an actual rewriting of the 1949 North Atlantic Treaty would be so politically perilous as to be almost inconceivable, NATO peace support beyond its core remit is in effect undertaken as a pre-existing and highly organised "coalition of the willing". The Coalition action in the 1990-91 Gulf Conflict which was functionally NATO-led, although not wholly NATO-composed, affords and example from the very outset of the post-Cold War era. The point, of course, is one of flexibility of approach and adaptability in a rapidly evolving international relations environment. This is a matter of profound importance for regional agencies and for the UN so far as an understanding of international law is concerned.

A brief digression into the basic, but often misrepresented, nature of international law is necessary here. Many lawyers, international and municipal, and not a few international relations specialists treat international law – and especially treaty law – as if it comprised fixed texts of certain meaning and application. Any law must, as writers as diverse as Karl N. Llewellyn [11] and Lon L Fuller [12] have emphasised, have at least a basic level of certainty if it is to succeed in its various normative and facilitative functions. The more extreme "black letter" approaches are, however, paradoxically destructive of this very aim in that an inability to achieve, sometimes radical, adaptations of understanding in new circumstances may lead at best to functional desuetude and at worst leave legal norms as a millstone around the neck of future ages which can only generate an unhealthy disrespect for the law itself. In practice all law, including municipal statute law, undergoes a process of adaptation and reorientation of understanding – anyone who doubts this should pause to consider the extraordinary gyrations inflicted upon the Princess Sophia Naturalisation Act [13] in *Attorney-General* v *Prince Ernest Augustus of Hanover* [14] by the three highest jurisdictions in England. If this is true of municipal law its is far more so, and more openly so, of public international law. International law is by its nature an expression of a formally binding consensus of nations. The sources of this law as they are set out for the purposes of the International Court of Justice in article 38 of the ICJ Statute [15] can all, with the exception of the subsidiary sources of judicial decisions and writings of publicists, most properly be seen as means of ascertaining the content of the consensus of States upon a given point. Treaties are in one sense the clearest case in so far as they essentially are formally written statements of agreement having in the case of large multilateral treaties, such as the UN Charter, a mixed contractual and quasi-legislative nature, including an eventual capacity to bind non-Parties by establishing general norms of international law. Consensus and circumstances may, of course, change and if this happens a treaty, or custom, may simply collapse into obsolescence or be suspended. It may also be reinterpreted in a context of more flexible understanding. This has very much been the case for the UN Charter, *inter alia*, in cases of defence and security concern.

It is a commonplace that the application of Chapter VII of the UN Charter was radically affected by the Cold War, clearly in the functioning of the Security Council under articles 39-42 and also in the effective obsolescence of the stand-by forces provision of articles 43 and 45. If it had been attempted to operate the Charter "as if" the post-War consensus of the 1940s still existed the system would swiftly have become unworkable. The post-Cold War era will also demand changes in application, albeit arguably in a less radical manner since many of the basic problems – including lack of resources – remain very real even if in somewhat varied forms. One area of immediate focus will inevitably be article 53. Here, fortunately, the omens are fairly positive. One key question for this purpose is the actual purpose of "regional arrangements or agencies". NATO, for example, does not consider itself, and in terms of general understanding is not, strictly a regional organisation. That it is more generally a regional "arrangement" is, in view of the almost infinite elasticity of the term, much more readily concluded. In practice, as remarked above, the Security Council has been pragmatic in its approach. It has called upon the assistance in peace support/enforcement measures of a range of groups and bodies, including formal alliances such as NATO and more *ad hoc* temporary groupings. In terms of a defined application of article 53 this would seem to be the only viable way forward. The issue returns, in fact, to the highly diverse nature of the agencies potentially concerned and an over-precise definition would seem to defeat the manifest intention of article 53 and therefore, *ex hypothesi*, to be an improper interpretation of the provision.

This leads in turn to a larger issue, that of the relation between Chapters VII and VIII and specifically between articles 42 and 53 of the Charter. The UN does not have, and never has had, the forces available itself to "take action" under article 42 and such action has, therefore, throughout the UN era been undertaken by mandated volunteer groups of Member States, whether as "Blue Helmet" forces in the strict sense or, as in the cases of Korea and the 1990-91 Gulf Conflict, in other formats. In short, UN-sponsored peace support and enforcement missions have from the outset involved entrustment of operations to a variety of temporary and permanent groups. Whether this is viewed as "action" under article 42 – usually referred to with deliberate vagueness as taken "under Chapter VII" – or "delegation" under article 53 must seem in principle a matter of very slight importance. This is especially the case granted that, whether action is taken under Chapter VII or Chapter VIII, it will equally fall within the remit of the Security Council. To this considerable extent the potential pattern of increased regionalism in post-Cold War peace support and enforcement suggests that the formal distinction between Chapter VII (in the article 42 sense) and Chapter VIII operations may have become unsustainable. Reference to "Chapter Six and a Half" measures, however inappropriately used, have been current for some time and the time has perhaps come for equal consideration of "Chapter Seven and a Half" operations at the more robust end of peace enforcement founded upon articles 42 and 53. In a situation in which, as is here suggested to be the case, the key peace support dynamic is one of appropriate resource selection, the two provisions can be seen inherently as points upon a continuous spectrum and not as categorically distinct norms.

There are, of course, practical distinctions to be borne in mind. The management of forces is a prime issue. The catastrophic command and control problems of the many Blue Helmet forces, up to and including UNPROFOR in former-Yugoslavia, clearly require address. The sort of problematic micro-management here in question is not required by the Charter, on the contrary, the UN Military Staff Committee is specifically tasked with strategic, but *not* tactical management of UN military operations. [16] The clear preference of an organisation like NATO for unambiguous strategic direction combined, subject to applicable international legal norms, with tactical flexibility in their achievement, seems an obvious lesson for both the utilisation of regional arrangements and for future "Blue Helmet" forces, if any. This would not involve, as such, a change in the Charter or its associated legal norms, but it would involve a radical, and long overdue, shift in the bureaucratic culture.

Such processes of adaptation to new circumstances are essential to the utility of international law and perhaps nowhere more so than in the defence and security sector. This is emphatically not a counsel of uncertainty or laxity and it is clear that such adaptation must take place within the constraints of certain fundamental norms. This phase of transition from the Cold War to the post-Cold War era involves some manifest dangers, exemplified in the NATO air strikes in the 1999 Kosovo crisis which fell into a legal limbo, being neither explicitly authorised nor expressly condemned.[17] The argument of "dissociation" needlessly advanced in the Kosovo context may be seen as especially dangerous as it was suggested in Chapter 9. Specifically, although this was not the idea in relation to Kosovo in 1999, the argument has an implicit resonance with Hitler's purported concern for the welfare of the *Ausland Deutsch* in territories which he planned to invade and occupy which implicitly poses a direct threat to the norms embodied in article 2(3)(4) of the UN Charter and the whole post-1945 international security order. This is a course which need not, and must not, be embarked upon.

THE POLITICAL AGENDA

The significant, and arguably distorting, effect of the Cold War ideological confrontation upon the UN system of collective defence and security has been outlined above. In particular the Cold War political dynamic operated to preclude the operation of the Security Council in the manner apparently intended by those who drafted the UN Charter. The relatively limited security function which the UN was, in this context, able to perform was undertaken by the General Assembly in the form of consensual peacekeeping operations with the constitutional limitations thereof. The end of the Cold War raised expectations of a renewed and efficacious UN activism which were raised to unrealistic levels by the successful UN-authorised Coalition action in the 1990-91 Gulf Conflict. Again, as remarked above, these anticipations were rapidly undermined by the subsequent experiences of former-Yugoslavia, Somalia and the African Great Lakes region, cases which demonstrated the inability of the UN to meet the increased demands placed upon it. The end of the Cold War was taken by many to signal a newly stable era of international relations which would involve a large downscaling of necessary defence preparedness and, therefore, expenditure. These twin expectations of a post-Cold War "peace dividend" together with increased UN peace support and enforcement activism proved, by their nature, to be incompatible. Contrary to these expectations the end of the relatively stable US-Soviet balance of power structure was replaced by a much less stable and predictable pattern in which smaller Powers, freed from the constraints of Cold War bipolar relations, were able to pursue policies which generated local, but nonetheless dangerous, confrontations and conflicts. Since the UN is dependent for any "military" action which it undertakes, or authorises, upon forces supplied voluntarily by Member States, the question of resources assumed a critical importance. In short, in a context in which in one way or another peace support rested ultimately upon "coalitions of the willing" the crucial issue became precisely that of the "willingness" of UN Members to make available the necessary resources and assets. The consequences of practical unwillingness became disastrously manifest in former-Yugoslavia, Somalia and the African Great Lakes. In all of these cases a combination of highly compromised mandates and under-resourced forces meant that the UN, at least initially, was unable to operate in the manner which the idealised post-Cold War vision seemed to anticipate. This problem was exacerbated by the fact that key actors within the Security Council proved more willing to advocate and secure UN mandates than to provide the practical means by which the objectives identified therein could be realised.

It was in this situation that recourse to regional agencies appeared to offer a solution to both the resourcing problem and, to some degree, that of political willingness. The expectation was that where a regional solution was sought to crises within that area the relevant Powers would be more highly motivated to make provision for an effective response. This was, not unreasonably, taken to be yet more the case in light of the fact that the end of the Cold War had freed regional Powers and organisations from the shackles of the former bipolar global security structures. The deployment of the NATO-led IFOR, SFOR and, later, KFOR forces in former-Yugoslavia lent a somewhat deceptive colour to these expectations. This appeared to reinforce the idea of a regional solution to regional problems, but upon closer examination this was far from the case. Europe, whether in the specific guise of the EU Powers or more generally, in fact signally failed to deal with the former-Yugoslav crisis and the effectiveness of the various NATO-led forces owed in practice a great deal to the actual and implicit power of the USA, from the brokering of the Dayton Peace Accords onwards. In short the role of the "Big Power" backer was, again, pointedly illustrated. The role of NATO in former-Yugoslavia sent out misleading signals not only in regard to the operations themselves, but also as a more general "regional" model. The atypicality of NATO amongst "regional organisations" has been remarked upon at several points in the foregoing analysis and it affords a most unsure foundation for general expectations of what can be achieved. It may be added that this does not devalue the regional option as such. NATO as a military alliance can clearly perform a useful military enforcement role, it does not, however, have any obvious role in peace and confidence building, unlike essentially non-military organisations such as, for example, ASEAN or the OAS, and it does not, indeed, aspire to such a role. Whether, in time, the OSCE might come to fulfil such a role in the Euro-Atlantic area remains to be seen, although at the close of the 20th century some scepticism would seem appropriate.

It is important to realise that the regional agencies are not only diverse in their constitutions and material capacities but are even more so in the political expectations and aspirations vested in them by their memberships. This reflects the diversity of the regions themselves and the international relations structures within them. The point is made plain by the regional analyses in foregoing chapters. It is, for example, plain that a focused military alliance such as NATO is expected to perform an entirely different function from the OAU which functions in a much larger "region", arguably in a group of regions, almost as a "miniature UN General Assembly". Attention may again be drawn to the fact that where inter-State relations within a region are dynamically unstable, it is unlikely that an effective regional security organisation will be able, or permitted, to develop, as is seen in the cases of the Arab League and SAARC. [18] The nature of intra-State relations is also highly significant, as regions comprising States whose major security concerns are internally rather than externally focused, as may be seen significantly amongst some of the Members of, for example, ASEAN, the OAS and the OAU, are unlikely to wish to engage in extensive extra-territorial peace support action. It may also be said that where internal civil-military relations are unstable or unclear, civilian governments are likely to be reluctant to participate in regional organisations which, in fact or appearance, appear to bolster an assertive military agenda.

A hypothetical "ideal" regional model might combine the qualities and capacities of the several regional agencies, combining peace and confidence building capacities with roles of increasing robustness up to and including military enforcement. In practice no region possesses such an ideal combination of resources or is politically likely to develop any such. As remarked above, the UN Security Council is therefore faced with the need to make choices amongst the available options in circumstances in which there may all too often be no evidently appropriate choice to make. It is in this that the future development of the role of the Security Council, including its potential reform, is of crucial importance. In this context any change must, whilst bearing in mind the need for genuine global representation, conserve the capacity for "prompt and effective" crisis management which was amongst the primary elements of the original *raison d'être* of the Council.

The vital point of emphasis is that the Security Council is, and is likely to remain, the only body which possesses the legal authority and, subject to debate regarding representation and domination by the Western Powers, the political legitimacy to authorise the international use of force, other than in an article 51 context. In the developing security architecture of the 21st century a key, but it must be stressed not exclusive, role of the Council will be to authorise enforcement action by regional agencies and "coalitions of the willing", but in so doing it must not be relegated to the role of a mere "rubber stamp" for the intervention of external actors. The dangers were, at least by implication, made clear in the cases of the US intervention in Haiti and the French-led "Operation Turquoise" in Rwanda, as well as the initial relations between NATO and the Security Council in the 1999 Kosovo crisis. The proper role of the Council may, thus, be perceived as one of positive and effective selection amongst peace support options rather than one of passive acquiescence in externally driven agendas. There is here, of course, the inevitable paradox, summarised in the maxim *quis custodiet ipsos custodes* (who guards the guards), of the fact that the possibly dangerous external agendas may actually be driven by one or more of the Permanent Members of the Security Council itself. This danger is, in effect, a peril of global he-gemonism which reflects the counter-danger of regional hegemonism. A possible, but remote, answer lies in the supposition of accountability through the General Assembly to the mass of smaller nations. The suggestion that another answer lies in the possibility of judicial review of Security Council action by the International Court of Justice may have a *prima facie* attraction. However, the Court is not well suited to make political and security decisions and could not realistically act beyond the level of the interpretation of the legal powers of the Council. The likelihood of "prompt and effective" action from the Court in the context of security crisis management may reasonably be doubted. One might say that, in this situation, a political solution must be found to political problems.

It must also be remembered that the political agendas within which the Security Council necessarily operates reflect the national political agendas of Member States. Because of its material power and influence this is most obviously true of the domestic political agendas of the United States, which are by no means necessarily favourable to the UN as an institution from both a financial and an ideological viewpoint – although this should not be taken to deny the pivotal role which the USA in fact plays in UN affairs. The relative breakdown of bipartisanship in matters normally ringfenced from domestic confrontations as a result of the bitter divisions between the Clinton Administration and the Congress adversely affected US engagement with the UN during the later 1990s, although this can be, and often has been, greatly overstated. The US financial contribution to the UN is of enormous signifi-cance and perceptions of default, primarily deriving from views generated during the Reagan Administration, are, in the 1990s, clearly outdated. This point is well illustrated by the fact that, in addition to making the most significant contributions to both the assessed and the peacekeeping budgets, the US is by the far the largest single donor in terms of voluntary contributions to departments such as the Department of Humanitarian Affairs (DHA). Unlike contributions to the peacekeeping budget, these payments have not, on the whole, attracted Congressional hostility, nor are they the subject of political interference since, whilst DHA must remain financially accountable, issues of command and control do not here arise.

The UN Security Council also operates as a stage upon which Member States play out global roles which may have complex domestic and historical roots. The post-1945 *Pax Americana* undoubtedly serves US national interests, just as the *Pax Britannica* served British interests in the 19th century, but the commitment of US economic, political and military power has undoubtedly supplied the major underpinning of the collective security, as well as balance of power, system for more than half a century. In the same way the commitment of States such as the UK and France combines genuine commitment to modern collective security with a consciousness of obligation and, not always appropriate, aspirations associated with the afterglow of Empire. The French-driven attempt to commit the WEU to security concerns in Francophone Africa may be seen as a less that positive example of this phenomenon. The desire of the UK and France to, in the words of Douglas Hurd, "punch above their weight" in world affairs, may be contrasted with the position of the PRC which shows little willingness to engage with security issues outsides its immediate sphere of influence. This, as remarked in Chapter 7, is in many ways a continuation of classical Chinese political positions which were also adopted by all the Imperial Dynasties, except the Mongol Yuan, after the T'ang. Whether this policy may change in the 21st century, especially if, as some contend, the PRC is inclined to adopt a more "Western" model of global affairs and influence, remains to be seen. The position of post-Soviet Russia is also interesting, in that there has manifestly been a loss of global influence which future Russian leaders may well desire to restore but do not necessarily have the economic base which would render this possible. The nature and sources of commitment of medium level and even small Powers are no less variable. Canada and the Scandinavian States stand out as nations which have, in effect, made a policy of principled commitment to peace support as such. It may also be said that some smaller States have also appeared to find a commitment to engagement with peace support action a means of securing international funding for the maintenance of large military establishments which are by no means necessarily of positive international or domestic impact.

Domestic agendas may also have a profound and often unhelpful effect upon the tactical conduct of peace support operations. It is arguable that during the NATO air strikes against Serbia during the 1999 Kosovo crisis the basic reasoning behind the decision to adopt high altitude bombing as a sole tactical method was founded upon a desire, understandable in itself, to minimise NATO casualties. There were strong political motivations for this, not least the sensitivity to "own" casualties which has come, somewhat unfairly, to be known as the "CNN Factor", which may be understandable but involves the creation of unreal and ultimately destabilising expectations of the nature of robust military action.

A final fundamental question arises in the appreciation of the very nature of "security". During the Cold War era security was perceived essentially in inter-state military terms and was pursued within the context of the bipolar ideological confrontation which came to shape, or at the very least influence, global politics and came to find its ultimate expression in the balance of (Super)power strategy of Mutual Assured Destruction (MAD). That this conceptualisation was ever adequate may be doubted, but at the end of the Cold War it is manifestly clear that it does not provide an appropriate basis upon which to theorise and practice international politics. Security has now necessarily come to be understood as covering a much wider spectrum of issues and actors. In general terms a former preoccupation with the military aspects of security has come to be superseded by a more holistic understanding which, while not seeking to negate the importance of military issues, nevertheless attempts to contextualise them through an appropriate consideration of economic, social and political factors. This new security agenda also acknowledges the importance of intra-State and trans-national actors and phenomena.

In the present context, the sense of security action as bound into the confines of military crisis management has become wholly inadequate. The necessities of both preliminary conflict aversion and post-intervention reconstruction and peace-building have come to be seen as having at least equal importance with any needful "enforcement" action. These phases are also not to be seen as discreet or freestanding phenomena, but rather as points upon a peace support continuum. The requisites of peace support neither commence nor end with military action. It is in this that, even from a strictly military perspective, the existence of an adequate exit strategy, defining in essence what the purpose of the operation is supposed to be, becomes of vital importance. As it has been put to the authors, the significant factor is not an arbitrary "end date" but a desired "end state", achievement of which will avoid the peril of early exit and rapid re-entry into a continuing crisis situation. A narrowly "military" analysis might suggest the advantages of a limited "surgical strike" operation and this may be supported by both political and economic factors. However, the more holistic analysis underlines the benefits of a more considered process of initial aversion and continuing peace support in the sense of peace building wherever and to whatever extent this is possible.

Within the specific context of the UN the broadened security agenda has unfortunately exacerbated "turf wars" between various elements of the Organisation and in particular as between the Security Council, the General Assembly and the Secretariat. As regards the relationship between the Security Council and the General Assembly the UN Charter is clear, notwithstanding the now largely historical complication of the Uniting for Peace Resolution, that primary responsibility for international peace and security rests with the former rather than the latter. However, as the concept of "security" has been broadened beyond that of inter-State conflict to cover intra-State issues of human and political rights, so the General Assembly has sought to counter this encroachment into areas previously seen as falling wholly within its remit. The area of actual and potential conflict between the Secretariat and the Security Council is somewhat different in character. The development within the Secretariat of departments such as those dealing with humanitarian affairs (DHA) and peacekeeping (DPKO) has received a generally positive response from within the Security Council and beyond. However tension has arisen between the Secretary General and particular Security Council members over issues of command and control of UN peace support operations to which they have made significant contributions.

STRATEGIC AND MILITARY DIMENSIONS

As has been noted above, the total spectrum of peace support action is by no means confined to "military" action by armed forces, it involves a wide range of civilian personnel as well as other disciplined services, including civilian police units. The more robust range of "enforcement" action is, however, inevitably vested primarily in military forces. Such use of national forces in "international policing" roles raises a number of questions which are hardly new to the post-Cold War era but remain of vital importance. As very broad categorisations these issues may be resolved into four broad areas, those of national defence interest, the utility of military force, command and control issues and material interoperability.

The primary legitimate function of any national military force is defence of the national territory against external aggression within the meaning of article 51 of the UN Charter. No responsible government could jeopardise the performance of this basic function by an over-commitment of armed forces to international security concerns. This means that although smaller Powers can and do contribute contingents to peacekeeping and peace enforcement forces, the major burden falls inevitably upon the larger Powers and pre-eminently upon the United States in many cases. This is not, of course, a universal axiom and it may be that in some instance the lead role will be played by a major regional Power, such as, for example, Nigeria in ECOMOG or Australia in the case of East Timor in September 1999. National military commitments without which such operations are impossible, turn upon availability and perceived policy interests. The realist school of strategic thought contends that no rationally governed state would, or should, commit its armed forces for any purpose other than the advance of its national interest. This argument may be, and often is, pushed to extremes but in essence it is correct. The key question is, of course, what is "national interest" for this purpose? It is part of the basic concept of global collective security as it is embodied in the UN Charter that an assault upon the security of any state is an assault upon the security of all. To this degree, therefore, it maybe argued that the maintenance of international peace and security is in the "real" national interest of all states. To some degree this is actually the case. The major powers, pre-eminently but not only the United States, have in many cases shown willingness to commit forces to peace support action where their direct political and economic interests are not necessarily at risk. The strategic concepts which underlie these decisions are inevitably the product of a complex mixture of motivations. Most powers will, of course, engage in peace support action where they have an immediate interest, of whatever sort, in positive crisis management. They may also do so in cases in which, as remarked above, they may have a variety of historical and/or ideological commitments. Such a combination of interests is not only inevitable but in itself entirely proper. A commitment to robust peace support is a commitment of soldiers lives and this, politically and ethically, must be founded upon a genuine interest which includes, but is not uniquely composed of, interest in collective security as such. Since, in the absence of article 43 and 45 commitments, all international peace support forces are contributed voluntarily, these processes of creation constitute a fundamental dynamic of the mechanisms of peace support choice. As commented above, a commitment to robust peace support will invariably involve a commitment is soldiers lives, but beyond this it will also place at risk the general population of the territory concerned. In calculating the utility of military intervention the potential levels of injury and damage inevitably associated with it must be weighed against the beneficial consequences anticipated. This involves a consideration both of the categoric viability of the policy of intervention and the practical likelihood of its success. These two issues do not reflect respectively matters of ethical theory and practice, it is rather the case that both are considerations within a process of ethical decision making. It should also again be remarked here that any idea that non-military sanctions are in some sense a "softer" option than military action, or one which avoids these ethical issues may be discounted in the light, for example, of the experience of post-1991 Iraq. This point is further reinforced, without overstating the case, by the fact that modern weapons systems allow a greater precision in targeting than was the case in earlier cases.

Once a decision has been made to commit forces to a peace support, and specifically a peace enforcement, mission, different but no less significant questions come into play. Prominent amongst these are the broad issues of command and control. UN Blue Helmet forces have suffered over the years from inappropriate strategic direction and even micro-tactical management, UNPROFOR in former-Yugoslavia may be taken as a classic case in point. Burdened with shifting, and in some cases mutually conflicting, mandates from the UNO in New York, it was expected simultaneously to carry out missions of humanitarian relief, peace making and, increasingly, quasi-enforcement. In addition to this, interference from afar by the UN in the detailed tactical management of its operations created an impossible command environment and, not surprisingly, a swift and destabilising throughput of force commanders. As it has been remarked above, the wonder in this context is less that UNPROFOR encountered so many problems than that it achieved relatively so much. It is not surprising that founded upon this and the much more positive IFOR/SFOR/KFOR experiences, the strong NATO preference is for a clearly expressed and mandated strategic goal, leaving, subject to the *jus in bello*, the tactical means for its achievement to the command structure on the ground. This said, the NATO militaries accept the primacy of civilian political leadership, although this cannot be said of all militaries. It should be added that the UN is not uniquely prone to inappropriate mismanagement. National governments have equal propensities in this direction and may be argued to have displayed them in aspects of the pre-KFOR NATO operations in the 1999 Kosovo crisis.

At the level of tactical command and control, practical mechanisms are necessarily left to be negotiated in each case. This fact is expressly recognised in the case of Blue Helmet forces by article 47(3) of the UN Charter which states that "Questions relating to the command of such forces shall be worked out subsequently". This reflects the inevitable sensitivity of any submission of national military forces to foreign command. Again, Blue Helmet forces have a particularly unfortunate history in this regard. National contingent commanders in such forces look not only to the force commander but also to their home governments which may have divergent views upon the purpose and conduct of the mission. As a result a UN force commander will in effect have to "negotiate" the implementation of his orders with national contingent commanders in a manner unthinkable in almost any other military situation. This is hardly conducive to operational efficacy either internally or by reason of the fact that, as in the case of UNPROFOR, divisions within the force will soon become clear to, and exploited by, opposing forces. Regional and *ad hoc* multi-national forces are by no means immune from such problems, but a number of factors tend to reduce their impact. For an established military alliance such as NATO, long joint operational experience and unified command structures largely avert such issues and whilst this will be less the case for *ad hoc* groupings it may still be hoped that more effective prior arrangement could be achieved in these cases also. The practical issue of material interoperability also arises and whilst this can never be the primary factor in structuring a force it may nonetheless be an important element in operational efficacy, as well as supply arrangements, and cannot wholly be left out of account.

CONCLUSIONS

The regional option presents neither a simple nor a singular solution to the problems of peace support in the 21st century. As the preceding analysis has sought to demonstrate, the regional agencies cannot safely be seen as a substitute for an ailing or inefficacious UN collective security system. To follow that path would involve an acceptance of regional hegemonisms leading ultimately to a power bloc structure with all the defects of the febrile international relations and security structures of pre-1914 Europe. It is rather the case that the end of the Cold War has created a positive opportunity for the regeneration of a genuine global collective security system in which the UN, manifestly, cannot be expected itself to be the unique source of peace support action, but will function rather as the mechanism through which a variety of resources will be deployed to that end in cases of need. Amongst these resources the regional agencies, in their diverse characters and situations, will almost certainly play a major role. It is essential, however, to note that the agencies have a highly diverse range of capacities, limitations, objectives and defects. An operation to which NATO might be suited is not one to which ASEAN would be attuned, and *vice versa*. Whether the demands of the new era will inspire further development, and proliferation, of agencies remains to be seen, but some developments, including those in Southern Africa, suggest that this may be the case.

However this may be, the relationship between the Security Council and the regional agencies, and other *ad hoc* actors will remain pivotal. As Boutros Boutros-Ghali remarked in *Supplement to Agenda for Peace*,

"The capacity of regional organizations for peacemaking and peace-keeping varies considerably. None of them has yet developed a capacity which matches that of the United Nations, though some have accumulated important experience in the field and others are developing rapidly. The United Nations is ready to help them in this respect when requested to do so and when resources permit. Given their varied capacity, the differences in their structures, mandates and decision-making processes and the variety of forms that cooperation with the UN is already taking ... it would not be appropriate to try to establish a universal model for their relationship with the United Nations. Nevertheless it is possible to identify certain principles on which it should be based. ... Such principles include: ... The primacy of the United Nations, as set out in the Charter ... . "[19]

It is indeed vital that the Security Council should actively exercise a positive choice amongst the available peace support options, including the significant regional agencies. This does not mean that Blue Helmet forces as such are a thing of the past, it is rather the case that they too are amongst the variety of options to be considered in any given case. Above all it will be essential in future peace support policy to make use of resources in the manner best fitted to their capabilities. None of this demands a legal revolution, the mechanisms of effective choice are not only made available by the UN Charter but, as notably for article 53, their operation is even made mandatory. The real question for the future from the UN, the regional and the national perspectives is one of effective political will in backing a viable collective security system using the resources which are actually available. The former League of Nations catastrophically failed this test, the United Nations has the opportunity to succeed in a context in which the price of failure is unthinkable.

NOTES

1. S/1995/1, 3 January 1995.
2. See Chapter 8.
3. See I. Claude, *Swords into Plowshares*, 4 ed., (McGraw-Hill, 1984).
4. For discussion see Chapter 6.
5. See Chapter 4.
6. See Chapter 7.
7. See Chapter 8.
8. See Chapter 7.
9. See Chapter 6.
10. See Chapter 5.
11. See K.N. Llewellyn, *The Common Law Tradition: Deciding Appeals* (Little, Brown & Co, 1960).
12. See Lon L. Fuller, *The Morality of Law* (Yale University Press, 1964).
13. 4 & 5 Anne, c.16.
14. [1957] AC 436.

15. I.e. Treaties, International Custom, Principles recognised by "civilised" nations, and judicial decisions and writings of qualified publicists.
16. See article 47, UN Charter.
17. For discussion see Chapters 4 and 9; also H. McCoubrey, "Kosovo NATO and International Law" (1999) XIV *International Relations* pp. 29-46.
18. See Chapter 8.
19. Paragraphs 87-88.

Select Bibliography

D. Ball, ed., *The Transformation of Security in the Asia/Pacific Region* (Frank Cass, 1996)

C. Baxter *et al*, *Government and Politics in South Asia*, (Westview Press, 1998)

P. Brogan, *World Conflicts* (Bloomsbury, 1992)

M.E. Brown, S. Lynn-Jones and S.E. Miller, *East Asian Security* (MIT Press, 1996)

G. Buzan, *People, States and Fear: An Agenda for International Security Studies in the Post-Cold War Era* (Harvester Wheatsheaf, 1991)

E.H. Carr, *The Twenty Years Crisis 1919-1939* (Macmillan, 1991)

M. Clark, ed., *New Perspectives on Security* (Brassey's 1993)

I.L. Claude, *Swords into Plowshares*, 4 ed., (McGraw-Hill, 1956, 1984)

I.L. Claude, *Power and International Relations* (Random House, 1962)

M.J. Davis, *Security Issues in the Post-Cold War World* (Edward Elgar, 1996)

R.J. Ellings and S.W. Simon, eds., *Southeast Asian Security in the New Millennium* (NBR/ME Sharpe, 1996)

T. Findlay (ed.), *Challenges for the New Peacekeepers* (Oxford, 1996)

S. Ganguly, *The Origins of War in South Asia; Indo-Pakistani Conflicts Since 1947* (Westview, 1986)

P.H. Gordon (ed.), *NATO's Transformation: The Changimg Shape of the Atlantic Alliance* (Rowman and Littlefield, 1997)

S.S. Harrison and M. Nishihara, *UN Peacekeeping: Japanese and American Perspectives* (Carnegie Endowment, 1995)

HMSO, *Britain, NATO and European Security* (HMSO, 1994)

T. Huxley, *Insecurity in the Asian Region* (RUSI, 1993)

S. Johal, *Conflict and Integration in Indo-Pakistan Relations*, (University of California Press, 1989)

Muhammad Khalil, *The Arab States and the Arab League: A Documentary Record*, 2 Vols., (Khayatys, 1962)

S.U. Kodikara (ed.), *South Asian Strategic Issues: Sri Lankan Perspectives*, (Sage, 1990)

R.W. Macdonald, *The League of Arab States* (Princeton University Press, 1965)

D. McGoldrick, *International Relations Law of the European Union* (Longman, 1997)

A. McGrew and C. Brook, *Asia-Pacific in the New World Order* (Routledge, 1998)

C. McInnes, ed., *Security and Strategy in the New Europe* (Routledge, 1992)

H.J. Morgenthau, *Politics Among Nations: The Struggle for Power and Peace* (McGraw Hill, 1993)

O.A. Otunnu and M.W. Doyle, *Peacemaking and Peacekeeping in the New Century* (Rowman and Littlefield, 1998)

W. Park and G. Wyn-Rees, *Rethinking Security in Post-Cold War Europe* (Longman, 1998)

I. Pogany, *The Security Council and the Arab-Israeli Conflict* (Gower, 1984)

S.E. Ratner, *The New UN Peacekeeping* (St. Martin's Press, 1995,1996)

T.W. Robinson and D. Shambaugh (eds.), *Chinese Foreign Policy: Theory and Practice* (Clarendon Press, 1997)

Bilveer Singh, *ZOPFAN and the New Security Order in the Asia-Pacific Region* (Pelanduk Publications, 1992)

P.B. Stares, ed., *The New Security Agenda: A Global Survey* (JCIE, 1998)

WEU Secretariat-General, *WEU Today* (WEU,. 1998)

A. Wolfers, *Discord and Collaboration: Essays on International Politics* (Johns Hopkins Press, 1962)

D. Wurfel and B. Burton, eds., *Southeast Asia in the New World Order* (Macmillan, 1996)

Index